GANDHI
AT FIRST SIGHT

Thomas Weber is an Honorary Associate, School of Social Sciences and Communications, La Trobe University, Melbourne, Australia. His most recent Gandhi-related books are: *Beloved Bapu: The Gandhi-Mirabehn Correspondence* (with Tridip Suhrud); *Going Native: Gandhi's Relationship with Western Women* (Roli Books); *The Shanti Sena: Philosophy, History and Action*; *On the Salt March: The Historiography of Mahatma Gandhi's March to Dandi*; *Gandhi, Gandhism and the Gandhians* (Roli Books); and *Gandhi as Disciple and Mentor.*

OTHER ROLI TITLES BY THOMAS WEBER

Gandhi, Gandhism and the Gandhians

Going Native: Gandhi's Relationship with Western Women

OTHER LOTUS TITLES

Adi B. Hakim Rustom B. Bhumgara Jal P. Bapasola	*With Cyclists Around the World*
Ajit Bhattacharjea	*Sheikh Mohammad Abdullah: Tragic Hero of Kashmir*
Amarinder Singh	*The Last Sunset: The Rise & Fall of the Lahore Durbar*
Amarinder Singh	*Honour and Fidelity: India's Military Contribution to the Great War 1914-18*
Anil Dharker	*Icons: Men & Women Who Shaped Today's India*
Aitzaz Ahsan	*The Indus Saga: The Making of Pakistan*
H.L.O. Garrett	*The Trial of Bahadur Shah Zafar*
Imtiaz Gul	*Pakistan Before and After Osama*
Khushwant Singh	*Train to Pakistan*
Kingshuk Nag	*The Namo Story: A Political Life*
Kuldip Nayar	*Beyond the Lines: An Autobiography*
M.J. Akbar	*Byline*
M.J. Akbar	*Blood Brothers: A Family Saga*
M.J. Akbar	*Have Pen will Travel: Observations of a Globetrotter*
Maj. Gen. Ian Cardozo	*Param Vir: Our Heroes in Battle*
Maj. Gen. Ian Cardozo	*The Sinking of INS Khukri: What Happened in 1971*
Madhu Trehan	*Tehelka as Metaphor*
Masood Hyder	*October Coup: A Memoir of the Struggle for Hyderabad*
Monisha Rajesh	*Around India in 80 Trains*
Nayantara Sahgal (ed.)	*Before Freedom: Nehru's Letters to His Sister*
Peter Church	*Added Value: The Life Stories of Indian Business Leaders*
Rajika Bhandari	*The Raj on the Move: Story of the Dak Bungalow*
S. Hussain Zaidi	*Dongri to Dubai: Six Decades of the Mumabi mafia*
Salman Akhtar	*The Book of Emotions*
Shantanu Guha Ray	*MAHI: The Story of India's Most Successful Captain*
Shrabani Basu	*Spy Princess: The Life of Noor Inayat Khan*
Vijay Kumar Singha	*Hindustani Classical Music: An Introduction*
Vir Sanghvi	*Men of Steel: Indian Business Leaders in Candid Conversations*

FORTHCOMING TITLES

Ajai Mansingh	*Firaq Gorakhpuri*
Peter Church	*Profiles in Enterprise: Life Stories of Indian Business Leaders*

GANDHI
AT FIRST SIGHT

Edited and Introduced
by
Thomas Weber

LOTUS COLLECTION
ROLI BOOKS

Lotus Collection

First published in 2015

The Lotus Collection
An imprint of
Roli Books Pvt. Ltd
M-75, Greater Kailash II Market, New Delhi 110 048
Phone: ++91 (011) 40682000
Fax: ++91 (011) 2921 7185
E-mail: info@rolibooks.com
Website: www.rolibooks.com
Also at Bengaluru, Chennai, & Mumbai

Cover Design: Sneha Pamneja
Layout: Sanjeev Mathpal
Production: Shaji Sahadevan

ISBN: 978-81-7436-997-0

Typeset in Centaur MT by Roli Books Pvt. Ltd.
Printed at Shree Maitrey Printech Pvt. Ltd., Noida

Books by Thomas Weber

Beloved Bapu
The Mahatma Gandhi/Mirabehn Correspondence
(edited with Tridip Suhrud)

Going Native
Gandhi's Relationship with Western Women

Gandhi, Gandhism and the Gandhians

The Shanti Sena: Philosophy, History and Action

Gandhi as Disciple and Mentor

On the Salt March
The Historiography of Gandhi's March to Dandi

Nonviolent Intervention Across Borders
A Recurrent Vision
(edited with Yeshua Moser-Puangsuwan)

Conflict Resolution and Gandhian Ethics

Hugging the Trees
The Story of the Chipko Movement

CONTENTS

Introduction I

A first sight of Gandhi
On first meetings and first impressions
The wages of history and the vicissitudes of memory
Who met whom?
Meeting the Mahatma
What is left

1904: Henry S.L. Polak 16
1905: Millie Graham Polak 24
1907: Joseph J. Doke 27
1909: T.S.S. Rajan 31
1914: Sarojini Naidu 36
1915: J.B. Kripalani 39
1915: G.A. Natesan 45
1915: Rajkumari Amrit Kaur 51
1916: Vinoba Bhave 56
1917: Rajendra Prasad 61
1918: R.R. Diwakar 65
1919: E. Stanley Jones 69
1924: G. Ramachandran 74
1925: Madeleine Slade 80
1926: Katherine Mayo 85
1926: Zakir Husain 89
1926: Muriel Lester 94
1927: Archibald Fenner Brockway 98

1928: Horace Gundry Alexander 101
1929: J.C. Kumarappa 106
1929: Sherwood Eddy 111
1930: Reginald Reynolds 114
1930: Newton Phelps Stokes II 119
1930: Negley Farson 124
1931: William Lawrence Shirer 129
1931: John Haynes Holmes 134
1931: Charlie Chaplin 143
1931: Jo Davidson 148
1931: Webb Miller 155
1931: Romain Rolland 160
1931: Mary Barr 167
1932: Dr Dinshaw K. Mehta 172
1933: Nilla Cram Cook 178
1934: Nirmal Kumar Bose 184
1935: Halide Edib Adivar 189
1935: Paramahansa Yogananda 195
1935: Margaret Sanger 202
1935: Yone Noguchi 209
1936: Shriman Narayan 214
1936: Herbert Fischer 219
1937: Joseph Jean Lanza Del Vasto 224
1942: Louis Fischer 228
1942: Edgar Snow 235
1945: Hermon Ould 240
1945: R.G. Casey 245
1946: Margaret Bourke-White 249
1946: Hallam Tennyson 255
1947: Lord Louis Mountbatten 260
1948: Vincent Sheean 264

Concluding Remarks 272
Acknowledgements 276

Gandhi at First Sight

A first sight of Gandhi

I had my first sight of Gandhi in London in late 1976. Well, at least a sight of his wax model at Madame Tussaud's museum; after all the Mahatma had been dead for over a quarter of a century by then. But even that sight moved me. That little brown man in a shawl, oversized nappy and carrying a stick – positioned among those gray men in gray suits or military uniforms, who were supposedly great world leaders – stood out. And needless to say, not just because of his dress. He was *Time* magazine's 'Man of the Year' in 1930 following his celebrated Salt March to the seaside village of Dandi to break the British salt laws and shake the foundations of the Empire. Seventy years later, he became runner up (to Albert Einstein) as *Time*'s 'Person of the Century'. He is one of the most recognised figures of recent history and has come to be seen not just as saintly politician and the 'Father of the Nation' of the world's largest democracy, but as the architect of mass nonviolent struggle and as the iconic godfather of things related to peace in general.

If I was moved by seeing a wax reproduction, how much stronger must the experience have been for those who met Gandhi in flesh and blood at the peak of his fame? The accounts presented here will show that for some of them the experience was profound and even life-altering.

On first meetings and first impressions

After a day or two of being in even the most beautiful of places, we tend to become complacent about our surroundings. First impressions, so the saying goes, are often lasting impressions. While with people, first impressions regularly prove to be totally misplaced, they are, at that time, real and raw, unshaped by later rationalisations. And, moreover, first impressions are often surprisingly accurate. In some cases, especially where there has been powerful anticipation, the impact of a first meeting can be overwhelming (as seems to have been the case with Madeleine Slade – Mirabehn, and Lanza del Vasto – Shantidas). Very often, those meeting Gandhi did not take long to comment that what you saw was what you got. Gandhi, it seems, was a well-integrated person who did not play games with those who sought him out (except to show very human and welcoming humour). Indeed, what his visitors saw *was* what they got. The first impressions were generally lasting.

Psychologists point out that we have an inbuilt bias to conflate the beautiful with the good. Many of Gandhi's first-time visitors (for example Nilla Cram Cook) mentioned that he was quite ugly to look at, but he was not a stranger with whom they locked eyes in a crowded room. People sought him out and these were not chance encounters. There were expectations, but still there do seem to be many cases of 'love at first sight' in the accounts. The lack of beauty certainly did not signal a lack of good. Several of those who sought his presence went on to dedicate themselves to the Mahatma and his cause after the first meeting. In essence, these first meetings with Gandhi took on life-changing attributes. For example, the impact of that first meeting on a group of young Bihari lawyers (including Rajendra Prasad) was truly life-altering. Many of them went on to be leading national activists, but one cannot help suspecting that if they had not met Gandhi at Champaran, most of them would have remained provincial attorneys. Prasad summed up these changes to the lives of the volunteers when he wrote:

> Most of us who joined Gandhiji in Champaran were lawyers and not one had joined him with the idea of giving up the profession. But when we started working in Champaran, our whole outlook changed. We found it impossible, once we had undertaken it, to go back to our avocation without completing the task at hand. Thus people who went there for a few days remained for months. When we had

> finished the work in Champaran, we returned home with new ideas, a new courage and a new programme. (Prasad, *Autobiography*, p.100)

While there is a large literature on the psychology of first meetings and impressions (often tendering advice for successful job interviews), I have no intention here of writing a scholarly introduction. This collection of first-hand writings on first meetings with Gandhi speaks for itself. It is merely a way to introduce Gandhi to a new audience and, because it presents the Mahatma in an unusual way, perhaps provide new insights for a more experienced audience.

When Gandhi was still an unknown young Indian in Rajkot, or a student in London, or even a lawyer in South Africa, who was there to write about him? Why would anyone record an everyday meeting? When he becomes famous, it is only natural for old memories to surface (and for the shadow of the current period to be cast backwards to contaminate those memories). Would T.S.S. Rajan have remembered the South African lawyer Mohandas Gandhi, who was a guest speaker at a London Indian students' dinner some forty years earlier, if that speaker did not go on to become *Mahatma* Gandhi? Many of us have shared houses during our student days, but how many of us would remember a first meeting with our house mates if nothing extraordinary had happened? For example, in Gandhi's case, fellow vegetarian, Doctor Joshua Oldfield shared rooms for a while with him in London and, first some forty and then sixty years later, tried to remember his friend. He comes up with little more than high praise for Gandhi's character and that he was a 'young, shy, diffident youth, slim and a little weakly'. (Oldfield, "My Friend Gandhi", p.187)

One of the first recorded meetings with Gandhi is that by Lionel Curtis, a young South African official who had to deal with the issues of immigration. He recalls that he met Gandhi the young Johannesburg attorney, the first Oriental he had come into contact with, around 1903. In his brief description, Gandhi 'was dressed in European clothes except for his Indian cap and gave me the impression of being an exceedingly able young lawyer. He started by trying to convince me of the good points in the character of his countrymen, their industry, frugality, their patience.' (Curtis, "Two Meetings", p.47) There is little texture here, no colourful story-telling.

Of course this book is not really about Gandhi at first sight. There are a great many accounts of seeing Gandhi giving a speech during a Congress session, having a glimpse of him as his train stopped at a railway station, or of taking his *darshan* while he was conducting a prayer meeting. But these more distant sightings, while they may tell us about their affects on the viewer, tell us little about the Mahatma. I have therefore restricted myself to including only actual first meetings which very often were in fact the first sightings. (I have cheated slightly in the case of Edgar Snow whose first encounter with Gandhi was very brief and superficial, unlike the second.) This allows those who were with Gandhi for the first time to describe not only their initial reactions, but also to describe the Mahatma, say something about his appearance and personality, and give an account of what was happening around him. All of the close to fifty accounts presented here are first-hand autobiographical accounts. There are many other accounts by third parties, but these have been excluded even where the reporter of the event assures the reader that he or she was told directly of the meeting. I simply had to draw the line somewhere.

THE WAGES OF HISTORY AND THE VICISSITUDES OF MEMORY

Memory is an interesting phenomenon. We selectively perceive what happens around us (far too much happens for us to take everything in) and then reconstruct this perception in accordance with our ideas of what is important at the present time. This is memory – a filtering process that has left us twice removed from the 'facts'. And, as legal officials who have to deal with evidence in legal cases know, time further corrodes memory (that is why police on the witness stand refer to their notes 'taken immediately after the incident'). Usually, the early accounts of meeting with Gandhi were written well after the event and well after he became famous. Then again, if Gandhi did not become famous, there would have been little reason to have written about the meeting at all.

This has led to some problems in making the selections for this book that details first-hand accounts of meetings. First, there is the already mentioned paucity of accounts written before Gandhi was well known. Secondly, the records of meetings that it is easy to get one's hands on are published records, and this means that those writing the accounts had enough personal clout to get their accounts into print. How many diary entries of the less well known must still be out there somewhere? Thirdly, it must be remembered that while there is a wide spread of accounts from most of Gandhi's life as a public figure, many of these published pen portraits were written years after the first meeting. And, of course, history does throw its shadow backwards, and has surely coloured the eventually published account. Although they are relatively few, I have tried, where possible, to include first glimpses that were written down soon after the event. However, most of the portraits are included in autobiographies which are generally written decades after the events they portray, or in collections brought out to commemorate some important date, such as the hundredth anniversary of Gandhi's birth.

To further potentially confuse this issue, as the lesser of evils, I have included the accounts of meetings strictly in the order in which they occurred, not in the order in which they were written (which in any case is probably not possible to determine for most of the accounts) or grouped around themes (spinning, silence days, prayers, interviews etc.). This of course presents certain problems alluded to above, but, unfortunately, they are unavoidable. Given this caveat, the primary function will be to illustrate how the meetings with Gandhi differed as his fame increased. At least in this order of presentation, the historical back story is chronologically rational. If only the protagonists had written about their first meeting with Gandhi immediately after it, and then published the unamended account soon thereafter, the problem of later knowledge shaping the narrative would not have been present.

WHO MET WHOM?

Early on, before Gandhi became anyone with whom a meeting would have been considered noteworthy enough to record, Gandhi himself, as junior partner in the encounter, was recording his own meetings with notables (e.g. Emily Hobhouse, Olive Schriener, Annie Besant, and Gopal Krishna Gokhale). For example, when he met Gokhale and Bal Gangadhar Tilak in Poona on 12 October 1896, while he was temporarily in India during his South Africa days, it was for Gandhi to wax lyrical. Although he says little about the meeting with Tilak in his *Autobiography*, he records his meeting with Gokhale thus:

> Next I met Gokhale. I found him on the Fergusson College grounds. He gave me an affectionate welcome, and his manner immediately won my heart. With him too this was my first meeting, and yet it seemed as though we were renewing an old friendship. Sir Pherozeshah [Mehta] had seemed to me like the Himalayas, the Lokamanya [Tilak] like the ocean. But Gokhale was the Ganges. One could have a refreshing bath in the holy river. The Himalaya was unscaleable, and one could not easily launch forth on the sea, but the Ganges invited one to its bosom. It was a joy to be on it with a boat and an oar. Gokhale closely examined me, as a schoolmaster would examine a candidate seeking admission to a school. He told me whom to approach and how to approach them. He asked to have a look at my speech. He showed me over the college, assured me that it was always at my disposal, asked me to let him know the result of my interview with Dr. Bhandarkar, and sent me away exultantly happy. In the sphere of politics the place that Gokhale occupied in my heart during his lifetime and occupies even now was and is absolutely unique. (pp.128-129)

As indicated above, the relatively young Gandhi spoke in hagiographical terms about his meetings with some of his heroes, as later many who met him would do. For example, in 1921, looking back to an earlier time in his life, he commented that:

> Discipleship, however, is a sacred personal matter. I fell at Dadabhai [Naoroji]'s feet in 1888 [while studying in London] but he seemed

to be too far away from me. I could be as a son to him, not disciple. A disciple is more than son. Discipleship is a second birth. It is a voluntary surrender. In 1896 I met almost all the known leaders of India in connection with my South African mission. Justice Ranade awed me. I could hardly talk in his presence. Badruddin Taiyabji fathered me, and asked me to be guided by Ranade and Pherozeshah. The latter became a patron. His will had to be law. [...] The lion of Bombay taught me to take orders. He did not make me his disciple. He did not even try.

I went thence to Poona. I was an utter stranger. My host first took me to Mr. Tilak. I met him surrounded by his companions. He listened, and said, 'We must arrange a meeting for you. But perhaps you do not know that we have unfortunately two parties. You must give us a non-party man as chairman. Will you see Dr. Bhandarkar?' I consented and retired. I have no firm impression of Mr. Tilak, except to recall that he shook off my nervousness by his affectionate familiarity. I went thence, I think, to Gokhale, and then to Dr. Bhandarkar. The latter greeted me, as a teacher his pupil.

'You seem to be an earnest and enthusiastic young man. Many people do not come to see me at this the hottest part of the day. I never nowadays attend public meetings. But you have recited such a pathetic story that I must make an exception in your favour.'

I worshipped the venerable doctor with his wise face. But I could not find for him a place on that little throne. It was still unoccupied. I had many heroes, but no king.

It was different with Gokhale, I cannot say why. I met him at his quarters on the [Fergusson] college ground. It was like meeting an old friend, or, better still, a mother after a long separation. His gentle face put me at ease in a moment. His minute inquiries about myself and my doings in South Africa at once enshrined him in my heart. And as I parted from him, I said to myself, 'You are my man'. (Gandhi, "A Confession of Faith")

It seems that he remembered the way he was treated by Gokhale; it is almost a template for how he established ease with his interlocutors at first meeting.

Interestingly, but perhaps not unexpectedly, some of those who were later to become his closest political co-workers had surprisingly little to say about what should have been their recorded historic first meetings. Nehru comes to mind. One would expect that a description of the Gandhi/Nehru first encounter would be well known in Indian history and feature prominently in a collection such as this one. Of course, Gandhi appears in Nehru's writings, but Nehru does not write the way that Gandhi's disciples do. He was Gandhi's closest political lieutenant, then co-worker and finally heir. However, he wrote surprisingly little about his first meeting with the Mahatma. At one place he merely tells his reader that 'My first meeting with Gandhiji was about the time of the Lucknow Congress during Christmas 1916. All of us admired him for his heroic fight in South Africa, but he seemed very distant and different and unpolitical to many of us young men.' (Nehru, *Mahatma Gandhi*, p.2), without further elaboration. In his conversations with Tibor Mende in 1955, Prime Minister Nehru talked briefly about being 'simply bowled over by Gandhi, straight off'. He 'worked as a kind of secretary to Gandhi'. Nehru further explains: 'I was searching for some method of action. And I did not agree with this business of throwing about bombs as some of our young men did. I thought it was silly. And now, he put forward a method of action. I jumped to it. I did not care for the consequences; I was enthusiastic.' (Mende, *Conversations*, pp.23-24) But there is never a single description of a first meeting, of circumstances or impressions. It is as though Gandhi was somehow always there.

Something similar is the case with Sardar Vallabhbhai Patel. He has a very interesting first sighting of Gandhi. However, it is recorded by others who were present, not by Patel himself. While Patel became Gandhi's right-hand man, he did not have long to live after the independence of India, and that time was taken up with the organisation of the new Indian state. There was no time for leisurely autobiography writing. Much to the pity, as the story of Patel's first encounter with Gandhi, as told by onlookers, is quite a colourful one. Patel was the leading lawyer of Ahmedabad, on the municipal council and a regular at the Gujarat Club. Gandhi had been in Ahmedabad for about a year and was slowly becoming noticed by the leading lights of the city.

There are several versions of the first encounter between the two. In one, the dapper, westernised, sardonic, chain-smoking lawyer was playing a game of bridge at the Club with G.V. Mavalankar (who was to become the first Speaker of the Lok Sabha of independent India) when Gandhi came to make a speech in the Club's hall. Mavalankar asked Patel if they should go over and hear what he had to say. Patel allegedly answered: 'who wants to listen to speeches? Let us have another round.' (Murti, *Sardar Patel*, p.110) Mavalankar noted that as an observer to the card game, he decided to go and listen to Gandhi. At this, Patel 'passed very sarcastic remarks, discouraging me from going [and] was very sceptical and critical about Gandhi's ideas and plans [and being] brutally blunt in expressing his view'. (Krishna, *Sardar Vallabhbhai Patel*, p.47)

In another version, in June 1916, Patel was playing cards with his friend Chimanlal Thakore when somebody invited them to listen to Gandhi talk about a national school. Patel continued his game, remarking that 'I have been told he comes from South Africa. Honestly I think he is a crank and, as you know, I have no use for such people.' (Ahluwalia, *Sardar Patel*, p.32)

Rajmohan Gandhi gives the most detailed version of this story: within a month of his return to India, Gandhi was being hailed as a Mahatma and Patel's response was that 'We already have too many Mahatmas'. Some members of the Club visited Gandhi's recently established ashram and brought back news of Gandhi's faith in nonviolence to secure India's freedom, as well as news that he wanted educated Indians to grind their own grain and to clean latrines. Patel was less than complimentary, ridiculing 'the crank' and passing sarcastic comments about Gandhi's 'brilliant ideas'. (Gandhi, *Patel*, pp.36-37) When Gandhi was invited to visit the Club, Patel resented the movement of people past his bridge table as they gravitated towards the lawn where the Mahatma was speaking. When he saw Gandhi coming, Mavalankar got up from his seat. Patel asked where his friend was going, only to be informed that it was to see Gandhi. Patel answered: 'You'll learn more if you watch our game. I can tell you what he'll say. He will ask you if you know how to sift pebbles from wheat. And that is supposed to bring independence.' (Gandhi, *Patel*, p.37)

Eventually, Gandhi and Patel came into contact through their welfare work and while Gandhi was in Champaran, the crops of Gujarat's Kheda district were washed away by floods, yet the government maintained high land taxes. Patel visited the affected villages on a fact-finding mission. Exchanging his flashy European dress for dhoti and kurta, and, quitting the Gujarat Club, he toured the villages with Gandhi's message on non-cooperation with the authorities. The struggle cemented the relationship between Gandhi and Patel, and under the Mahatma's spell, the pompous lawyer became a pre-eminent fighter for the people in Gandhi's causes. (Weber, *Gandhi as Disciple*, pp.145-148)

Several of the other heavyweights of the Indian national movement, for example Annie Besant, Mohammed Ali Jinnah, B.R. Ambedkar, and Jayaprakash Narayan say nothing, or at least nothing much, about their first meeting with Gandhi and even some of his closest friends and confidants seem not to have marked the occasion by a serious application of pen to paper. Often, there is little more than a Nehruvian in passing 'I first saw Gandhiji at the so and so Congress' and later we learn how they worked with the Mahatma. Surprisingly, we get little from his secretaries Mahadev Desai and Pyarelal, from his backers Jamnalal Bajaj and G.D. Birla, or from his close friends such as Rabindranath Tagore (although many of his students wrote about Gandhi's arrival at Shantiniketan) or Kaka Kalelkar.

Meeting the Mahatma

This of course does not mean that only those of less historical consequence recorded their first meetings. The following accounts contain the recollections of Sarojini Naidu, J.B. Kripalani, Rajkumari Amrit Kaur, Rajendra Prasad, and Lord Louis Mountbatten. There are many others also: South African colleagues such as Henry and Millie Graham Polak; celebrities such as Charlie Chaplin, Pramahansa Yogananda, Margaret Sanger, and Margaret Bourke-White; some of his closest devotees such as Vinoba Bhave, Mirabehn, and J.C. Kumarappa; religious figures such as Joseph Doke, E. Stanley Jones, and John Haynes Holmes; internationally renowned (or budding) writers and journalists such as Webb Miller, Louis Fischer, Vincent Sheean, Halide Edib, Negley Farson, Yone Noguchi, Katherine Mayo, Edgar Snow, and William Shirer; and well-known pacifists such as Romain Rolland, Muriel Lester, Lanza del Vasto, Horace Alexander, and Reginald Reynolds; politicians such as Fenner Brockway and R.G. Casey; and an assortment of others who captured their first sighting of Gandhi in memorable prose in a way that added to our knowledge of the Mahatma. And the 'flavour' of the memorable prose of the journalists was quite different from that of the religious seekers or the merely curious.

One of the interesting details that seem to come out of the collection of first-hand accounts of first meetings with Gandhi is the number of them that occur on his day of silence. We have to assume that the supplicants were not just unlucky, pulling the short straw out of seven. In his later life, Gandhi was an extremely busy person whose time was rationed. Those who knew him at all well knew that Mondays were his days of silence and so would not request interviews on that day. Novices, one presumes, put in their requests for some time with the Mahatma to whoever was present from Gandhi's secretariat. More than likely, they would not feel that they were in a position to request certain times and presumably would have been delighted to have some time in the near future locked in for an interview with the Mahatma. One can only wonder if Mahadev Desai or Pyarelal warned them of the periods of silence, or merely had a small inward laugh as they gave them the next available (Monday) time.

It would not be an unreasonable assumption to think that most people who met Mahatma (as opposed to Mohandas) Gandhi recorded it somewhere. There are probably attics all over the world with boxes of personal paper, including diaries, which are gathering dust even though they record some remarkable events, even meetings with the Mahatma.

Reporters who interviewed Gandhi of course wrote about their experience for publication. Politicians, especially those Indian ones who were involved in the freedom movement, or British ones who fought against the tide, commonly wrote memoirs mentioning their relationship with Gandhi. In fact there is no shortage of material detailing meetings with the Mahatma. Celebrities who met Gandhi often went on to pen autobiographies where the event is recounted. Those known to have had a personal association with Gandhi were frequently asked to provide essays for various commemorative volumes. In short, the problem is more one of selection than of finding sufficient usable material in the first place. Here I have restricted myself to first-hand accounts of first meetings rather than merely biographical ones. But even this category can be too broad. A great many people, who were not well known or important in Indian political history, who were not literarily overly proficient, or who simply had nothing new to say, could have been included here. However, that would have given us more brief stories that went along the lines of: 'I entered the room and saw a dark semi-naked figure sitting on the floor plying a spinning wheel. He had a shaven head, large ears, a beak-like nose and protruding lower lip. He could not have been called handsome. Then he looked up at me and smiled. Everything suddenly changed. His beauty shone through. And (if it was not his day of silence) he said, "So, you have come", and beckoned me to sit by him.' This is then frequently followed by a record of a conversation. Many of these simply had to fall by the wayside. Nevertheless, some that did little more than this have been included because the accounts were those of significant people or were representative of a period in time.

WHAT IS LEFT

The accounts of first meetings presented here vary in length. While some writers put down their reminiscences in greater detail than others, occasionally I have used editorial discretion to shorten the passages. At times the writers slipped into a discourse on Gandhian philosophy or a history of Gandhi's political activities in the midst of the meeting story and, in these cases where necessary, I made cuts in order to keep the human drama alive.

The desire to provide a spread of first meetings over as large a period of Gandhi's life as could be covered by representative accounts could not always be fulfilled. For the early Gandhi, obviously, there simply are no accounts. Family members may describe other family members, but records of first meetings are not the usual way of doing this. However, even for later periods of the Gandhi saga, the accounts are still bunched together at certain times and missing from others. The years he was in prison saw a drop off in the numbers. There are seven first meetings for the year 1931. Although this is a large amount, still others could have been included. Gandhi's trip to London, and then the Continent on the way home, opened him up to a spate of new visitors. Many of these people (for example Charlie Chaplin) were celebrities in their own right and many told interesting stories of the meeting. I simply did not feel that I could drop more of these. There were periods when Gandhi was serving lengthy prison terms, for example almost all of 1922 and 1923, most of 1932 until the middle of 1933, and from late 1942 until mid-1944, when he had relatively few visitors and those that were allowed to visit him were generally old colleagues and friends, not first-time *darshan* seekers.

Someone who met Gandhi in the early South African days (such as the Polaks and Doke) met an impressive youngish local political activist. Many of those who came after reading Romain Rolland's book left a spiritually disillusioned Europe following the slaughter of the First World War seeking new spiritual guidance or even a master. Those who met Gandhi after his Empire-shaking Salt March and Civil Disobedience campaign were meeting perhaps the most famous person on the planet. Their experiences had to be different. Hopefully in the accounts reproduced here there are more than vague clues to how something of the change in Gandhi's recognition and fame affected the meetings, while the circumstances of the meetings themselves often illustrate this change. As one reads the following accounts, given the limitations described above, it may be valuable to look for what changes and what remains constant in Gandhi.

The stories presented in this book are the very best of that writing in English that I have managed to uncover. (However, it should be remembered that an equally impressive collection could be compiled from either Hindi or Gujarati writings, and that there are also collections of unpublished sources, such as the Oral History Transcript series at the Nehru Memorial Museum and Library, Teen Murti, that cover accounts of first meetings with Gandhi.)

Each of the accounts presented here starts with a brief introduction to the person whose first meeting with Gandhi is being reproduced. This is followed by the autobiographical account of the meeting (with a reference to the source). After each account I have provided a postscript where I have added further information. This could be a different account of the meeting, an even more interesting second meeting, something about the context in which the meeting occurred, or the significance of the meeting. Each account finishes with a list of suggested further readings that may give an insight into the life of the non-Gandhi protagonist, for example additional biographies or autobiographies, or sources about the themes raised in the meetings.

As a last word, I would like to thank Priya Kapoor of Roli Books for suggesting the project to me and Neelam Narula for shepherding the book so expertly through the publication process; Lisa Donnelly from La Trobe University's Borchardt Library for helping me track down obscure sources with such efficiency and good humour; Marja Koskela and Delene Hutchins for proofreading the manuscript; Charles DiSalvo for making several valuable suggestions (not least about the conclusion); Shashi Joshi, who while working on a similar project, was encouraging and generous with advice; and Dennis Dalton, Rajmohan Gandhi and Tridip Surhud for their kind words about the book.

References:

Ahluwalia, B.K., *Sardar Patel: A Life*, New Delhi: Sagar, 1974.

Curtis, Lionel, "Two Meetings with Gandhi", in S. Radhakrishnan (ed.), *Mahatma Gandhi: Essays and Reflections on His Life and Work*, Bombay: Jaico, 1956, pp.47-48.

Gandhi, M.K., *An Autobiography or The Story of My Experiments with Truth,* Ahmedabad: Navajivan, 1940.

Gandhi, M.K., "A Confession of Faith", *Young India,* 13 July 1921.

Gandhi, Rajmohan, *Patel: A Life,* Ahmedabad: Navajivan, 1991.

Krishna, B., *Sardar Vallabhbhai Patel: India's Iron Man,* New Delhi: HarperCollins, 1996.

Murthi, R.K., *Sardar Patel: The Man and His Contemporaries,* New Delhi: Stirling, 1976.

Nehru, Jawaharlal, *Mahatma Gandhi,* New York: Asia Publishing House, 1949.

Mende, Tibor, *Conversations with Mr. Nehru,* London: Secker & Warburg. 1956.

Oldfield, Joshua, "Gandhi as I Knew Him", *John O'London's Weekly,* 29 March 1930, pp.1000-1004. Reprinted in Joseph John (ed.), *Gandhi as Others See Him,* Colombo: Bastian, 1930, pp.16-24.

Oldfield, Joshua, "My Friend Gandhi", in Chandrashanker Shukla (ed.), *Reminiscences of Gandhiji: By Fortyeight Contributors,* Bombay: Vora, 1951, pp.187-189.

Prasad, Rajendra, *Autobiography,* Bombay: National Book Trust, 1957.

Weber, Thomas, *Gandhi as Disciple and Mentor,* New Delhi: Cambridge University Press, 2004.

1904

HENRY S.L. POLAK

Henry Salomon Leon Polak was born into a Jewish family in Dover in 1882. He was educated in London and Switzerland (where he studied the works of Tolstoy) and became the Assistant Secretary of the Society of Chemical Industries in London. For reasons of health, he went to South Africa in 1903 with an uncle who was in the chemical business. Around this time, before the start of his satyagraha campaign for the rights of South African Indians, Gandhi was already a successful lawyer and lobbyist. In 1904, the thirty-five-year-old Gandhi met fellow 'New Age' vegetarian Theosophist, and reporter for the *Transvaal Critic,* the twenty-two-year-old Henry Polak. Polak gave Gandhi a copy of John Ruskin's book *Unto This Last* which led to the founding of Gandhi's first ashram: The Phoenix Settlement (to which, according to Gandhi, Polak took to 'like a duck takes to water'.) Polak took over the editorship of Gandhi's paper *Indian Opinion* in 1906 while Gandhi was visiting England. He became a full-fledged attorney-at-law in 1908 after completing his articles with Gandhi. He was arrested after the Gandhi-organised 'Great March' into the Transvaal in 1913. After 1915, Gandhi resided in India and Polak, as a journalist and lawyer, in England. However, their friendship remained until Gandhi's death. Henry Polak died in 1957.

Not long before I first met Gandhiji, in Johannesburg in 1904, I had joined the editorial staff of the *Transvaal Critic*. Until then I had no knowledge of the existence in South Africa of an important Indian community. I had come to learn of it from reading, among the exchange papers that came to me, *Indian Opinion* (then published in English, Gujarati, Hindi, and Tamil) which, I later came to know, Gandhiji had financed and which was largely under his control, though he never edited it. From it I gathered some valuable information concerning Indian culture, history, and political affairs. Moreover, I discovered mainly from this interesting source that there was a local Indian problem, and that the Indian community was complaining loudly of the many disabilities imposed upon it. Its leader and spokesman was Gandhiji, who had just come prominently before the Johannesburg public once more because of his outspoken criticism, in a newspaper controversy with the Medical Officer of Health, of the Johannesburg Municipality of its serious neglect of the Indian Location of the city, where the Indians were segregated, resulting in a bad outbreak of plague. This he had ascribed to the denial to his countrymen of the municipal vote, despite their payment of rates and taxes in common with the white population. I thought that he had the better of the argument, and, as a faithful journalist, I wanted to see him and to find out more of the Indian community and its needs.

My desire was increased when he was pointed out to me one day by a friend as we entered a vegetarian restaurant shortly after my conversion to a non-flesh diet by the great Russian, Tolstoy. He was a pleasant-looking man, sitting alone. Apart from his black, lawyer's turban and his rather dark complexion, there was nothing specially to mark him out. I could not guess that I was then gazing at the man who was to become the best-known Oriental of his time.

A few days later, I mentioned my desire to meet this interesting personality to the proprietress of another vegetarian restaurant which I frequented. It was my lucky day. She responded immediately. 'That's easy,' she said; 'come by my "at home" tomorrow night. He always comes, and I will introduce you to him.' So we met, and the meeting changed the current of both our lives. I did not then know, as I came to know later when I had become closely associated with him, that, being himself an ardent vegetarian Gandhiji had largely helped to finance these two restaurant-keepers, and when subsequently they failed in business, he lost heavily thereby.

Strangely enough, my real card of introduction to him was not that of a journalist, but because I was almost the only other person he had met who had read a book on the subject of nature-cure of disease by one Adolf Just, entitled *Return to Nature*. Upon learning this, he welcomed me with open arms, and we had a long talk on this and cognate subjects. He was interested in my vegetarianism and was delighted to learn that, like himself, I was an ardent admirer of Tolstoy. 'I have a shelf full of his books at my office. Come and look at them,' he said. I took the opportunity of his cordial invitation to ask for an early appointment, in order to learn from him more of the Indian question and of India, and to make a certain suggestion that I had been turning over in my mind for some time.

Gandhi was then practising as an attorney (solicitor) of the Transvaal High Court. Though a barrister of the Inner Temple, he had chosen a branch of legal practice which brought him into direct contact with the lay client. I had already heard that he was held in high esteem by his fellow-lawyers and with respect by the Courts before whom he practiced. Later I came to know that he would never sue a client for his unpaid fees or take a case involving appearing in Court without first warning the client that he reserved the right to return the 'brief' if he should find that the client had been deceiving him. He held strongly that, as an officer of the Court, which had confidence in him, he could be no willing party to deception. [...]

At the time of our first meeting, as his family was still in India, he was living in a modest room behind his chambers in Rissik Street. A little later, and when he had settled down with the family as a small householder, he offered me its use, which helped to bring me into closer contact with him.

The day of our appointment arrived, and he received me in his office. As I sat down, I drew a mental picture of my host's surroundings, a picture which presently became so familiar to me that it remains unblurred to this day. Above his desk I noticed a large and beautiful picture of Jesus Christ. This at once indicated to me where some, at least, of his sympathies lay. Though I knew already that he was a Hindu, I at once realised that he was very tolerant in his religious approach. On the political side of his interests, another wall held large portraits of Dadabhai Naoroji, Renade, and Gokhale – his political *guru*. If my memory does not deceive me, there was also a fine portrait of Tolstoy. In a small bookcase beside his chair were a number of volumes very familiar to me, but also some as yet unknown. There were the Bible, Arnold's *Song Celestial* (the *Bhagavadgita*), and an array of Tolstoy's works, many on non-violence. I also noticed a copy of *India: What Can it Teach Us?*, by Professor Max Muller, which I quickly borrowed.

Gandhiji welcomed me pleasantly and with what I presently came to recognise as traditional Indian courtesy. His manner at first was quiet and restrained. As he told me something of the background of the South African Indian question, however, he warmed up. His voice took on a more serious tone when he described some of the hardships and disabilities under which his countrymen lived in this land of their exile. He told me how by their labour, originating in the evil indentured labour emigration system, and by their varied enterprise during nearly half a century, they had helped actively in the country's development and had saved Natal from economic ruin. [...]

Gandhiji, in those early days had a curious hesitation in rapid speech, which took the form of a slightly sibilant in drawing of the breath, as he sought for the right expression. Later, when I had come to know him well enough to do so, I drew his attention to this, and I suggested that it would be useful to correct it in public speech so as not to distract attention from his argument. He promptly took the matter in hand, and the peculiarity soon disappeared.

Throughout our conversation, I never heard him utter one angry word or make an attack upon any individual, though several anti-Indian personalities were mentioned between us. I soon learnt that he had no animus against individuals and that, though he could be indignant at injurious action or policy, he was always objective and impersonal in his exposition of its background. To him the Indian question was a human problem, like so many others, and I heard no hint in his tone or language, either then or later, of any bitterness at the many affronts that had been put upon himself because of his race and colour. His philosophic self-control aroused great admiration and respect among the few Europeans who knew him well as a man. It was never difficult to get close to him, for he was of a simple, friendly, and informal nature. But his mind worked with a political astuteness and a metaphysical subtlety which often baffled even his closest associates.

I had already told him that, even before going to South Africa, I had been attracted to Indian culture and philosophy by some books that I had bought at a second-hand book-shop in London. I mentioned some of them that I had brought with me overseas – Dutt's summaries of the *Mahabharata* and the *Ramayana* and Arnold's *Light of Asia* among them – and he had been delighted to hear this. He now showed me many more works along the same lines of thought.

I informed him that I had lately become deeply interested in Indian political problems, both in the Motherland and in South Africa, as I had seen them discussed in *Indian Opinion*. I told him that I had strongly differed from my own paper's policy on the Indian question, and that I had taken up the matter with my editor who, after listening to my objections, had generously informed me that I need not write in support of the paper's policy on racial and colour questions. Gandhiji beamed as I told him this, and congratulated me warmly upon my independent stand. I also told him that I had agreed with his side of the published correspondences with the Medical Officer of Health on the causes of the spread of the plague outbreak. He then told me many details which had not appeared in the press; but never a word did he utter of the great risks which he had personally taken in nursing plague-patients – of which I learnt indirectly only later – though he had much to say on the self-sacrificing service of others of his countrymen.

Having by now reached the stage of mutual understanding, I felt the time had come to offer him my services as a writer for *Indian Opinion*, though at the same time I had no intention of giving up my regular job on the *Critic*. He said that, if I were willing to do so without remuneration, which his paper could not afford, my contributions would be very welcome. As no thought of payment had entered my mind, I told him that I should be proud to do something to help to make the South African Indian question better understood among my own countrymen, both here and in England, with which I had professional contacts, as well as through the recognised organ of the Indian community. So began an editorial association with the paper which lasted till I left South Africa twelve years later.

From: H.S.L. Polak, "Some South African Reminiscences", in Chandrashanker Shukla (ed.), *Incidents of Gandhiji's Life, by Fifty-Four Contributors*, Bombay: Vora, 1949, pp.230-247 at 230-235.

POSTSCRIPT:

Gandhi remembered the meeting a little differently. It occurred in the restaurant where Polak sent Gandhi his card and expressed a desire to talk to him. He was invited to join Gandhi at his table. The young journalist wanted to talk to the Indian community leader about the plague. Gandhi later recalled that he was quick to sum up his new young friend:

> Mr. Polak's candour drew me to him. The same evening we got to know each other. We seemed to hold closely similar views on the essential things of life. He liked simple life. He had a wonderful faculty of translating into practice anything that appealed to his intellect. Some of the changes that he had made in his life were as prompt as they were radical. (Gandhi, *Autobiography*, p.219)

This clearly indicates that the process of recognition went both ways. It was not only Polak who saw something of great value in Gandhi. Gandhi also recognised his own strong desire to befriend Polak. Just over a dozen years after their first meeting, Gandhi related the event to his secretary Mahadev Desai, and explained how he managed to 'capture' Polak:

> I can judge people in a very short time. I judged Polak within five hours. He read my letter published in a newspaper and wrote me a letter. He then came to see me and I at once saw what he was, and since then he became my man. He married and started his practice as a pleader only after he joined me. He told me before marriage that he must earn a little for his children. I told him plainly, 'You are mine and the responsibility to provide for you and your children

is mine, not yours. I am getting you married, as I see no objection to your marrying.' His marriage was celebrated at my residence. (Gandhi, "Talk with Mahadev Desai", 31 August 1917)

FURTHER READING:

Gandhi, M.K., *An Autobiography or The Story of My Experiments with Truth*, Ahmedabad: Navajivan, 1940.

Gandhi, M.K., *Satyagraha in South Africa*, Madras: Ganesan, 1928.

Polak, H.S.L., H.N. Brailsford and Lord Pethick-Lawrence, *Mahatma Gandhi*, London: Odhams Press, 1949.

Weber, Thomas, *Gandhi as Disciple and Mentor*, New Delhi: Cambridge University Press, 2004.

West, Albert, "In the Early Days with Gandhi", *The Illustrated Weekly of India* (1965), vol.86, no.40, pp.30-31, 33.

1905 MILLIE GRAHAM POLAK

Gandhi's best friend and assistant, Henry Polak was engaged to Millie Graham Downs, whom he had met at the London Ethical Society, before going to South Africa. Millie was a Scottish Christian who had no concerns about marrying the Jewish Henry. Gandhi assured Millie's worried family that she would be well looked after if she joined Henry. Millie and Henry married at the end of 1905 with Gandhi serving as best man. Through her book *Mr. Gandhi: The Man,* Millie gives us a very personal glimpse into the life of the South African Gandhi. Millie was certainly not overawed by, the not yet Mahatma, Mohandas Gandhi. She often disagreed with him fearlessly, but it did not dent their relationship, instead she fulfilled the role of a loving but challenging sister. Following Gandhi's return to India and their return to London, the Polaks kept up a correspondence with Gandhi until his death. He always signed his letters to them as Bhai (brother), rather than Bapu (father).

Two or three other friendly letters passed between us, and then, at six o'clock on the morning of December 30, 1905, I arrived at Jeppe Station, Johannesburg, and I found Mr. Gandhi and Mr. Polak waiting on the platform for me.

My first impression of Mr. Gandhi was of a medium-sized man, rather slenderly built, skin not very dark, mouth rather heavy lipped, a small dark moustache, and the kindest eyes in the world, that seemed to light up from within when he spoke. His eyes were always his most remarkable feature and were in reality the lamps of his soul; one could read so much in them. His voice was soft, rather than musical, and almost boyishly fresh. I particularly noticed this as we chatted of the little things of my journey and proceeded to his home.

The house was situated in a fairly good middle-class neighbourhood, on the outskirts of the town. It was a double-storied, detached, eight-roomed building of the modern villa type, surrounded by a garden, and having, in front, the open spaces of the kopjes. The upstairs verandah was roomy enough to sleep on it, if one wished to do so, and, indeed, in the warm weather, it was often so used.

The household, I learned, consisted of Mr. Gandhi, his wife and three sons, Manilal, aged eleven, Ramdas, aged nine, and Devdas, aged six, a young Englishman engaged in the telegraph service, a young Indian ward of Mr. Gandhi's, and Mr. Polak. My addition to the family completed its possibilities of accommodation.

From: Millie Graham Polak, *Mr. Gandhi: The Man*, London: Allen & Unwin, 1931, pp.18-19.

Postscript:

From the first, it was obvious that Millie Graham was going to be the type of woman Gandhi approved of: she married Henry immediately after her arrival in South Africa without even the necessity of 'a special dress' or religious rites – their 'common religion' being 'the religion of ethics'. Having a 'coloured' person as best man, combined with Polak's habit of referring to himself and friends as 'we Indians', meant that the ceremony at the registry office had to be delayed, 'pending inquiries', to ensure that it was not a mixed marriage. Gandhi had to intervene and obtain a note from the Chief Magistrate to clear up the 'amusing incident'. (Gandhi, *An Autobiography*, p.227)

Further Reading:

Gandhi, M.K., *An Autobiography or The Story of My Experiments With Truth,* Ahmedabad: Navajivan, 1940.

Polak, Millie Graham, "Gandhi and Women", in Chandrashanker Shukla (ed.), *Gandhiji as We Know Him, by Seventeen Contributors,* Bombay: Vora, 1945, pp.47-51.

Polak, Millie Graham, "In the South African Days", in Chandrashanker Shukla (ed.), *Incidents of Gandhiji's Life, by Fifty-Four Contributors,* Bombay: Vora, 1949, 247-251.

Watson, Francis, and Hallam Tennyson, *Talking of Gandhi,* New Delhi: Sangam, 1976.

Weber, Thomas, *Going Native: Gandhi's Relationship with Western Women,* New Delhi: Roli Books, 2011.

1907

JOSEPH J. DOKE

The English Baptist minister, Joseph J. Doke made the acquaintance of the young barrister Mohandas Gandhi in mid-1907 following his interest in Gandhi's 'passive resistance' movement against the discrimination suffered by South African Indians. Six months later, following a vicious assault on Gandhi by an enraged Pathan who thought that Gandhi had given in to the authorities, he convalesced at the Doke household where the daughter, Olive, sang *Lead, Kindly Light* to him. (It was to become one of Gandhi's favourite hymns.) In 1909, Doke wrote the landmark first biography of Gandhi. While the strength of the biography stems from the author's intimate relationship with his subject, it also gives us a picture of how Gandhi wanted to present himself. It seems that Gandhi more or less dictated the book to the writer, and it was Gandhi who arranged for its publication. Immediately after the book had appeared, Gandhi sent a copy to the great Russian author and pacifist, Leo Tolstoy, who commented that Doke's work gripped him and gave him a chance to know and better understand Gandhi.

It was late in December, 1907, when I saw Mr. Gandhi for the first time. Rumour had been very busy with his name. The Passive Resistance movement had come into prominence. Some small stir had been made in the newspapers by the imprisonment of a Pundit, and in one way or another, Mr. Gandhi's name had been bandied from lip to lip. One evening, a friend raised the Asiatic Question at the supper-table, and as we were comparatively new to Johannesburg, although not new to the country, he told us what he thought of the Indians. His account was so strange and so completely opposed to all our previous experience, that it made us curious, and more than anything else decided me to interview the leader.

The office, at the corner of Rissik and Anderson Streets, I found to be like other offices. It was intended for work and not for show. The windows and door were adorned with the name of the occupant with the denomination of Attorney attached to it. The first room was given up to a lady-typist; the second, into which I was ushered, was the SANCTUM SANCTORUM. It was meagrely furnished and dusty. A few pictures were scattered along the walls. They were chiefly photographs of no great merit. The Indian Stretcher-bearer Corps was in evidence – photographs of Mrs. Besant, Sir William Wilson Hunter, and Justice Ranade – several separate Indian portraits – and a beautiful picture of Jesus Christ. Some indifferent chairs, and shelves filled with law books completed the inventory.

All of this I confess to have noted afterwards. Just then, my whole attention was centred in the man who greeted me, and in an effort to readjust my ideas to unexpected experiences. Having travelled in India, I had almost unconsciously selected some typical face and form as likely to confront me, probably a tall and stately figure, and a bold, masterful face, in harmony with the influence which he seemed to exert in Johannesburg. Perhaps a bearing haughty and aggressive. Instead of this, to my surprise, a small, lithe, spare figure stood before me, and a refined, earnest face looked into mine. The skin was dark, the eyes dark, but the smile which lighted up the face, and that direct fearless glance, simply took one's heart by storm. I judged him to be of some thirty-eight years of age, which proved to be correct. But the strain of his work showed its traces in the sprinkling of silver hairs on his head. He spoke English perfectly, and was evidently a man of great culture.

Asking me to be seated, he listened to an explanation of my visit, noting the points raised with a nod of the head, and a quick 'Yes', until I had done. Then he went straight to the mark. Using his fingers to emphasize his thoughts, he gave the most luminous statement of the Asiatic position, in a few crisp sentences, that I have ever heard. I was anxious to know what the religious elements in the struggle were, and he gave them with convincing clearness, explaining patiently every little involved issue, and satisfying himself that I understood each before dealing with the next. Once, when he paused longer than usual, to see whether I had grasped the thought or had only assented for the sake of courtesy, I closed my note-book, thinking he had finished. 'Don't close it,' he said, 'the chief point is yet to come.'

There was a quiet assured strength about him, a greatness of heart, a transparent honesty, that attracted me at once to the Indian leader. We parted friends.

From: Joseph J. Doke, *M.K. Gandhi: An Indian Patriot in South Africa*, Rajghat, Varanasi: Akhil Bharat Sarva Seva Sangh, 1956, pp.7-9.

POSTSCRIPT:

Interestingly, in his biography of the not yet Mahatma Gandhi, Doke notes that he 'is not a Christian in any orthodox sense', adding that

'Perhaps orthodox Christianity has itself to blame for this' because orthodox Christianity practised discrimination against Indians. (Doke, *M.K. Gandhi*, p.148) This refers back to the period of 1893, Gandhi's first year in South Africa. At this time, strenuous efforts had been made by nonconformist Christians to secure Gandhi's conversion. It seems that, at least for a short while, they may have come close as Gandhi toyed with the idea. With some humour, Gandhi reported that 'These people loved me so well, that if it would have influenced me to become a Christian, they would have become vegetarians themselves!' (Doke, *M.K. Gandhi*, p.58)

FURTHER READING:

Doke, Olive C., "Reminiscences of M.K. Gandhi", in Chandrashanker Shukla (ed.), *Incidents of Gandhiji's Life, by Fifty-Four Contributors*, Bombay: Vora, 1949, pp.42-46.

Mahadevan, T.K., *The Year of the Phoenix: Not a Novel*, New Delhi: Arnold-Heinemann, 1982.

Malhotra, S.L., "A Study of Gandhi's Biographies – Joseph J. Doke and Romain Rolland", *Gandhi Marg* (1985), vol.6, no.12, pp.845-861.

1909

T.S.S. RAJAN

T.S.S. Rajan was born in 1880 and following his medical studies in Madras moved to Burma to practice in Rangoon. In 1907 he went to London for higher qualifications. He obtained his M.R.C.S. degree in 1911 and, after a stint in Middlesex Hospital, returned to Burma. After several years of medical practice he went home to India and in 1914 he joined the Indian National Congress, becoming General Secretary in 1922. He set up his own clinic the following year. He was the Secretary of the Tamil Nadu Provincial Congress Committee for many years, and was imprisoned by the British in all three of Gandhi's national campaigns for freedom. He translated for Gandhi on the Mahatma's tours of Tamil Nadu and operated on Gandhi's son Devadas. In the mid-1930s he was a member of the Central Legislative Assembly and in the later 1930s, and again after independence, was a minister in the Madras Government (as Minister for Food and Public Health). He retired from public life in 1953 and died from complications following appendix surgery two years later.

Vanity is a part of human nature. We always like to exhibit ourselves to our best advantage, particularly when we happen to be on view. True greatness rarely exhibits itself in such a way. God's good man never seeks occasions to display his good nature. It is inherent in him. This was the lesson I learnt when I happened to meet Mahatma Gandhi, a plain Mr. Gandhi, South African barrister Gandhi if you like it, in about the year 1909 in London. I was merely a medical student – one of the many that flocked to the London University even in those days. I had no occasion to know or see Mr. Gandhi. Like many other young men, I felt I was intensely patriotic if I joined any movement, national in outlook, which had for its motive the freedom of India. To have the courage to talk of Indian freedom in those days was a great patriotic act, and I had a great veneration for those young men who talked loudly of revolution leading to freedom for India. A handful as we were, we became a dreaded lot in the Indian world that lived and moved about in London. Vinayak Damodar Savarkar was our chief, and the late V.V.S. Ayyar his lieutenant. We decided on bringing together all Indian students scattered about Great Britain just to remind ourselves of our national solidarity in an alien land. A search was made amongst the leading Indian front-rank politicians who had then congregated in London, to request them to preside and take part in the function. We had a categorical refusal from every one of them till at last it was left to Mr. Gandhi to agree to our request but with a condition.

The function consisted of a dinner and a post-dinner talk. Over one hundred and twenty five students agreed to partake in the subscription dinner, and it was to have been arranged in some hotel or restaurant in London. But the chief guest of the function, Mr. Gandhi, our last hope as a president, would not have anything of the kind, and insisted on a pukka vegetarian Indian dinner, to be managed in whichever way we thought best.

The condition was agreed to, and we straightway engaged a hall, bought provisions, and decided to cook various Indian dishes for the function. A part of us volunteered to do the cooking, and we entered on our duties in the underground cellar and kitchen of the building early in the day so that we might be ready to lay the table at 7.30 p.m. – our dinner time. At about 2 p.m. a small, thin, wiry man with a pleasant face joined us in work and was making himself very useful. He volunteered to do the washing of plates and cleaning of vegetables with such gusto and willingness that we were only too willing to give him the joy of his performance. Hours rolled on, and there was no abatement in the work turned out by this man. Later in the afternoon when Mr. Ayyar turned up in the kitchen, did we come to know that our unannounced worker was Mr. Gandhi, the great man of Indian South Africa, the president of our evening function. It took my breath away to see the great man of whom we had heard so much and to witness his utter humility and willingness to share with us the work we were engaged in. Our importunity in dissuading him from his services did not prevail, for he continued his work well on into the evening when he helped us to lay the tables and the plates, and serve the dinner we had prepared. At long last after strenuous work of hours did he consent to sit at the head of the table and preside over the function. At the beginning of his speech, a very simple and hesitant one, he told us how pleased he was to see us tuck up our sleeves and do the work in the way that we had done. He said he knew the difficult task we had undertaken, and was agreeably surprised to know that the Indian students in London, sons of well-to-do parents, did not consider it mean to serve their fellow-men in the way we had done, and that it augured well for the future of our land. He spoke of many other things besides, but I have forgotten them all now. What persists in my mind even at this distance of time is the picture of my first meeting the Mahatma in the underground kitchen cellar of a London restaurant. I have often been a prisoner in the jails of our country during the many occasions of the satyagraha struggle conducted by Gandhiji; and during all those occasions I have found myself voluntarily working in the kitchen. During our last internment, Rajaji [Chakravarti Rajagopalachari] made a casual remark about me, saying: 'Rajan, how is it that I find you gravitating to the kitchen whenever you happen to be imprisoned?' Has Gandhiji's example in the kitchen cellar in London got into my blood and stuck there? I do not know. But I do remember I found greatness in the Mahatma of the future years, long before the world knew of him.

From: T.S.S. Rajan, "Since My Student Days", in Chandrashanker Shukla (ed.), *Incidents of Gandhiji's Life, by Fifty-Four Contributors,* Bombay: Vora, 1949, pp.259-264 at 259-261.

POSTSCRIPT:

In 1939 Dr. Rajan visited Gandhi at Sevagram. It was Gandhi's day of silence and Rajan received a note which informed him that the silent day had become a health necessity for the Mahatma. This got doctor Rajan thinking about the physical health implications of silence. Later, he wrote to Gandhi's secretary to provide a record of Gandhi's personal experience as 'a piece of scientific information'. In particular he wanted to know if during Gandhi's periods of silence there was a visible drop in his blood pressure, whether he had an increase of energy afterwards, and whether he felt mentally more alert afterwards. He asked that if the answers to his questions were worthwhile, that they be published in Gandhi's weekly *Harijan.* Gandhi responded in his paper, pointing out that the periods of silence were no strain or effort for him, if fact he was so tired of arguing and talking that he was silent for most of the time making exception generally only for visitors with appointments or in cases of sickness. In answering the questions, Gandhi noted that there was a perceptible drop in his blood pressure during his periods of silence, that there was absolutely no doubt that he felt recuperated and had greater energy for work following periods of silence, in fact his output of work was much greater during his silence periods, that his mind enjoys peace during silence periods, that silence sooths him, that it lifts burdens off his mind and does so better than any drug can do and, in addition, it induces sleep. However, there was also a caution: 'I have noticed in the jails that prisoners get moody when, deprived of company, they have to observe enforced silence. To produce the effect I have described, silence has to be liked. No one, therefore, need be silent out of love of imitation or merely for the knowledge that it produces on me the effect described by me. The best thing would be to take silence on medical advice. Needless to say that here I do not refer to the spiritual need and effects of silence.' (M.K. Gandhi, "Virtues of Silence", *Harijan,* 28 October 1939.

FURTHER READING:

Rajan, T.S.S., *Ninaivu Alaigal [Autobiography]* (Tamil), Madras: Kalaimkal Karyalayam, 1947.

Rajan, T.S.S., *Tamil Nattil Gandhi* (Tamil), Madras: Kalaimkal Karyalayam, 1954.

1914

SAROJINI NAIDU

Known as 'The Nightingale of India', the poet, political activist and then politician, Sarojini Naidu was born to Bengali Brahmin parents in 1879 in Hyderabad. She studied in Madras, London and Cambridge, and married the doctor Govindarajulu Naidu in 1898. She published her first book of poetry (*The Golden Threshold*) in 1905 and became a feminist, social reformer and close confidant of Gandhi. In 1925 she was appointed as the first Indian female president of the Indian National Congress (a position held by Annie Besant eight years earlier). She toured the United States in the cause of Indian independence in 1928-1929 and was by Gandhi's side when he broke the salt laws following the celebrated Salt March to Dandi in 1930. After Gandhi's arrest, she led the first raid on the salt works at Dharasana. Naidu accompanied the Mahatma to London in 1931 for the second Round Table Conference on India's future and was imprisoned several times for her civil disobedience during India's freedom struggle. Her English-language poetry collections attracted a large English and Indian readership. After independence, in 1947 she became the first governor of the United Provinces (now Uttar Pradesh), a post she held until her death in 1949.

Curiously enough, my first meeting with Mahatma Gandhi took place in London on the eve of the great European War of 1914, when he arrived fresh from his triumphs in South Africa, where he had initiated his principle of passive resistance and won a victory for his countrymen, who were at that time chiefly indentured labourers, over the redoubtable General Smuts. I had not been able to meet his ship on his arrival, but the next afternoon I went wandering around in search of his lodging in an obscure part of Kensington and climbed the steep stairs of an old, unfashionable house, to find an open door framing a living picture of a little man with a shaven head, seated on the floor on a black prison blanket and eating a messy meal of squashed tomatoes and olive oil out of a wooden prison bowl. Around him were ranged some battered tins of parched groundnuts and tasteless biscuits of dried plantain flour. I burst instinctively into happy laughter at this amusing and unexpected vision of a famous leader, whose name had already become a household word in our country. He lifted his eyes and laughed back at me, saying: 'Ah, you must be Mrs. Naidu!' Who else dare be so irreverent? 'Come in,' he said, 'and share my meal.' 'No thanks,' I replied, sniffing; 'what an abominable mess it is!' In this way and at that instant commenced our friendship, which flowered into real comradeship, and bore fruit in a long, loving, loyal discipleship, which never wavered for a single hour through more than thirty years of common service in the cause of India's freedom.

From: "The Father of Modern India: An Appreciation by Her Excellency Sarojini Naidu", in H.S.L. Polak, H.N. Brailsford and Lord Pethick-Lawrence, *Mahatma Gandhi*, London: Odhams Press, 1949, pp.6-8, at p.7.

POSTSCRIPT:

The closeness between Gandhi and Sarojini Naidu, and the humour inherent in their relationship, is well illustrated by the way they addressed each other personally and in correspondence. In her letters, she wrote to the Mahatma 'from the Wandering Singer to the Spinner-Stay-At-home' and signed off letters with sentences such as 'salutations to the "Mystic Spinner" from the Wandering Singer.' Gandhi would reply with lines such as 'Lovingly yours, Matter-of-Fact (Not Mystic) Spinner.' In other places he addressed her as 'Dear Bulbul', 'Dear Old Singer', and 'Dear Sweet Singer', and signed his correspondence to her as 'Little Man' or 'Spinner.' Naidu jokingly was known to describe Gandhi as 'Mickey Mouse' and at one stage famously quipped, in response to the trouble that had to be taken for Gandhi to be able to travel in third-class train compartments, that it cost the nation a great deal to keep Gandhi in poverty!

FURTHER READING:

Ali Baig, T., *Sarojini Naidu*, New Delhi: Publications Division, Ministry of Information and Broadcasting, Government of Indian, 1974.

Naidu, Sarojini, *The Feather of the Dawn*, New York: Asia Publishing House, 1961.

Naidu, Sarojini, *The Sceptred Flute: Songs of India*, New York: Dodd, Mead & Co., 1928.

Naravane, V.S., *Sarojini Naidu: Her Life, Work and Poetry*, New Delhi: Orient Longman, 1980.

Paranjape, Makarand, R. (ed.), *Sarojini Naidu: Selected Letters 1890-1940s*, New Delhi: Kali for Women, 1996.

Paranjape, Makarand, R. (ed.), *Sarojini Naidu: Selected Poetry and Prose*, New Delhi: Rupa, 2010.

Rajyalakshmi, P.V., The *Lyric Spring: The Poetic Achievements of Sarojini Naidu*, New Delhi: Abhinav, 1977.

Sahukar, Nimeran, *Sarojini Naidu: The Nightingale of India*, New Delhi: Rupa, 2003.

Sengupta, Padmini, *Sarojini Naidu*, Bombay: Asia, 1966.

Weber, Thomas, *On the Salt March: The Historiography of Mahatma Gandhi's March to Dandi*, New Delhi: Rupa, 2009.

1915

J.B. KRIPALANI

Jivatram Bhagwandas Kripalani (born in 1888) was an academic at the Government College in Muzaffarpur when he visited Gandhi at Rabindranath Tagore's school, Shantiniketan, near Calcutta. Later he joined Gandhi in the Champaran Satyagraha campaign. For some years, he served as the principal of the Gujarat Vidyapith, an educational institution founded by Gandhi in Ahmedabad. From 1927 onwards, he dedicated his life to the Congress and constructive work. He was imprisoned in each of Gandhi's three major campaigns for independence. In 1946 he was elected president of the Congress, but following differences with other leading figures left to edit a weekly magazine, *Vigil*, and founding or working with various socialist parties. He served several terms as a Lok Sabha member and died in 1982.

Gandhiji finally left South Africa in the latter part of 1914. Before coming to India he went to England to meet Gokhale who was then there. He had sent before him such members of his two ashrams in South Africa, the Phoenix Settlement, and Tolstoy Farm, as had wanted to return to India. They had established themselves at Shantiniketan. Gandhiji was to go there and join them when he returned to India from England. As soon as I heard this, I wrote to Kaka Saheb Kalelkar, who was then known as Brahmachari Dattetreya and who was temporarily an inmate of Santiniketan, to inform me of the arrival of Gandhiji. I had visited Santiniketan a few times before and I had put my nephew Girdhari for his education there. As soon as I was informed in March 1915 that Gandhiji had reached the Poet's [Rabindranath Tagore] home I took a week's leave from the college and went there. I was then a professor at Muzaffarpur (Bihar). I had heard of Gandhiji in connection with his unique struggle in South Africa to safeguard the dwindling rights of his countrymen settled there.

The political condition of India was extremely depressing at the time. After the Surat split in the Congress, it was deprived of its active and radical elements. The Government had managed to rally the moderates or liberals, as they called themselves, to its side by the so-called Minto-Morley Reforms. The authorities had succeeded in suppressing the extremists or nationalists, as they were called, by its repressive policy. Tilak had been exiled to Mandalay for six years. Aurobindo had gone to Pondicherry to practice yoga, Lala Lajpatrai was in America. Bipin Chandra Pal had retired from active politics. The terrorist movement had been suppressed. The country was without any effective leadership. The Congress in the hands of the moderates was no longer a vital force.

For a young man like me, interested in the freedom of the country, there seemed no scope for any effective political work.

I wanted to see if Gandhiji's idea and method held any hope for organising the country for the freedom struggle. I had heard of his political faith. He of course did not believe that British rule in India was a matter of 'divine dispensation'. Yet he held with the moderates that British rule was on the whole for India's good. He believed that the British people would do the right thing by India whatever injustice might be perpetuated by the white bureaucracy here. In spite of this belief of Gandhiji and his declaration that Gokhale was his political guru, I wanted to meet him and judge for myself. There was also the curiosity to meet one who believed that politics could be given a moral basis. I was a student of history. Its heroes were all men of blood and iron. I had never read in history of a national struggle carried on non-violently.

Arriving at Santiniketan, I was taken straight to Gandhiji. It was evening. Gandhiji was sitting on a low platform, his unshod feet dangling down to the ground. He wore a shirt open at the neck and a dhoti. He was taking, as I learnt afterwards, his last meal of the day. He welcomed me with a broad smile and said that he was expecting me, having been informed by Dattetreya of my desire to meet him. I was to be his guest and not of the Poet. I readily accepted his hospitality and thanked him. I then observed the meal he was taking. It consisted of nuts. I had never seen a man of the upper class taking a meal of nuts. He seemed to be enjoying his food, masticating it slowly. There was nothing abstemious or ascetic about his food. He seemed to have a good appetite. He kept talking with me while eating.

On this first meeting all our talk was personal. There was no exchange of political views. I asked him about his programme. He said that from Santiniketan he had to go to Calcutta to fulfil an engagement. His first object then would be to find a suitable place for his ashram. He and his companions could not stay at Santiniketan indefinitely. As for his public activity, he said he would do nothing for one year but go around the country and study the situation, in accordance with the promise he had given to Gokhale.

We met off and on during my one week's stay there. He talked of his new technique of truth and non-violence for the redress of political wrongs. He related some of his experiences in South Africa. I made no secret of my own views on the subject. I was by now convinced that little could be accomplished through political murders. But I was sure that some day, somehow, the nation would have to use violence to achieve national independence. I could not say how violence would be possible for an unarmed nation! Perhaps the army might revolt or military help might come from outside, as had happened in some other countries. I also told him that I did not believe in the good intentions of 'Perfidious Albion', 'the nation of shopkeepers' as England was known on the Continent. Further, those very moderates, who had praised his methods and work in South Africa, would be the very persons who would denounce them when introduced in Indian politics. If he got any recruits for satyagraha, it would be from the camp of Tilak.

But more important than these talks was the way he roused the inmates of Santiniketan to see some shortcomings from which their institution suffered and the way they could be corrected. He was not satisfied with the hygiene of the place and its arrangements for the preparation of food in the general mess. He pointed out the defects to the teachers and the pupils and said that they would not improve these conditions if they relied on cooks and servants. They must cooperatively attend to the hygiene and cook their food themselves. He induced them to dispense with the services of the cooks and servants. His proposals were accepted and Santiniketan was soon buzzing with new life. This experiment, though it was soon abandoned, gave me an idea of Gandhiji's reforming zeal, his organising capacity and his powers of persuasion. To rouse the land of lotus-eaters, as Santiniketan was sometimes called, was not an easy task. But he did it in three or four days.

The general impression left on me by my first acquaintance with Gandhiji was that he was a man of integrity, putting his heart and soul into any work that he undertook. Also, when convinced of the rightness of a cause, he would try to give it effect, whatever be the difficulties in the way. He would not be affected by the favours of friends and the frowns of opponents. He could, if need be, walk alone – '*Akele chalo*'. He was sincere and serious. He was simple in his habits but not a puritan who would interfere with the legitimate enjoyments of others to convince himself of his superiority. He was also full of humour and laughter. He was a friend of the poor and was trying to live like them to the extent it was possible in India. Before I took leave of him, I told him that he could avail himself of my services in anything that he understood in the way of political work or work for the poor and downtrodden of India. I was a free man without any encumbrances.

This was my first meeting with Mr Gandhi – he had not yet become Mahatma.

From: J.B. Kripalani, "My First Meeting with Gandhiji", *The Illustrated Weekly of India* (1969), vol.90, no.22, p.17.

POSTSCRIPT:

Kripalani's next meeting with Gandhi was far more eventful. Almost three years later Gandhi was visiting Muzaffarpur in the Champaran district of Bihar to look into the grievances of the indigo planters. Kripalani was hostel warden at a local college at the time. The Mahatma telegrammed ahead that he was coming. News got out and the students decided not just to accompany Kripalani to receive the distinguished guest, but to give 'a fitting reception in the Indian style by performing an *arati*'. Flowers were collected and Kripalani climbed a coconut tree to obtain the necessary coconuts. When Gandhi was finally found among the crowds thronging the station, the *arati* was performed. Kripalani noted that 'the ceremony seemed to embarrass Gandhiji, perhaps because *arati* is performed before the gods. But in India he had to get used to it. The Hindus make little distinction between gods and their great men.' A carriage had been procured to take Gandhi to Kripalani's residence but the students had unhorsed it, determined to honour the Mahatma by pulling the carriage themselves. Gandhi protested and, refusing to enter the carriage if they pulled it, threatened to offer satyagraha if they persisted. Gandhi and Kripalani finally got into the closed carriage and fell into conversation. As they proceeded, Kripalani realised that he 'did not hear the sound of the hoofs of the horses. I understood that the students had not carried out Gandhiji's instructions. We arrived at the hostel. When Gandhiji got out of the carriage, he said he had been deceived. If he had known that the students were pulling the carriage, he would have got down and walked.' (Kripalani, *Gandhi*, p.60)

FURTHER READING:

Kripalani, J.B., *Gandhi: His Life and Thought*, New Delhi: Publications Division, Ministry of Information and Broadcasting, Government of India, 1970.

Kripalani, J.B., *My Times: An Autobiography*, New Delhi: Rupa, 2004.

Tandon, P.D., *Acharya J.B. Kripalani – A Symposium*, Bombay: Hind Kitabs, 1948.

1915

G.A. NATESAN

Ganapati Agraharam Annadhurai Ayyar Natesan was born 1873 in Thanjavur district in Madras Presidency. He was a writer, publisher, nationalist, and politician. After graduating from Presidency College, Madras, the twenty-one-year-old joined the *Madras Times* and in 1897 started his own publishing company. In 1900 he launched the English language monthly, the *Indian Review*, which covered economic, social, literary and nationalist issues. He raised funds for Gandhi's campaign in South Africa from as early as 1910 and assisted his countrymen who were deported back to India. Gandhi stayed at his home for three weeks during his tour of Madras soon after returning to settle in India. Natesan was the first to publish Gandhi's writings in India, including the first Indian edition of Gandhi's seminal work *Hind Swaraj*. Later he switched his allegiance from the Congress Party to the more pro-British Indian Liberal Party which opposed Gandhi's major campaigns for independence. He became joint secretary of the Liberal Party in 1922, but maintained his friendship with Gandhi till the end. He died three months after the Mahatma.

I came to know him personally only after his return to this country from South Africa in 1915. As Secretary of the Indian South African League in Madras, it was my privilege to be in frequent correspondence with him. [...]

He arrived in Madras one fine April evening accompanied by his wife. There, on the platform was a strong contingent of leading citizens waiting with garlands to welcome them, and a great cheering crowd had gathered outside the station, waiting for *darshan*. Gandhiji, in those days, was not so sparsely dressed as now. He was wearing his white homespun in true Gujarati fashion and his head was draped in a prodigious turban. The two alighted from a third-class compartment with a bundle of clothes as though they were no more than a family of poor peasants come to see the city from the interior. It was all so unlike what was expected of the hero of a hundred adventures in a far-away land.

It was my privilege to be his host. In spite of all that we had read of him, we had no precise idea of the utter simplicity of his way of life. With due care and many consultations and anxious thought for his comforts, I had furnished his apartments in my office premises in Esplanade with what seemed to me the minimum requisites of decent accommodation – two cots, a cushion-chair, a table and a desk. When I showed him his rooms, he stood gazing for a while and then burst into a loud laugh. He asked for the removal of the cots and the rugs covering the floor and all the furniture from Kasturba's quarters. They preferred the bare unfurnished rooms – and not until these emblems of luxury were removed, would he make himself at home.

The citizens of Madras gathered to do honour to the Gandhis on their homecoming at a great demonstration held at the Victoria Public Hall on April 21. Sir S. Subramanya Ayyar presided. I recollect an eloquent message from the Rt. Rev. and Lord Bishop of Madras, President of the Indian

South African League, conveying his deep sympathy with the meeting to welcome Mr. and Mrs. Gandhi 'who had carried on their noble struggle in South Africa on behalf of their fellow-countrymen'. As Secretary of the League, it fell to me to read the address which was couched in beautiful terms: 'In the ample roll of those that have served this common motherland of ours few can rival and none can excel you in the record of the things accomplished. [...] You embody to the present generation the godliness and profound wisdom of the saint. Mrs. Gandhi is to us the incarnation of wifely virtue, living in and for her husband and following him like a shadow in plenty and in poverty, in joy and tribulation, at home, in gaol, and on the march.'

Gandhiji's reply to the address was remarkable for its earnestness and simplicity. For the first time, we heard him speak on a public platform. There was no thunder in his eloquence, no passion, no demonstration in his utterance. The voice was even and the manner grave, and the words fell with simple grace and dignity. But there was something in the speech that went home to the hearts of the listeners as no finished oratory could do. And when he passed on to recount the exploits of the brave martyrs from Madras, the effect was tremendous:

'Sir, if one-tenth of the language that has been used in this address is deserved by us, what language do you propose to use for those who have lost their lives, and therefore finished their work on behalf of your suffering countrymen in South Africa? What language do you propose to use for Nagappan and Narayanaswamy, lads of seventeen or eighteen years, who braved in simple faith all the trials, all the sufferings, and all the indignities for the sake of the honour of the Motherland? (Cheers) What language do you propose to use with reference to Valliamma, that sweet girl of seventeen years who was discharged from Maritzburg prison, skin and bone, suffering from fever to which she succumbed after about a month's time?' (Cries of 'shame')

'It was the Madrasis who of all the Indians were singled out by the great Divinity that rules over us for this great work. Do you know that in the great city of Johannesburg, it is considered among the Madrasis to find a single Madrasi dishonoured if he has not passed through the jails once or twice during this terrible crisis that your countrymen in South Africa went through during these eight long years? You have said that I inspired these great men and women, but I cannot accept that proposition. It was they, the simple-minded folk who worked away in faith, never expecting the slightest reward, who inspired me, who kept me to the proper level, and who compelled me by their great sacrifice, by their great faith, by their great trust in the great God to do the work that I was able to do. (Cheers) It is my misfortune that I and my wife have been obliged to work in the limelight, and you have magnified out of all proportion (Cries of "No, no") this little work we have been able to do.'

'They deserve the crown which you would seek to impose upon us,' he continued: 'These young men deserve all the adjectives that you have so affectionately, but blindly, lavished upon us. It was not only the Hindus who struggled, but there were Mohammedans, Parsis and Christians, and almost every part of India was represented in the struggle. They realised the common danger, and they realised also what their destiny was as Indians, and it was they, and they alone, who matched the soul-force against the physical force.' (Loud applause)

It was a new experience for Madras: the words were few but thrilled us through and through. There was not much in the manner, but a great deal in the matter of his speeches. He seldom repeated second-hand opinions and his views on every subject were refreshingly original. Whether he spoke in denunciation of anarchical crimes or on loyalty to the British Raj, there was always something out of the common, and the attractive turn he gave to his thoughts was a perpetual surprise to his audience.

> He bought a fresh mind to play upon the problems of the old country and his solutions were a continual surprise.

From: G.A. Natesan, "Reminiscences", in D.G. Tendulkar (ed.), *Gandhiji: His Life and Work*, Bombay: Keshav Bhikaji Dhawale, 1944, pp.208-215, at pp.208-211.

POSTSCRIPT:

The *Hindu* newspaper, in its 19 April edition, covered Gandhi's arrival in Madras and his being taken to the home of Natesan in colourful language:

> Mr. and Mrs. M.K. Gandhi arrived in Madras last Saturday evening from Hardwar by the Delhi Express. [...] A little disappointment was in store for the people, however. When the train arrived, they searched all the first- and second-class compartments, but in vain, and they were inclined to think that Mr. Gandhi and Mrs. Gandhi had not come. But a guard told them that Mr. and Mrs. Gandhi had come by that train and they were in a compartment at the end of the train. A long search discovered Mr. and Mrs. Gandhi sitting in a third-class compartment. Mr. Gandhi looked thin and emaciated, a loose shirt soiled by four days of continuous travel covered his body and a pair of trousers similar in appearance covered his legs. There was a rush to that compartment and the crowd was such that about a dozen policemen who had been there found themselves powerless to manage the crowd and had to leave it to shift as best it could. [...] Shouts of 'Long live Mr. and Mrs. Gandhi', 'Long live our hero', and 'Bande Mataram' rang from the crowd. Mr. Gandhi bowed to them in acknowledgement and was conducted to the carriage. The students who had gathered in large numbers unyoked the horse and volunteered to drag the carriage. The carriage was taken, dragged by the students, to the premises

of Messrs Natesan & Co., Sunkurama Chetty Street, Mr. Gandhi being cheered all along the way, Mr. and Mrs. Gandhi standing in the carriage and with hands cooped acknowledging the greetings.

On arrival at Messrs Natesan & Co., where he will be stopping during his stay in Madras, Mr. Gandhi stood up in the carriage and in a loud and clear voice said that he was exceedingly thankful to them for the expression of their love to him. He was fagged on account of the four days continuous journey and wished to be allowed to say good night. He would, however, be free to see them during his stay here between three and five o'clock on all days and discuss questions affecting their common good. Mr. and Mrs. Gandhi expect to stay in Madras for a fortnight. Mr. Gandhi desires to visit the places in the South wherefrom the bulk of South African Indian settlers have been drawn in order to meet such of the passive resisters as have settled in India.

FURTHER READING:

Natesan, B., *Sixty Years After: Souvenir of the Sashriabdha-Poorthi of the Hon. Mr. G.A. Natesan,* Madras: G.A. Natesan & Co., 1933.

Natesan, G.A., *What India Wants: Autonomy Within the Empire,* Madras: G.A. Natesan & Co., 1917.

1915 RAJKUMARI AMRIT KAUR

Rajkumari Amrit Kaur was born in 1889, the only daughter of Raja Sir Harnam Singh of Kapurthala state in the Punjab. She was brought up as a Christian in surroundings of luxury at the Jullundur palace. Rather than being married off in childhood, she was sent to England for education. She (called 'rebel' by Gandhi) remained unmarried and was drawn to the Mahatma (whom she called 'tyrant'), becoming one of his closest co-workers. She held various offices in all-India organisations for women after 1930 and, in 1934, she joined Gandhi's Ashram at Wardha and from then on served periodically in his secretariat. A fervent nationalist, she was arrested during the Salt Satyagraha in 1930 and again during the Quit India Movement in 1942. She was a member of the Indian Delegation to UNESCO in 1945 and 1946 and was the first minister for health in the Indian cabinet from 1947 until 1957. She was elected to the Lok Sabha in 1952, where she served until 1957, and thereafter was a member of the Rajya Sabha until 1962. During her life she was committed to working for women's causes and continued her involvement with medical and health organisations to the end. She died in 1964.

The late Shri Gokhale was an honoured friend of my father and often used to stay at our home. I may say that the flames of my passionate desire to see India free from foreign domination was early fanned by contact with him. He once said to me: 'One day soon you will, I hope, see a man who is destined to do very great things for India.' With this at the back of my mind I seized the very first opportunity I could of being presented to Gandhiji. This was in 1915 at the Bombay Congress when Lord Sinha was presiding. Gandhiji was more or less an unknown factor in the political life of India at that time. The tumultuous ovation went to the great Tilak who had just returned from the Andamans. Gandhiji spoke a few words about Indians in South Africa. With no loud speakers in those days his speech was more or less inaudible except to those on the dais or in the front rows of the audience. But there was a quiet strength, and earnestness and a deep humility about him that went straight to my young heart; and I feel I have owed allegiance to him and his way of life ever since, even though circumstances did not permit my actually joining him till much later.

He came to Jullundur after the massacre of Jallianwalla Bagh. By then he was the idol of the people. The undisciplined crowds had trodden on him. At 6 p.m. he was suffering from a badly bruised foot and high fever. My doctor brother, who happened to be the Civil Surgeon there, begged him to postpone his journey by 24 hours. 'How can I break my faith with so many who are waiting for me at various places?' came the quick reply. 'And I assure you I shall be free from fever by 10 p.m. which is when my train leaves.' I sent him a hot water bottle and begged of him to take it with him for the journey. The next morning the bottle came back with a note of thanks written by Mahadev Desai in which he said 'You will be glad to know that the fever went before he left Jullundur so he had no need of the bottle afterwards'.

His second visit to Jullundur the same year brought him to see me because he had heard I was ill. He asked me to give all my 'foreign finery' to him to burn and take to 'Khadi'. I stoutly denied having such 'foreign finery'. I said I now bought only Swadeshi. 'That is finery too'. I pleaded that burning was quite wrong. His reply was: 'Not even when these things stand for the chains of our slavery? But if you will not burn, at least give it to me, and I will send it to poor Indians in South Africa and you take to spinning and Khadi'. Alas! that his words, at that time, fell on more or less stony ground. I tried to wear Khadi but found it too coarse for my fastidious tastes. In those days there were none of the fine Andhra or Bihar muslins such as there are today. Because his words carried power in them, however, I learnt how to spin and used to give my yarn to be spun for cloth for a poor child or woman. I began buying Khadi for dusters, towels and for any rough use in the house. Afterwards Gandhiji said to me: 'Many people have used Khadi as a door mat but they do not realise how they have thus wronged it and all it stands for!' Later when the realisation of what Khadi embodies dawned upon me I understood what he meant by calling any cloth that was not Khadi as part of that which was contributing to keep us slaves. Years later, when I came to live with him in Maganwadi, he saw or sensed, perhaps, my inability to rid myself of some of the comforts to which my sheltered life had accustomed me and how understanding he was! He would not allow me at first to sleep on the ground. I was not made even to wash up my own plates etc. I was willing to do everything and pleaded with him to be allowed to do so – but Gandhiji, while he has the enviable capacity of drawing people to him, has also the even greater capacity of keeping them with him. It is because he leads gently over the rough places that he evokes complete loyalty from all and sundry.

From: G. Borkar (ed.), *Selected Speeches and Writings of Rajkumari Amrit Kaur*, New Delhi: Archer, 1961, pp.1-4.

POSTSCRIPT:

Gandhi and Rajkumari Amrit Kaur maintained a relationship that often had light-hearted moments. For example in commenting on the khadi sales Amrit Kaur organised in Simla, where she had her main residence, Gandhi noted that 'Your sales of khadi certainly went beyond even my expectations. All this due to the effort of a mere woman – frail in body and idiot mentally!!! No, wonder poor khadi workers in Simla are trembling over the prospect of your absence during the next Simla season. But we need not worry about the future which is in God's hands. *You* will give a good account of yourself no matter where you are.' He also allowed her certain latitude in her behaviour given her background, but nudged her in the direction he wanted her to take: 'You were extravagant in buying the thermos, the magnificent apples. But you would not be a Rajkumari if you were not extravagant. You are none the less so because you spend on others. If you counted yourself a trustee, as you should, of all you possess including your body, you would be balanced in using them even for your trust. You may not philosophically smile this simple truth away. Remember the value of a rupee in terms of the poor. It means 64 solid meals which millions do not have. Many in Segaon live on a rupee per month, i.e., only two meals a day costing one pice each. But millions do not get this much. How can you and I, knowing this as well as that I am writing this, mis-spend a pice? Will you be wise for a while? If you will become the – or a – woman of my imagination, you will have to develop all your faculties, not excluding account-keeping.' (Gandhi to Amrit Kaur, 7 November 1936)

FURTHER READING:

Gregg, Richard B. (ed.), *Letters to Rajkumari Amrit Kaur,* Ahmedabad: Navajivan, 1961.

Lok Sabha Secretariat, *Eminent Parliamentarians Monograph Series: Rajkumari Amrit Kaur,* New Delhi: Lok Sabha Secretariat, 1992.

1916

VINOBA BHAVE

Vinoba Bhave is generally considered the greatest post-Gandhi Gandhian. He is known as Gandhi's moral or spiritual heir and his land-gift Bhoodan movement of the 1950s and 1960s was a major experiment in nonviolent politics. He visited Gandhi soon after the latter's return from South Africa and instantly fell under Gandhi's spell, and a bond of love that was to last throughout their lives quickly developed. In 1921, Vinoba founded a branch of Gandhi's ashram at Wardha. Although he mostly worked outside the political arena, he was arrested six times between 1923 and 1942 and served five and a half years in jail. When Vinoba set out for the 1951 annual conference of Gandhian workers, he resolved to cover the 250 miles on foot and to return through an area of Communist insurgency. As he toured Telengana district, a landowner offered to donate some land to the landless and the Bhoodan movement was born. Vinoba, 'the walking saint', spent the next twelve years on the march throughout India, as he said, 'looting with love'. Vinoba retired to his ashram in 1970, directing the Gandhian movement from the sidelines. Weak and unwell, in November 1982 at the age of eighty-seven, he declined to take food or liquids for ten days until he passed away in the mode of an ancient Hindu sage.

During my boyhood I had already been attracted by Bengal and the Himalayas, and dreamed of going there. On the one hand I was drawn to Bengal by the revolutionary spirit of [the nationalist song] *Bande Mataram,* while on the other hand the path of spiritual quest led me to the Himalayas. Kashi [Varanasi] was on the way to both places, and some good *Karma* has brought me as far as that. I went to Gandhiji, and found with him both the peace of the Himalayas and the revolutionary spirit of Bengal. Peaceful revolution, revolutionary peace: the two streams united in him in a way that was altogether new.

When I had reached Kashi the air had been full of a speech which Bapu had delivered at the Hindu University there. In it he had said a great deal about non-violence, his main point being that there could be no non-violence without fearlessness. The violence of the mind, shown in violent attitudes and feeling was, he said, worse than open, physical violence. [...] This had all taken place a month before I arrived, but it was still the talk of the town. I read the speech, and it raised all kinds of problems in my mind. I wrote to Bapu with my questions and received a very good reply, so after some ten or fifteen days I wrote again, raising some further points. Then came a postcard. 'Questions about non-violence,' he wrote, 'cannot be settled by letters; the touch of life is needed. Come and stay with me for a few days in the Ashram, so that we can meet now and again.' The idea that doubts could be set at rest by living rather than by talking was something that greatly appealed to me.

Along with the postcard came a copy of the Ashram rules which attracted me still more. [...] That was what drew me to Bapu. Here was a man, I felt, who aimed at one and the same time at both political freedom and spiritual development. I was delighted. He had said 'Come' and I went.

I alighted at Ahmedabad railway station on June 7, 1916. I had not much luggage, so I put it on my head and started out, asking my way as I went. I crossed Ellis Bridge and reached the Ashram at Kochrab [it was moved to Sabarmati in the following year] about eight in the morning. Bapu was told that a new man had come, and sent word for me to meet him after I had taken my bath. I found him busy cutting vegetables. This too was something new; I had never heard of any national leader who occupied himself with such a job, and the sight of it was a lesson in what was meant by bodily labour. Bapu put a knife in my hand, and set me to work at a job I had never done before. That was my first lesson, my 'initiation'.

As we sat cutting the vegetables Bapu asked me some questions, and then said: 'If you like this place, and want to spend your life in service, I should be very glad to have you stay here.' Then he went on: 'But you look very weak. It is true that those who seek self-knowledge are not usually physically robust, but *you* look ill. Those who attain self-knowledge never fall ill.' That was my second lesson! I can never forget what Bapu said to me then.

After that, I had no more talks with Bapu except about the immediate work in hand. I was usually fully absorbed in my work, but I also used to listen to his conversations with the many people who came to see him. He knew that I was a well-intentioned lad, though others were apt to consider me rather a dullard. During one of these conversations Bapu had commented that some remark was 'just a secondary expression'. I interrupted. 'No,' I said, 'it's the language of devotion.' 'You are right,' said Bapu at once. 'The language of knowledge and the language of devotion are not the same.' It was just like him to listen with respect to someone like me, hardly more than a child, and accept what I said. Others too began to listen to me after that.

From: Vinoba Bhave (Marjorie Sykes trans. and Kalindi ed.), *Moved By Love: The Memoirs of Vinoba Bhave,* Dartington UK, Green Books Limited (www.greenbooks.co.uk), 1994, pp.64-66.

POSTSCRIPT:

According to Gandhi, it was not only Vinoba who gained by joining Gandhi's ashram. Gandhi hailed Vinoba as 'one of the rare jewels of the Ashram', adding that 'he has come to purify the Ashram with his own religious merit: he has come not to receive but to give'. (Quoted in Shah, *Vinoba,* p.32) Later when Gandhi selected Vinoba ahead of luminaries such as Jawaharlal Nehru, as the first satyagrahi of his Individual Satyagraha campaign of 1940-41, he introduced Vinoba to the Indian public in the most glowing of terms:

> Who is Vinoba Bhave and why has he been selected? He is an undergraduate having left college after my return to India in 1915. He is a Sanskrit scholar. He joined the Ashram almost at its inception. He was among the first members. In order to better qualify himself he took one year's leave to prosecute further studies in Sanskrit. And, practically at the same hour at which he had left the Ashram a year before, he walked into it without notice. I had forgotten that he was due to arrive that day. He has taken part in every menial activity of the Ashram from scavenging to cooking. Though he has a marvellous memory and is a student by nature, he has devoted the largest part of his time to spinning in which he has specialized as very few have. He believes in universal spinning being the central activity which will remove the poverty in the villages and put life into their deadness. Being a born teacher he has been of the utmost assistance to Ashadevi [Aryanayakam] in her development of the scheme of education through handicrafts. Shri Vinoba has produced a text-book taking spinning as the handicraft. It is

original in conception. He has made scoffers realize that spinning is the handicraft *par excellence* which lends itself to being effectively used for basic education. He has revolutionized *takli*-spinning and drawn out its hitherto unknown possibilities. For perfect spinning probably he has no rival in all India.

He has abolished every trace of untouchability from his heart. He believes in communal unity with the same passion that I have. In order to know the best mind of Islam he gave one year to the study of the Koran in the original. He therefore learnt Arabic. He found this study necessary for cultivating a living contact with the Muslims living in his neighbourhood. ('Civil Disobedience', *Harijan*, 20 October 1940)

FURTHER READING:

Deshpande, Nirmala, *Vinoba,* New Delhi: National Book Trust, India, 2002.

del Vasto, Lanza, *Gandhi to Vinoba: The New Pilgrimage,* London: Rider, 1956.

Nargolkar, Vasant, *The Creed of Saint Vinoba,* Bombay: Bharatiya Vidya Bhavan, 1963.

Ram, Suresh, *Vinoba and His Mission,* Varanasi: Sarva Seva Sangh, 1962.

Shah, Kanti, *Vinoba: Life and Mission [An Introductory Study],* Varanasi: Sarva Seva Sangh, 1979.

Shepard, Mark, *Gandhi Today: A Report on Mahatma Gandhi's Successors,* Arcata, Calif.: Simple Productions, 1987.

Weber, Thomas, *Gandhi as Disciple and Mentor,* New Delhi: Cambridge University Press, 2004.

1917 RAJENDRA PRASAD

Born into a traditional Hindu landed family in 1884, following a brilliant academic career, Rajendra Prasad practiced law in Calcutta until 1916 when he transferred to the Patna High Court in Bihar. Not long after, peasant representatives had convinced Gandhi to look into their grievances at the hands of British indigo planters in the Champaran district. Because Gandhi's knowledge of Hindi was not adequate, he recruited local interpreters and assistants. Prasad was one of the young lawyers who answered the call. Rather than enquiring about their legal expertise, Gandhi asked if they were prepared to go to jail. In 1920 Prasad gave up his law practice to join the Noncooperation Movement and was imprisoned several times by the British. In 1946 he was sworn in as minister for food and agriculture in the interim government preceding full independence. For the next three years he presided over the Indian Constituent Assembly, helping to shape the Constitution. In 1950 he was unanimously elected the first (and became the longest serving) president of the Republic of India. As a staunch Gandhian, he declared that his presidential salary and allowances were too high and had them reduced by 80 per cent.

This was my first meeting with Gandhiji; the first time, too, that I spoke to him. I was not particularly affected by this meeting, nor did I feel that it would lead to a complete change in my outlook and my life.

Years before, I had met the late Shri Gokhale, who had advised me to join the Servants of India Society. We had talked it over for a fairly long time. I was considerably attracted by this suggestion and spent much anxious thought on it for a number of days. Ultimately, however, I decided that I could not accept his advice. I do not know, therefore, how it came to pass that I accepted, without thought, Gandhiji's suggestion and decided to go to jail. That was the only question he had posed and we had all answered it in the manner I have indicated, though, at the time, there was no question of our devoting our whole life to the service of the county.

This idea of voluntarily going to jail was a novel one, not only for me but for the whole country as well. Till Gandhiji came, we did not do anything that would, in the ordinary course, entail imprisonment. Rather, we thought that it would be a piece of cleverness on our part to do things in such manner as would enable us to avoid going to jail. If we wanted to talk sedition, we would do it; but even while we did so, we would think of Section-A of the Indian Penal Code and would use such language as would enable us to keep out of trouble. We wanted to kill the snake but, at the same time to preserve the club with which we wanted to kill it; and he who could do this successfully was looked upon as a clever person. The revolutionaries carried their lives in their hands; but, at the same time, they would, as far as they could, keep open for themselves the door of escape. Nobody deliberately wanted to jump into the fire. If a man was prosecuted, lawyers were called in to defend him, and everything necessary was done to get him off. Hardly anyone ever admitted his guilt. This was the only method we knew. Never had we knowingly taken upon ourselves the kind of risk we did at the instance of Gandhiji. Personally, I was a man of moderate views. I am still a man of moderate views. I do not know, therefore, how, and in what way, I suddenly took the decision I did, which was not only a novel thing in my personal life but also opened up a new way for public workers in the country. True, I had before me the example of our two friends – Babu Dharnidhar and Babu Ramnavami Prasad. But those who had come with me – Mazhar-ul-Haque Sahib and Babu Brajkishore – were considered to be much bigger persons. Did they also allow themselves to be influenced by the example of those two friends? Did they also take the decision to follow Gandhiji without weighing the consequences? Were they, too, following him blindly?

The analytical process of thought, however, came later. So far as I know, I was not at all conscious of it at my first meeting with Gandhiji, which as I have already mentioned, did not make any very significant impression on my mind – certainly not of the kind that my meeting with the late Shri Gokhale did. Perhaps it was some magnetic quality of Gandhiji's which, without any awareness on our part at that time, exercised a kind of irresistible fascination on us and impressed us to follow him unquestioningly.

From: Rajendra Prasad, *At the Feet of Mahatma Gandhi,* New York: Philosophical Library 1961, pp.18-19.

POSTSCRIPT:

In fact Prasad should have met Gandhi some time earlier than he actually did. A Champaran cultivator and client and friend of Prasad's, Raj Kumar Shukla, was to escort Gandhi from a Calcutta Congress meeting to Patna.

The young lawyer Prasad, who was to meet them as Gandhi came out of the session, was delayed and did not know about the Patna plan. Rajendra Prasad recounts the discomforting outcome: 'Raj Kumar took Gandhiji to my house in Patna. Only my servant was there and thinking that Gandhiji was a village client he put him up in an out-house and showed him no respect at all. Meanwhile, Mazharul Haq [Bihar's representative on the Imperial Legislative Council] heard of his visit and hastened to my house to take Gandhiji to his own residence.' When Gandhi and Prasad were finally introduced to each other, Gandhi 'who had a simple kurta (shirt) on, smiled and said: "So, you have come. You know I had been to your house." I had already heard a little of it and was embarrassed on account of my servant's behaviour.' (Prasad, *Autobiography*, pp.83-84)

FURTHER READING:

Prasad, Rajendra, *Autobiography*, Bombay: National Book Trust, 1957.

Prasad, Rajendra, *Satyagraha in Champaran*, Ahmedabad: Navajivan, 1949.

Rajendra Prasad, "Since he Came to Champaran", in Chandrashanker Shukla (ed.), *Incidents of Gandhiji's Life, by Fifty-Four Contributors*, Bombay: Vora, 1949, pp.264-277.

Punjabi, Kewal L., *Rajendra Prasad: First President of India*, London: Macmillan, 1960.

Weber, Thomas, *Gandhi as Disciple and Mentor*, New Delhi: Cambridge University Press, 2004.

1918

R.R. DIWAKAR

Ranganath Ramchandra Diwakar, was born in 1884 and, having completed his studies, spent two years as a teacher, and then, in 1921, became a journalist working for the freedom movement under Gandhi's leadership. He spent two years 'underground' with a large reward for his capture during the early 1940s and was imprisoned several times, spending a total of six years in detention under British rule. Following the advent of Indian independence, Diwakar served as member of the Constituent Assembly, as minister for information and broadcasting and as governor of Bihar. Retiring from politics and government administration, from the late 1950s until his death in early 1990, Diwakar returned to his first passion: the spreading of the Gandhian message. He served as chairperson of the Gandhi Peace Foundation and the Gandhi Smarak Nidhi (Gandhi National Memorial Trust). He was one of the founders of the World Conference of Religion and Peace, and was a writer of repute, authoring books on Aurobindo, Ramakrishna and the Buddha, as well as countless books, forewords to books, pamphlets, and articles on Gandhi and Gandhian techniques.

Yes, it was the month of May 1918. I had returned to Hubli, my home, after appearing in Bombay for two examinations of Law and Master of Arts. I learnt from the newspapers that the Bombay Provincial Conference was being held in Bijapur. I thought it a good opportunity to spend my time there. After the examinations, I had nothing else to do. I had to wait for the results till July. I made up my mind to go to Bijapur for the conference held on May 5-6. I expected a number of leaders to attend it. It would be an opportunity to see them all in one place for one purpose.

On going to Bijapur I got myself enrolled as a volunteer for sundry duties in connection with the function. I was assigned the duty of attending on important leaders who were there. Fortunately for me, Gandhiji was one of them. He was still wearing the Kathiarwari *pugree* those days and had not yet attained eminence. But his name had registered respect in my mind. So, I was happy to know that I had an opportunity to attend on him among others.

As things had it, the volunteers working there were not a very trained and disciplined lot. In the morning the captain of the volunteers had a wordy altercation with Srinivasrao Kowjalgi, Chairman of the Reception Committee. Kowjalgi was a prominent leader of Karnataka and a patriot of respect. Our captain took offence and called on all of us to strike work! Word reached me at about 11 am at the leaders' camp where I was posted. I was embarrassed beyond measure. How could I dare convey this strike notice to the leaders there! I thought I should not inconvenience them in any way. I took the decision to see that lunch was properly served to the guests after which I could inform them about the strike.

After lunch, I went up to Gandhi very hesitantly and said that according to orders of my captain, I was to stop serving him. He looked at me with a gaze I cannot forget. 'What kind

> of volunteers are you?' he asked. 'At any rate, I do not require the services of people like you. You speak of a strike. Volunteers never strike. It is labourers who work for wages that strike.' I was ashamed. What he said stuck in my mind.
>
> Fortunately, our captain apologized to Kowjalgi and called off the strike. So, I was saved further embarrassment. [...]
>
> In the evening after the conference was over, a special meeting had been arranged, the subject being 'Removal of Untouchability'. Gandhi had been invited to speak. After the introductory speeches, he was requested to address the audience. Gandhi stood up and simply said, 'Those who are looked down upon as "untouchables" please raise your hands.' None did so. None had been invited! Gandhi sat down, saying 'Whom am I to speak to?'

From: R.R. Diwakar, *My Encounter with Gandhi*, New Delhi: Gandhi Peace Foundation, 1989, pp.23-24.

POSTSCRIPT:

It seems that one of Diwakar's final meetings with Gandhi changed his life as much as the first one did. He was 'underground' for two years (from August 1942 to August 1944 with five thousand rupees on his head). This was after the arrest of Gandhi and the leaders of the Congress following the passing of the Quit India Resolution. Although Diwakar noted that 'Satyagraha can never reconcile itself either with secrecy or with going underground', following Gandhi's proclamation of the slogan 'Do or die', it seems that there was some confusion about the program of action. He continues the story:

> Many had the impression that sabotage and such other paralysing activities which involve injury to government property were

> permissible. I was one of those who was misled in that way and went underground. Along with some colleagues I tried to direct the underground movement in the Karnataka districts. Six months later, when Gandhi fasted in the Aga Khan Palace, in February, 1943 I contacted him through his youngest son, Devdasji, and submitted to him the report of Karnataka activities. Gandhi sent word that injury to property was as bad as injury to person, and that injury to property was sure to lead to injury to person on either side or on both sides. We took the cure and stopped all those underground activities and instructed the batches of workers that overt nonviolent action and open civil disobedience were the only things permitted. But somehow some of my colleagues and myself persuaded ourselves that our continuance underground was necessary for organising even the open defiance activities by others. [...]
>
> It was only after Gandhi's release in 1944 that I contacted him again personally and he made it clear that secrecy had no place either in his philosophy or in his tactics and that I should discover myself. So I did on the 9th of August 1944 by openly offering myself to the police authorities.

In a self-deprecating way, R.R. Diwakar notes that 'in spite of this personal lapse' on his part, it was corrected by Gandhi himself. And this led him to writing his early study of the principles and practices of satyagraha. (Diwakar, *Saga of Satyagraha*, pp.viii-ix)

FURTHER READING:

Diwakar, R.R., *Glimpses of Gandhiji*, Bombay: Hind Kitabs, 1949.

Diwakar, R.R., *Saga of Satyagraha*, New Delhi: Gandhi Peace Foundation, 1969.

1919

E. STANLEY JONES

Eli Stanley Jones was born in Baltimore in 1884. He became a missionary of the Methodist Episcopal Church in India from 1907 and a pastor of the English Church of Lucknow. On his arrival in India he set about learning Hindi and commenced working with outcastes and those of low caste. His approach was not typical as instead of attacking Hinduism and Islam, he preached a gospel which aimed to make Christianity an equally Indian religion, rather than one that kept Christ tied to Western culture. He became a close friend of Mahatma Gandhi. Jones conducted mass meetings in major cities, becoming known as the Billy Graham of India. In 1928 he declined the office of Bishop of Kansas City in order to continue his Indian missionary work. He was a prolific writer and his books were translated into numerous languages and sold in the millions of copies. In 1930, he established an ashram in the Himalayas, and, later, one in Lucknow which in 1950 added a psychiatric centre. Since then the model has been copied around the world as the 'Christian Ashram Movement'. His 1948 book on Gandhi was said to have been a major influence on Martin Luther King Jr. After the Second World War, he divided his time between America and India, where he died in 1973.

I was giving an address in St. Stephen's College, Delhi, and the Principal Rudra said, rather casually: 'Mr. Gandhi (that is before he became Mahatma—"The Great-souled") is upstairs; would you like to see him?' This was all in great contrast with later years, for in later years the house would have been surrounded night and day with a curious crowd, and to get an interview with him would not have been easy, for people from all over the world would be pressing him for interviews. But here I was being asked if I would like to see him! He was seated on a bed, surrounded by papers, and he greeted me with an engaging and contagious smile. Without preliminaries, I went straight to my question: 'How can we make Christianity naturalised in India, not a foreign thing, identified with a foreign government and a foreign people, but a part of the national life of India and contributing its power to India's uplift? What would you, as one of Hindu leaders of India, tell me, a Christian, to do in order to make this possible?' He responded with great clarity and directness: 'First, I would suggest that all of you Christians, missionaries and all, must begin to live more like Jesus Christ. Second, Practice your religion without adulterating it or toning it down. Third, Emphasise love and make it your working force, for love is central in Christianity. Fourth, Study the non-Christian religions more sympathetically to find the good that is within them, in order to have a more sympathetic approach to the people.' A few days later I quoted these four things, which the Mahatma had suggested, to a British High Court Judge, and he remarked: 'That's genius—to pick out four things like that is genius.' It was. For he had put his finger unerringly on the four weak spots in our individual and collective lives. [...]

I wish we could leave the whole of the relationships of the Mahatma with Christianity at this point. It is so wholesome, so sincere and so deeply needed by us. I am sorry to have to leave this period of simple, unrestrained relationships to take up a

> period when we, the missionaries, who seem to have a natural affinity with the Mahatma, often found ourselves at cross-purposes with him through many years. Yet I, for one, clung to him through these clouded years and loved and defended him, even when I couldn't always follow his reasoning. Something held my heart even when the mind couldn't follow. As I look back I see that much of the blame must fall on us as missionaries, and we would do well to take his criticisms to heart and mend our ways and attitudes.

From: E. Stanley Jones, *Mahatma Gandhi: An Interpretation,* London: Hodder and Stoughton, 1948, pp.69-70, 73.

POSTSCRIPT:

In an earlier book on the uptake of Christianity in India, written after Gandhi had been painted as something of a failure after the Non-Cooperation Movement of the early 1920s, Jones notes that much of the popularity of Jesus can be attributed to Gandhi:

> While a Christian lecturer was commenting on this remarkable permeation of the atmosphere of India with the thought and spirit of Jesus, a Hindu turned and said to me, 'Yes, but he failed to say that Mahatma Gandhi was responsible for a great deal of this new interest in Jesus,' I could only agree with him that the criticism was just.
>
> Mahatma Gandhi does not call himself a Christian. The fact is that he calls himself a Hindu. But by his life and outlook and methods he has been the medium through which a great deal of this interest in Christ has come.
>
> He saw clearly that there were two ways that India might gain her freedom. She might take the way of the sword and the bomb — the way that Mohammed Ali and Shankat [sic] Ali, the

Mohammedan leaders, untamed by Gandhi, would have taken; and the way that the Bengal anarchists have actually taken. The fires of rebellion were underneath. The flash of a bomb here and there let the world see in that lurid light what was there. Gandhi brought all this hidden discontent to the open. A member of the secret police told me that it was comparatively easy for them now since Gandhi's advent, that they simply went to the Non-Co-operation Headquarters and asked what would be the next step in their programme in the fight with the Government and they told him just what they would do next. Gandhi turned the streams of discontent and rebellion into open and frank channels.

He rejected both the sword and the bomb, not because it was expedient, but because he believed with all his soul in something else, in another type of power — soul force or the power of suffering — and another type of victory being the precursor of the outward national victory. In the fires of that suffering there would come the inward freedom, the purification of the social and political life from within.

Now for the first time in human history a nation in the attainment of its national ends repudiated physical force and substituted the power of soul or soul force, and has made inward national regeneration a vital part of its programme. This is certainly an infinitely more Christian way than we have ordinarily taken in the West. Had the Indian people really caught the ideal on a national scale and put it into practice, as an inner circle caught and practised it, they would have risen to almost unparalleled moral heights. As one English writer, who is not supposed to be sympathetic, put it, 'Had India really practiced Gandhi's programme, no nation on earth could have denied to India the moral leadership of the world'. They would have shown us a way out of the vicious circle into which militarism has got us. They would have demonstrated what we all vaguely feel, that the final power of the world resides in the soul. (Jones, *The Christ of the Indian Road,* pp.86-89)

FURTHER READING:

Graham, Stephan A., *Ordinary Man, Extraordinary Mission: The Life and Work of E. Stanley Jones,* New York: Abbington, 2005.

Jones, E. Stanley, *Along the Indian Road,* New York: Abingdon, 1939.

Jones, E. Stanley, *The Christ of the Indian Road,* London: Hodder and Stoughton, 1926.

Jones, E. Stanley, "My Conversion to Non-Violent Non-Cooperation", in S. Radhakrisnan (ed.), *Mahatma Gandhi 100 Years,* New Delhi: Gandhi Peace Foundation, 1969, pp.171-179.

Martin, Paul A.J., *The Missionary of the Indian Road: The Theology of E. Stanley Jones,* Bangalore: Theological Book Trust, 1996.

1924 G. RAMACHANDRAN

G. Ramachandran, born in Kerala in 1904, joined Rabindranath Tagore's Visva Bharati University at Shantiniketan as a sixteen-year-old and became one of its earliest honours graduates. Not long after, he became an inmate of Gandhi's Sabarmati Ashram. Zakir Husain, the Vice Chancellor of the Jamia Millia Islamia, asked Gandhi to send Ramachandran to his university to help organise khadi work. Following that, he went to Tamil Nadu to work with nationalist leader Chakravarti Rajagopalachari. He became an anti-untouchability campaigner and a tireless worker in Gandhi's constructive programs. He was arrested eleven times, spending seven years in prison under British rule. In 1947, with his wife he founded Gandhigram near Madurai. The small rural khadi centre grew into a deemed university with a broad syllabus combining tertiary studies with practical community work and peace activism. In 1959, he sponsored Martin Luther King Jr.'s visit to India. At various times he was a member of the Rajya Sabha, general secretary of the Gandhi Smarak Nidhi, founder secretary of the Gandhi Peace Foundation, the first editor of the journal *Gandhi Marg*, and chairperson of the All India Khadi and Village Industries Commission. The last fifteen years of his life were dedicated to the Madhavimandiram Loka Seva Trust, a self-sustaining village for women and children, which he founded in 1980.

The year was 1924 and I was then a student in the Visva Bharati University in Santiniketan. The late C.F. Andrews was my favourite professor and I lived very close to him in mind and spirit. I could not then have been more than 20 years of age. Something suddenly happened in my life which gave it a turn from which I never could come away in all the rest of my life.

In those days in the Visva Bharati I had set myself up as an intellectual and I loved nothing better than to challenge every kind of ideology and concept. I found endless delight in posing as an agnostic and held that the very idea of God was anti-reason. God was not needed at all to make men and women good. In fact, God had never succeeded in doing that yet! The moral and spiritual life was largely the artistic life of poise, dignified behaviour and intellectual clarity. I was always debating and arguing with vehemence. It was into this life of mine that something came like a flash of lightning, illuminating my inner world and changing it forever.

C.F. Andrews suddenly received a hundred-worded telegram from Maulana Mohammad Ali who was then President of the Indian National Congress. The telegram conveyed the news that Mahatma Gandhi had gone on a fast of 21 days in Delhi to bring about unity between the Hindus and Muslims and that a great conference of the leaders of all the communities was being summoned in the same city. Maulana Mohammad Ali had asked C.F. Andrews to come to Delhi immediately and to take care of Gandhi during the fiery ordeal. The whole of Santiniketan was plunged into gloom. Never before had Gandhi undertaken such a long fast. He was also reported to be in indifferent health. Could he survive such a long fast? Even if the mind was strong would the frail body stand the test? There was a crowded meeting of students and teachers in the library hall in Santiniketan at which Andrews spoke with deep feeling. He caught the night train for Delhi. I lost my sleep. I was thrilled and shattered at the same time. Two days later, Andrews summoned me to Delhi to come and help him. There was an excited meeting of the students who gave me a touching send-off. Within the next 48 hours I reached Delhi. The Delhi Railway Station was full of Khadi-clad and white-capped Congress volunteers. From every part of India, Congress leaders and workers were pouring into Delhi. The mighty pull of the moral conscience associated with the Gandhian fast was stirring in the souls of vast numbers of men and women in India. Within a few days, Delhi had become the centre of many cross-currents of pilgrimage from every part of India. One of the Congress volunteers identified me, drew me out of the station, put me into a tonga and we went straight to 'Dil-khush', a beautiful, quiet house on the edge of the city in which Gandhi lay fasting. As our tonga neared 'Dil-khush', we passed through growing crowds of men and women and as we turned at the gate, I saw some five to six thousand people sitting in solemn silence on the roadside and on the lawns and in the shade of the trees. A deep anxiety hung in the air like some heavy rain-cloud of July.

Many wonderful things happened during the next few days. Andrews occupied a small room on the ground floor opposite to the staircase which led up to the first floor and it was in a room on the first floor that Gandhi lay fasting. I was kept busy day and night helping Andrews wash his clothes, bring his food, sweep and tidy his room and last, but not least, deal with his correspondence and the unending stream of visitors who filled the small room all the time. So far as Gandhi was concerned, Dr Ansari had forbidden all visitors except a few of his closest co-workers. It was in that small room of Andrews that I saw for the first time the Roman figure of Motilal Nehru, prince-like Jawaharlal, sharp and ascetic Rajaji, dynamic Chittaranjan Das, the immense Ali brothers, tall and valiant Swami Shraddhananda, and a host of others. For more than a week, I did not get even a glimpse of Gandhi. I was a prisoner in that room on the ground floor. And then, one evening, Andrews asked me to accompany him to attend Gandhi's evening prayers and I felt the thrill of the thought that at last and for the first time I was going to see Gandhi at close quarters.

The sun had just set as I climbed the stairs behind my venerable professor. By the time we reached Gandhi's room, it was full of silent figures sitting on the carpet on the floor. The electric lights had been switched off. In the dim light of evening I could only see a thin and indistinct figure on the cot wrapped in folds of snow-white Khadi. I knew that was Gandhi. He looked a frail figure etched in delicate, peaceful lines, against the indistinct evening light which came in through the open window. I could also distinguish the faces of the leaders of Muslim, Christian, Sikh and Hindu communities sitting around the cot with bowed heads. Then someone suddenly struck up the cadences of the prayer, the pattern of which has become classical in later years in the history of India. Again and again the voices of prayer rose and fell inside that room. There was complete silence after the prayers; no one spoke a word.

I watched that scene and heard the prayers with all the critical and intellectual attitude I could summon. I said to myself that I must not be swept away. I tried to keep a hold on myself. But, even as the prayers were going, something began to pound inside me. It was not a physical experience, but a mental one absolutely. I saw the frail figure on the bed and looked at the many mighty men of India's destiny sitting with heads bowed in reverence around the central figure on the cot. The question came to me, how did this little man succeed in becoming the unquestioned leader of a political revolution and how on earth did he perform the magic of linking that revolution with non-violence. How could at all a man of prayer become the leader of a revolution? All distinctions of caste, religion and creed melted in the power of devotion to the unseen God. My mind caught fire. The truth came to me in a flash that God existed and ruled the conscience of humanity. The intellect might not touch God and reason might also fail to reveal God. But, God did exist. No myth could hold and rule the hearts of men and women. God was truth and love in one and he who lay on the bed fasting, so that Hindus and Muslims might come together in goodwill and in understanding, was the symbol of that truth and love. The spirit of God appeared to hover close within that room. A man had brought God into the room. I felt it unmistakably with the touch of my mind. I said to myself, I may never see God or know God fully, but this human symbol proved the truth of Godhood. I would follow the man who had brought God into the room. I took a silent vow.

From: G. Ramachandran, "My First Darshan", *Gandhi Marg* (English) (1957), vol.I, no.I, pp.43-46, at pp.43-45.

POSTSCRIPT:

Through Gandhi, G. Ramachandran found not only God but a wife. Married very young and widowed in her teens, Soundaram Iyengar later attended Lady Hardinge Medical College in Delhi. One of her college friends was Sushila Nayyar, sister of Gandhi's later secretary Pyarelal. Soundaram graduated at age thirty-two in 1936 as one of the first woman doctors in India, and through her Gandhian connections was to meet and fall in love with Ramachandran. They wanted to get married but Ramachandran had taken a vow not to marry until he had turned thirty-five and her family was vehemently opposed to the union. After all, she was a Brahmin and he was not. Inter-caste marriages were strongly disapproved of and widow remarriage was socially unacceptable (except on Gandhi's ashram). Gandhi advised them to remain apart for a year and if their desires for a formal union were still there he would bless the marriage. On 7 November 1940, Gandhi gave the bride away in a simple ceremony in Sevagram.

Further Reading:

Banerjee, Samir, *Notes from Gandhigram: Challenges to Gandhian Praxis*, New Delhi: Orient BlackSwan, 2009.

Ramachandran, G., *Adventuring with Life*, Trivandrum: S.B. Press, 1984.

1925

MADELEINE SLADE (MIRABEHN)

Born in 1892, Madeleine Slade, the daughter of a British admiral, was a devotee of the music of Beethoven. She became fixated on Gandhi after reading Beethoven chronicler Romain Rolland's biography of the Mahatma in 1923. After a year of physical preparation she left England and, on 7 November 1925, arrived at Gandhi's Sabarmati Ashram to devote her life to her spiritual master. She was given the name Mirabehn and became Gandhi's best known European disciple. She lived with Gandhi at his various ashrams and other more temporary residences, travelled with him to the London Round Table Conference on the future of India in 1931, and had the privilege of sharing an almost two year imprisonment with him in the Aga Khan's palace in Poona in the early 1940s. Following Gandhi's assassination in January 1948, she remained in India, doing the work of her master in the Himalayan foothills. In 1959 she returned to Europe, to the woods where Beethoven had strolled. She died in Vienna in 1982.

I boarded the P & O liner on October 25, 1925, and the voyage began. The weather was fair and the moon was waxing. Each evening, as it rose in the east and shed on the ocean a path of light along which the ship travelled, I gazed upon it as an emblem of what I was approaching. And day by day I wrote down my thoughts and feelings to be posted to Villeneuve [the home of Romain Rolland] as soon as I reached India. On November 6th the ship came alongside the dock in Bombay. As had been promised, friends were there to meet me. They took me to the Nairojees' house on Malabar Hill, where the brother and sisters, grandchildren of Dadabhai Nairojee, pressed me to stay and rest for at least twenty-four hours. But I had no thought for anything but to reach Sabarmati without delay. In the afternoon, Devadas Gandhi, Mahatma Gandhi's fourth and youngest son, came in and he too pressed me to stay, but, seeing my determination to go on at once, he finally arranged for my departure by the Ahmedabad train that night.

The train steamed into the Ahmedabad station next morning November 7th, exactly on time, and as it drew to a standstill, a smiling bespectacled person looked in at the window. In half a minute another, also smiling but of quite a different character, looked over his shoulder, and a third was in the background. They all seemed to know that I was the person they were looking for, and introduced themselves – Mahadev Desai (secretary and right-hand man of Mahatma Gandhi); Vallabhbhai Patel (later to become first Home Minister of Free India); and Swami Anand (manager of the weekly *Young India*). Even at that moment of concentrated anticipation I noted the masterful manner of Vallabhbhai, who turned to Mahadev and said, 'You two look after the luggage and I'll take her off in the car'. And before I knew where I was I found myself being swept away in the car, this new acquaintance sitting by my side. I looked at his clean-shaven face and was struck by its power curiously intermingled with a kindly and humorous expression. The car turned into a courtyard and drew up in front of a house.

'This is not the Ashram, is it?' I exclaimed.

'No, no,' he said, 'this is the All-India Spinners' Association Office.'

As he spoke, someone came out and had a few words with him through the window, all in Gujerati, and I could not understand anything. I looked inquiringly at him as we drove off again.

'That was the All-India Spinners' Association Secretary,' he said, 'Shankarlal Banker.'

Now we passed out of the city and over a bridge to the other side of the Sabarmati River. I was gazing out of the window in tense suspense. I saw buildings ahead.

'Is that the Ashram?' I eagerly asked.

'Not yet,' he replied, and I noticed the quizzical look in his expression. Then in a few minutes he remarked, 'You see those trees and some buildings beyond? That's the Ashram.'

By this time I had lost any sense of physical being. All was concentrated in the thought of what was approaching. In a minute or two the car drew up at a gate under a big tamarind tree. We got out and went along a narrow brick path which passed through a custard-apple orchard. Then a little garden gate led to a small enclosure where a simple building stood. We stepped up onto the veranda. I felt encumbered with the bag in my hand and hurriedly handed it to my companion. He took it and, standing a little to one side, ushered me into the room. As I entered, a slight brown figure rose up and came toward me. I was conscious of nothing but a sense of light. I fell on my knees. Hands gently raised me up, and a voice said: 'You shall be my daughter.' My consciousness of the physical world began to return, and I saw a face smiling at me with eyes full of love, blended with a gentle twinkle of amusement. Yes, this was Mahatma Gandhi, and I had arrived. He went back to his white gaddi behind a little desk, and I sat down on the floor in front of him.

People began coming in and out of the room, and I noticed everyone spoke of 'Bapu'. Here there was no Mahatma Gandhi, only Bapu, meaning in Gujerati, Father. But in this case it had a meaning all its own, just as he whom it described was unique.

Bapu now said, 'Come along, let's go to see Ba (Mother),' and he took me onto the veranda and on into the kitchen.

Bapu introduced me jokingly in Gujerati, but I could understand he was telling Ba she would have to bring out her best English. Ba, very small and dignified, folded her hands and said sweetly, 'How do you do.' But she kept looking at my feet.

'She is looking at your shoes,' said Bapu, 'because our custom in India is to take off our shoes before coming into a kitchen.'

I rushed out onto the veranda and took mine off at once. Bapu laughed.

Thus my new education began.

From: Mira Behn (Madeleine Slade), *The Spirit's Pilgrimage*, Utah: Great River Books, 1995, pp.65-67.

POSTSCRIPT:

About ten years before she penned her autobiography, Mirabehn edited a volume containing over half of all the letters that Gandhi had written to her. In her introductory essay to *Bapu's Letters to Mira* she describes her meeting with the Mahatma in even more reverential terms than in the above extract:

> We passed through a small gate, then up two steps to a verandah and through a door into a room. As I entered, I became conscious of a small spare figure rising up from a white *gaddi* and stepping

> towards me. I knew it was Bapu, but, so completely overcome was I with reverence and joy, that I could see and feel nothing but a heavenly light. I fell on my knees at Bapu's feet. He lifted me up and taking me in his arms said, 'You shall be my daughter.' And so has it been from that day. (Mirabehn, *Bapu's Letters to Mira,* p.6)

FURTHER READING:

Gupta, Krishna Murti (ed.), *Mira Behn: Gandhi's Daughter Disciple: Birth Centenary Volume,* New Delhi: Himalaya Seva Sangh, 1992.

Mirabehn (ed.), *Bapu's Letters to Mira [1924-1948],* Ahmedabad: Navajivan, 1949.

Suhrud, Tridip and Thomas Weber (eds.), *Beloved Bapu: The Mahatma Gandhi/Mirabehn Correspondence,* New Delhi: Orient BlackSwan, 2014.

Weber, Thomas, *Going Native: Gandhi's Relationship with Western Women,* New Delhi: Roli Books, 2011.

1926 KATHERINE MAYO

Katherine Mayo was an American writer who is best known for her landmark book *Mother India.* Mayo insisted that her book was to be an impartial study of India for an American audience which only knew that 'Mr. Gandhi lived there; also tigers...' She interviewed Gandhi for the book on 17 March 1926. The book caused uproar in India when it was published the following year. It strongly backed British imperialism to reform India from what she saw as debased Hindu social customs such as child marriage. The book went through twenty-seven editions, becoming one of the most popular books on India in the first half of the last century. The Anglophile Mayo pleased the British rulers, outraged Indian public opinion (many rejoinder volumes were published), and discredited Gandhi (who responded with an article entitled 'Drain Inspector's Report'). Gandhi had hoped that she would repent for what she had written. She did not, and followed up with two further books on the same theme that were so obviously propaganda pieces that even the British authorities distanced themselves from them.

A small stone house, such as would pass unremarked in any small town in America. A wicket gate, a sun-baked garden, a bare and clean room flooded with light from a broad-side of windows. In the room, sitting on a floor cushion with his back to a blank wall, a man. To his right two younger men, near a slant-topped desk perhaps eighteen inches high. To his left, a backless wooden bench for the use of western visitors. If there are other objects in the room, one does not see them for interest in the man with his back to the wall.

His head is close-shaven, and such hair as he has is turning grey. His eyes, small and dark, have a look of weariness, almost of renunciation, as of one who, having vainly striven, now withdraws from striving, unconvinced. Yet from time to time, as he talks, his eyes flash. His ears are large and conspicuously protruding. His costume, being merely a loin cloth, exposes his hairy body, his thin, wiry arms, and his bare, thin, interlaced legs, upon which he sits like Buddha with the soles of his feet turned up. His hands are busy with a little wooden spinning-wheel planted on the ground before him. The right hand twirls the wheel while the left evolves a cotton thread.

'What is my message to America?' he repeated, in his light, dispassionate, even voice. 'My message to America is the hum of this spinning-wheel.'

Then he speaks at length, slowly, with pauses. And as he speaks the two young men, his secretaries, lying over their slant-topped desk, write down every word he says.

The wheel hums steadily on. And the thread it spins for America appears and reappears in the pages of this book.

From: Katherine Mayo, *Mother India,* London: Jonathan Cape, 1927, p.201.

POSTSCRIPT:

Gandhi had been long battling against most of the customs Mayo abhorred; the real problem with her book was that it impugned Hinduism which Gandhi celebrated while trying to eradicate its blemishes. *Mother India* championed British colonialism which Gandhi was attempting to dismantle. Whatever truths there may have been in the book, it had slandered Gandhi's people. His "Drain Inspector's Report" titled review was angry, but it was also ambiguous, leaving the impression that it was a difficult document for Gandhi to write. In his review he notes:

> The book is cleverly and powerfully written. The carefully chosen quotations give it the appearance of a truthful book. But the impression it leaves on my mind is, that it is the report of a drain inspector sent out with the one purpose of opening and examining the drains of the country to be reported upon, or to give a graphic description of the stench exuded by the opened drains. If Miss Mayo had confessed that she had gone to India merely to open out and examine the drains of India, there would perhaps be little to complain about her compilation. But she says in effect with a certain amount of triumph, 'The drains are India'. [...] Her case is to perpetuate white domination in India on the plea of India's unfitness to rule herself. [...] Whilst I consider the book to be unfit to be placed before Americans and Englishmen (for it can do no good to them), it is a book that every Indian can read with some degree of profit. We may repudiate the charge as it has been named by her, but we may not repudiate the substance underlying the many allegations she has made. It is a good thing to see ourselves as others see us. We need not even examine the motive with which the book is written. A cautious reformer may make some use of it. [...] But let us not resent being made aware of the dark side of the picture wherever it exists. Overdrawn her pictures of our insanitation, child marriages, etc., undoubtedly are. But let them serve

> as a spur to much greater effort than we have hitherto put forth in order to rid society of all cause of reproach. (M.K. Gandhi, "Drain Inspector's Report", *Young India,* 15 September 1927)

Gandhi supporter, the French intellectual Romain Rolland summed up Gandhi's critique by asking, 'Suppose I come to London and visit nothing but the slums, the brothels and the clinics catering for serious illnesses, and then say, "This is England!" Would that be honourable?' (Rolland to Renée Thiesson, 2 October 1927)

Further Reading:

Athiyaman, P., and A.R. Venkatachalapathy, "Debate: On Gandhi, Mayo and Emilsen", *South Asia* (1989), vol.12, no.2, pp.83-90.

Emilsen, William W., "Gandhi and Mayo's 'Mother India'", *South Asia* (1987), vol.10, no.1, pp.69-81.

Field, Harry H., *After Mother India,* New York: Harcourt, Brace and Company, 1929.

Jha, Manoranjan, *Katherine Mayo and India,* New Delhi: People's Publishing House, 1971.

Seshachari, C., *Gandhi and the American Scene: An Intellectual History and Inquiry,* Bombay: Nachiketa, 1969.

Weber, Thomas, *Going Native: Gandhi's Relationship with Western Women,* New Delhi: Roli Books, 2011.

1926

ZAKIR HUSAIN

Born in Hyderabad in central India in 1897, Zakir Husain attended the Anglo-Mohamedan Oriental College (later Aligarh Muslim University) where he became a well-known student leader, obtaining his B.A. with honours in 1918. Following Gandhi's call for the youth of India to boycott state-run institutions, he became one of the founders of what was to become Jamia Millia Islamia (National Islamic University). After completing an M.A., he went to Berlin where he obtained a Ph.D. in economics in 1923. When the Jamia was facing closure for lack of funds, Husain asked for it to be kept open until he returned to India. The university moved to Delhi and was supported by Gandhi. On his return, at the age of twenty-nine, he became the vice-chancellor, staying in the position for twenty-one years. Husain became one of the leading educational thinkers in the country and turned the Jamia into a reputed centre of learning. After Indian independence, he became the vice-chancellor of Aligarh Muslim University providing stabilising leadership during a time of communal tensions. He became a member of the Rajya Sabha in 1956, and the governor of Bihar the following year. He served as the second vice-president of India between 1962 and 1967 when he was elected the third (and first Muslim) president of the Republic, a post he held until his death in 1969.

It was a morning in June, 1926. Three of my colleagues of the Jamia Millia Islamia and I had come to Sabarmati Ashram to meet Gandhiji. We had arrived rather late the previous night and arrangements had been hastily made to put us up. We were told that we would have breakfast in Gandhiji's hut, and were now seated there, four in a row, facing the kitchen, with Ba serving out food. Suddenly we heard a voice behind us:

'How lovely!'

We all turned, to see Gandhiji striding towards us. He came and sat on his cot, gracious and smiling, and talked and laughed as if he had known us for years.

Gandhiji was much talked about in Germany, where the translation of Romain Rolland's book had a record sale. I had brought out a book on him myself while I was there and also delivered speeches on his message of non-violence. But this was the first time I met him. During the two or three days I was at the Ashram, I had fairly long talks with him. I was already committed to working in the Jamia Millia. This commitment had brought me into close personal contact with many eminent [Muslim leaders], and I was naturally anxious to find out how much guidance and support I would get from them, and which method of approach would yield the best results. My motive in coming to see Gandhiji was the same. I wanted to know what Gandhiji thought and felt about the Jamia Millia and in what way he would be willing and able to help in its maintenance and expansion. He had served it once, in 1924, when quite a number of its influential supporters had declared or implied that its continuation was no longer necessary or possible. What would he do for it now?

It seemed he could do very little, because of the prevailing suspicions and tensions. But I was more deeply moved and inspired with a greater confidence than I would have been if he had expressed himself in a different way and promised liberal financial assistance. I would have got money, but I would also have felt that it was money that would make the Jamia Millia and not men. It was just the way he said things, the way he looked when saying them, that impressed me. I was not carried away. I did not feel that life would be easier for the Jamia Millia or for me. But I became more determined to do what I had decided to do.

What was this due to?

It seemed quite clear from the way Gandhiji talked that he was searching for the truth, the truth that would govern his relationship with the Jamia Millia. There was no uncertainty. Gandhiji wanted the Jamia Millia to take root, to grow strong, to represent an idea that was clear in his mind. But it would have to make itself, and not be made by him. He would be deeply concerned, he would watch, he would hope. But he would do nothing by way of help that would involve risk of the Jamia Millia losing its freedom to develop its own identity. Institutions, like men, must make themselves into what they want to become. I was profoundly impressed by what Gandhiji said. And I could see why. His thought and speech expressed his whole personality, and his personality was not an accident of nature, or a product of inherited culture; it had been fashioned by himself, in accordance with a moral design. He had worked on it like a craftsman, long and patiently, and was still far from satisfied. He had worked, not in seclusion or solitude, but, as it were, in the market-place of life, where all could see the unwavering determination and tireless energy with which he gave it the form that he desired and could test its strength. His smile, his laughter, his charm were essential elements of the design; so were his sincerity and humility. He did not talk like one who thought he had finished what he had set out to do, but like one who was still engaged in it, who could still commit mistakes, lose his grip over his tools, or falter in his resolve. Perfect accord between principle and practice is not achieved once for all. It requires continuous effort, continuous self-examination and in the process sincerity and humility acquire a certain rare quality. Gandhiji's sincerity was not only obvious; it was a challenge to me to be equally sincere. And I felt that I had to approach my task with a spirit of reverence, to be humble because the greater the task the more exacting would be its demands. One had to be worthy of one's task in every way and all the time.

From: Zakir Husain, "Moral Awareness", in S. Radhakrishnan (ed.), *Mahatma Gandhi 100 Years,* New Delhi: Gandhi Peace Foundation, 1969, pp.123-128 at pp.123-125.

POSTSCRIPT:

While Husain and Gandhi trusted each other and there was obvious affection between them (Husain even called Gandhi his guru), he was not exactly a follower of Gandhi in the strict sense. He may have been strongly influenced by the Mahatma: he wore khadi, at Gandhi's request prepared a syllabus based on Gandhi's scheme of what became known as 'nai talim' or 'basic education' that linked intellectual with practical work, he requested Gandhi to send G. Ramachandran to the Jamia Millia Islamia to teach khadi, and asked Gandhi for help with his Muslim educational institutions when assistance was required. However, he was independent minded and did not accept everything that came from Gandhi's lips unquestioningly. Although head of Islamic educational institutions, Husain held strongly to the Gandhian vision of a secular India. As Rajmohan Gandhi notes, 'That a Muslim convinced about Hindu-Muslim unity was in charge of Jamia pleased Gandhi; and Zakir Husain was glad to find that the Mahatma trusted him and offered no advice on how the Jamia should be run.' For Husain the idea of the Jamia was to create a feeling of Indian nationhood in a way that did not lead

Muslims to lose their Islamic identity. In this it was probably closer to the Gandhian spirit than any other Islamic institution. This close relationship and what it entailed was not always recognised or welcomed by others. At times Husain was accused of not being Muslim enough, and to some Hindus the mere fact that he was a Muslim caused concern, nevertheless he noted that while the Jamia was a Muslim institution with Islamic ideals he would not allow narrow or false interpretation of those ideals turn the university into a breeding-ground of communalism. Because of his personality and the fact that the roles he engaged in were not overtly political, he was spared outright attacks from the orthodoxy (although it is clear that Muhammad Ali Jinnah did not trust him and others thought that he may have been sacrificing his faith to accommodate the Hindus). This allowed him to end his life as the highly respected president of the Republic of India.

FURTHER READING:

Gandhi, Rajmohan, *Understanding the Muslim Mind,* New Delhi: Penguin, 1987.

Mujeeb, M., *Dr Zakir Husain: A Biography,* New Delhi: National Book Trust, 1992.

Ruhela, S.P., and Ikram Ahmad, *Uniqueness of Zakir Husain and His Contributions: Birth Centenary Volume,* New Delhi: Regency, 1997.

1926

MURIEL LESTER

From a wealthy family, Muriel Lester left school at age eighteen in 1902 seemingly headed for the life of the idle rich. However, Tolstoy's writings led her to pacifism, and a visit to a Factory Girls' Club, founded by Annie Besant, further changed her life. Muriel and her sister Dorothy devoted their lives to social work in London, eventually founding Kingsley Hall, a social gathering place for those living in the surrounding overcrowded slums. Eventually it became what has been called a 'veritable Christian ashram'. In 1919, Muriel came across Gandhi's writings and she visited Gandhi in 1926 at the Sabarmati Ashram. She developed a close friendship with Gandhi and hosted him when he was in London during the Round Table Conference in 1931. She returned to India and joined Gandhi's Harijan tour in 1934 and visited him on several further occasions. Following the Second World War, Muriel Lester devoted her life to the International Fellowship of Reconciliation, travelling the world as its secretary until she was in her eighties.

It is a hot October afternoon, 1926, in his first ashram. My nephew and I are naturally nervous. We have been practicing the India greeting. Hurriedly we kick off our western shoes, feeling self-conscious.

But here is Gandhi striding across the room, as thin as we expected, and a little stooped. Smiling, he shakes us by the hand, thoroughly pleased to see us. He seats us by him (we creak a little on our ankles). He devotes his entire attention to us, not because we are any different from the rest of the world, but because we are people, humans, children of God like himself.

After a few minutes we are shown to our rooms, in a row of little sheds with mud floors. Inside each room there is a cot, a table, a few pegs on the wall. We squat on the mat on the cool floor, breathing deeply from the impact of the vitality we experienced in him a few moments before. We feel an inrush of confidence, a sense of stability, such as some tree lovers get from a deep rooted, wide spreading oak.

A young man comes and asks us to choose what work we wish to do while here. Of course everybody looks after his room, and stands daily washing his clothes in the river, sweat pouring from his nose, fish who apparently love the taste of soap, nipping at his shins. But, what are we going to do for our fellows? I choose spinning. My nephew chooses the job of cleaning the latrines. But he is in luck! There is no plumbing – everything has to be done by hand. Before long he finds that the other man with whom he will work is Gandhi!

I still remember the unwelcome yet exotic sound of the gong booming out the call to get up a quarter to four next morning. Someone calls for me and shows me how to swing my lantern close to the ground as I walk so that any snakes or other things in the path may be warned to get out of the way. The other side of the garden is the praying ground about the size of a tennis court and all sand. We turn down our lanterns, take off our shoes and squat in the darkness. The Indian instruments, either the zittar or the bina prepare the way for prayer. At first it sounds a wailful, mournful sort of music, but one soon comes to love it. Gandhi sits near the musicians and the ashram children are ranged just in front of him, quite close. A little thread of silver, a waning moon, appears above his head.

Gradually we learn the rules by watching the other hundreds of folks trying to keep them. We are ashamed of the feeling but are deeply relieved to find that some of them fail, as often as we do.

From: Muriel Lester, *Gandhi's Signature,* New York: Fellowship of Reconciliation, 1949, pp.5-7.

POSTSCRIPT:

Sometimes second and subsequent meetings are even more memorable than the first. Unlike her nephew who cleaned latrines with the Mahatma, Muriel Lester had trouble establishing a close relationship with him. While friends encouraged her to talk to Gandhi, she was hesitant because he was constantly surrounded by admirers who were hanging on his every word. For almost a month they exchanged the usual pleasantries without any deep contact. Shortly before she was to leave the Ashram, friends ushered her into Gandhi's room. The Mahatma was silently spinning. To overcome the embarrassing silence, Lester blurted out that it would be important for Gandhi to come to England. Gandhi responded by pointing out that his success in nonviolent methods had not reached the stage where he had anything to teach peace advocates like her. She responded by explaining that she didn't want him to come to England 'to teach us. I want you to come and learn from us.' Gandhi, who always favoured those who challenged rather than those who venerated him, burst out laughing, and they became close friends. (Lester, *It Occurred to Me,* p.135)

FURTHER READING:

Deats, Richard, (ed.), *Ambassador of Reconciliation: A Muriel Lester Reader,* Philadelphia, PA: New Society Publishers, 1991.

Lester, Muriel, *Entertaining Gandhi,* London: Nicholson and Watson, 1932.

Lester, Muriel, "Gandhiji: 1926-39", in Chandrashanker Shukla (ed.), *Incidents of Gandhiji's Life, by Fifty-Four Contributors,* Bombay: Vora, 1949, 143-148.

Lester, Muriel, *My Host the Hindu,* London: Williams and Norgate, 1931.

Lester, Muriel, *It Occurred to Me,* New York: Harper and Brothers, 1937.

Wallis, Jill, *Mother of World Peace: The Life of Muriel Lester,* Enfield Lock, Middlesex: Hisarlik Press, 1993.

Weber, Thomas, *Going Native: Gandhi's Relationship with Western Women,* New Delhi: Roli Books, 2011.

1927

ARCHIBALD FENNER BROCKWAY

Born to missionary parents in Calcutta in 1888, Fenner Brockway discovered an interest in pacifism while at school in London. He became a journalist and member of the Independent Labour Party and by his mid-twenties was a committed pacifist. He spoke out against British involvement in the First World War and was arrested and imprisoned for long periods for his anti-conscription activities. Following his release, in 1919 he joined the India League which advocated Indian Independence. In the 1920s and '30s, he was a member of the British Parliament and chairperson of War Resisters' International. Although he lost his absolute pacifism during the Spanish Civil War, after the Second World War he was one of the founders of the Campaign for Nuclear Disarmament and again a Member of Parliament. In 1964 he accepted a life peerage and sat in the House of Lords as The Baron Brockway. He was active in peace and disarmament causes well into his late '80s. He died in 1988 just short of his hundredth birthday. Brockway, who had been in mail contact with Gandhi for half a dozen years, was badly injured in a motor car accident while visiting India in 1927 at the invitation of the National Congress and the Trade Union Congress.

I was fortunate in having many interesting visitors. Indeed, the visitors were so many that a large notice had to be displayed prohibiting them without permission of the Resident Medical Officer. [...]

Most of all I appreciated the visits of Mahatma Gandhi. He was in Madras for four days and gave me half-an-hour each day. He came in a white loin cloth with a loose white garment over his shoulders. His personality was much more vital and genial than I expected. His eyes twinkled with the joy of life as he smiled, his walk and movements were vigorous. I was both fortunate and unfortunate, because I found the influences of his personality always stilled my feverishness and helped me in conquering pain; unfortunate because I was unable to discuss with him as fully as I should have liked the problems of India and the implications of our common pacifist philosophy.

One day he was observing as 'Silence' day; he did not speak, but, taking my hand in his, seemed to pour out the essence of his personality with healing influence. I was interested to note that, while no words passed his lips, he wrote down a question for me: How was I sleeping? He had instinctively found the difficulty which was troubling me most; for three weeks I had had no natural sleep.

Another day I discussed with him the influence of drugs. I had been given bromide, and it had had a startling effect. I felt as though my personality was divided into two parts. My mind was exceptionally clear and sane, as though liberated from the influence of emotion or the senses. But beneath it was a second personality, vicious and violent, full of bitterness and anger. That evening I had heard that the Indian nurses had had no Christmas privileges and that they had to work overtime whilst the Anglo-Indian nurses had had their party. My second personality concentrated upon this grievance, and got into an amazing passion over it. It made me want to do violence to the hospital authorities; an overwhelming desire for sheer physical assault surged up within me. At the same time I had this feeling, my sane mind was contemptuous of it. It realised that the violent emotions were due to the drug and sought only to throw off its influence. I felt as though I were imprisoned in a net and I struggled to break through it. When at last normal consciousness came, I found a nurse, a ward-boy and a doctor were holding me down! Gandhi was greatly interested in this experience, but acknowledged that he had not considered with any thoroughness the question of drugs and their physical and psychological effects.

From: A. Fenner Brockway, *A Week in India (and Three Months in an Indian Hospital)*, London: The New Leader, 1928, pp.76-79, Independent Labour Publications (ILP).

POSTSCRIPT:

In another version of the meeting with Gandhi in Madras Hospital on the Mahatma's silence day, Brockway notes that 'He jotted down a few lines of enquiry on a piece of paper, and I told him that I was not sleeping at night owing to the pain. He took my hand, and an extraordinary calm came over me. That night I slept without a drug for the first time.' (Brockway, "My Personal Memories", pp.35-36)

FURTHER READING:

Brockway, Fenner, "My Personal Memories", in Chandrashanker Shukla (ed.), *Reminiscences of Gandhiji: By Forty-eight Contributors*, Bombay: Vora, 1951, pp.35-37.

Brockway, Fenner, *The Indian Crisis*, London: Victor Gollancz, 1930.

1928

HORACE GUNDRY ALEXANDER

Born in 1889, the English Quaker Horace Alexander was educated at Cambridge University, graduating with a degree in History in 1912. With the outbreak of the First World War, he served on several anti-war committees and then, as a conscientious objector to military service, instead of joining the army he started his career as a teacher. He first met Gandhi on a trip to India in 1928 and had frequent contact with him while Gandhi was in England in 1931 attending the Round Table Conference on India's future. He then became one of the founders of the India Conciliation Group as an intermediary between Gandhi and the British Government. He also had contact with Gandhi while he was stationed in India serving with the Friends' Ambulance Service in 1942-1943, visiting the imprisoned Gandhi in Poona. He returned to India in 1946 at Gandhi's insistence to work in the Indian section of the Society of Friends, and saw the Mahatma regularly in Calcutta (he accompanied Gandhi on part of the Mahatma's Noakhali pilgrimage) and New Delhi in the period leading up to his assassination. In 1984 he was awarded India's highest honour available to a non-Indian civilian, the Padma Bhushan. Throughout his life he was a dedicated bird-watcher. He died in 1989.

In 1927-28 I had the opportunity to visit India and to spend some months travelling about the country. I was introduced to India by C.F. Andrews, so it was natural that I should plan to spend some time at the Ashram of his intimate friend, Mahatma Gandhi. Indeed, I had hoped to visit him soon after my arrival in India, but at that time he was touring in the South, so I postponed my visit to the Sabarmati Ashram till the spring, just before my return to England.

So one day late in March, 1928, I arrived at Sabarmati railway station, and found a tonga which drove me to the Ashram. I had been expected, and within a very short time I was being looked after by Mahadev Desai, who then handed me over to a young member of the Ashram, whose name, I am sorry to say, I now forget. He explained the local arrangements and left me in my room. Later, he took me over to the evening prayers.

When we were all assembled, Gandhi himself came quickly walking, sat down, and the prayers began. That was my first sight of him. At the end of the prayers, while the members of the Ashram gave their reports, the children began to run about. They had a little game of running past Gandhi's seat, and he put out his hand as if to catch them as they ran past him. So the first thing I learnt about him was that he enjoyed the company of children.

Next day, it was arranged that I should have a talk with him at, I think, three in the afternoon. I arrived a minute or so before three. Mahadev looked in to see if Gandhi was ready for me and came back to say: 'Would you mind waiting a few minutes?' Of course not. Why should such a busy man be expected to be ready on the dot? I had had plenty of occasions for sitting, waiting for appointments, perhaps fifteen or twenty minutes, without even the suggestion that it was unusual. A few minutes later, I was asked to go in. There I was immediately met by two small surprises: first, I had been in India long enough to learn the Indian salutation, putting my two hands together. But Gandhi insisted on shaking hands: the small but simple courtesy of using a Western salutation to greet a Westerner. Then he said: 'Please excuse me for keeping you waiting. At four minutes to three I asked if you had come; as you had not, I decided that I had better have my milk first, so that our talk need not be interrupted. But I am sorry to have kept you waiting.' What wonderful courtesy; and what an example of the virtue of punctuality! I was to learn quickly how it was that his friends said that he was 'the slave of his watch'. 'Slave', is, of course, quite the wrong word. He had more to do in every 24 hours than almost any other man; so he had learnt how to pack the most into every minute. Yet he never gave the impression of being hurried. You never felt that he was impatiently waiting for the visitor to depart.

The only other thing that I recall from our first talk was an incident when a local man, obviously not a member of the Ashram, came into the room. He prostrated himself on the ground, with his forehead in the dust. I could not understand what Gandhi said to him in Gujarati; but he spoke very sharply to him and was obviously displeased at this lowly obeisance.

I stayed for a week at the Ashram, and I soon learnt that, every morning, Gandhi spent half an hour helping some of the women to cut up the day's vegetables. I did not much like being a useless member of the community, even for a week; so I said to him: 'Would you allow me to help with this work each morning?' 'Yes, certainly,' he replied. 'But you will have to get up half an hour earlier.' Which, of course, I readily did.

My first morning of vegetable cutting happened to be Gandhi's silent day. This created some problems, as I was a 'new boy' who did not know what to do. But he made various signs and gestures, and I tried to copy him, so I think there was no major disaster.

I will not describe the other details of those days, but two things stand out in my memory. They have been recorded in print elsewhere; but they are worth repeating. When I was about to leave, Gandhi said to me: 'You have spent a week with us here, so I expect you may have seen things that you think might be done better. If so, please write and tell me what you would suggest. We are not above learning from our visitors. There are many things that I know are not satisfactory. But we are short of money. We shall remedy them when we are able to.' Then he pointed to a place where water ran out from a tap, under which we washed our hands after each meal. 'As an Englishman,' he said, 'you are likely to have noticed that there is no drainage under that tap. That is bad hygiene. I hope to put it right soon.' I protested that I should not bother him over a little thing like that. 'You call it a little thing,' he said, 'but I do not agree with you. Hygiene is very important. Anyway it is against our philosophy here to divide things into big and little. If a thing is badly done, that is a serious fault, and it cannot be dismissed as merely a "little thing".'

During my last talk with him, I told him that I should soon be returning to England. If I had the opportunity to tell public meetings about my experiences, what should I say? First,' he said, 'we want you to get off our backs.' I had not expected such a sharp expression. But it was unforgettable.

From: Horace Alexander, "My First Meeting with Gandhiji", *Illustrated Weekly of India* (1969), vol.90, no.17, p.17.

Postscript:

On his return to England, Horace Alexander still did not want to bother Gandhi about what he considered small issues like dripping taps and hygiene, instead, in a letter to Gandhi he suggested that it might prove to be beneficial to introduce a period of silence, in the Quaker mode, into the daily prayers at the ashram. (Alexander, *Gandhi through Western Eyes,* p.190) Gandhi considered it seriously, remembering such meetings he attended in South Africa. He understood the theory behind the practice but believed that in India it would fall flat. He noted that as there are many ways of worshipping there was no reason to take on new ways if the old ones were adequate. (See Gandhi's letter to Horace Alexander, 22 June 1928) The recitations and singing of bhajans continues, at Sevagram at least, to this day.

FURTHER READING:

Alexander, Horace, "At Sabarmati", in Chandrashanker Shukla (ed.), *Gandhiji as We Know Him, by Seventeen Contributors,* Bombay: Vora, 1945, pp.68-76.

Alexander, Horace, *Gandhi through Western Eyes,* Bombay: Asia, 1969.

Alexander, Horace, *The Indian Ferment: A Traveller's Tale,* London: Williams and Norgate, 1929.

Carnall, Geoffrey, *Gandhi's Interpreter: A Life of Horace Alexander,* Edinburgh: Edinburgh University Press, 2010.

1929 J.C. KUMARAPPA

Born in Tanjore into a devout Christian family in 1892, Joseph Cornelius Kumarappa went to London to study economics and chartered accountancy in 1913. He remained until after the war, returning to India in 1919 only after much pleading by his mother. A decade later he went to the United States to study business administration at Syracuse University and public finance at Columbia University where he also completed an M.A. dissertation on the causes of Indian poverty. This turned him into a nationalist. Soon after meeting Gandhi he became a professor at the Gandhian nationalist university, the Gujarat Vidyapith in Ahmedabad, not far from Gandhi's Sabarmati Ashram. He edited Gandhi's journal *Young India* during the Salt Satyagraha and was imprisoned in 1932-34 and 1942-45 as part of Gandhi's campaigns. In the mid-1930s he became secretary of the All India Village Industries Association in Wardha and, after Indian independence, worked for the Planning Commission of India in the areas of agricultural policy and rural development. Although he formally retired in 1953, he kept disseminating his message of 'Gandhian Economics' till the end. He died in early 1960.

In the year 1929, I returned from the United States where I had made a study of public finances, and wrote out the story of the British exploiting India through their taxation policy in the form of an essay. It was suggested that I should publish this. I was negotiating with some of the publishers in India in this regard when I was told the subject was one in which Gandhiji would be intensely interested, and I was urged to submit the manuscript to him first. At the time Gandhi was merely a name to me. It was hardly associated with any definite ideas. The person who was responsible for this suggestion was very persistent about my getting in touch with Gandhiji. Gandhiji was passing through Bombay towards the end of April that year after his South Indian tour. I was then practicing as an Auditor in Bombay. I was directed to go and see Gandhiji at Mani Bhuvan, Laburnum Road, Gamdevi, which was his usual Bombay residence at that time. I went in European clothes up the staircase, and the door was answered by someone whom I took to be a servant clad in dhoti and shirts. I asked him if I could see Gandhiji, and I was told that Gandhiji was busy in a Working Committee meeting, and that he would not be able to see me just then. I had taken my manuscript with me, and marking that the person who was talking to me was able to speak good English, and thinking he might be worthy of taking a message, I left the manuscript with him and asked him to give it to Gandhiji. (This person later turned out to be Gandhiji's Secretary Pyarelal.) Pyarelal telephoned to my office address later to say that Gandhiji would want to see me in Ahmedabad after he had had a look at the essay, and suggested that I see him at Sabarmati on the 9th of May, 1929 at 2.30 p.m. I reached Sabarmati accordingly that morning, and went to the Ashram where I was horrified by the emptiness of the so-called guest room. It was devoid of all furniture excepting a charpai, though glorified by the designation of a guest room.

Squatting toilet arrangements further made me anxious to get away from the place at the earliest moment. With these personal difficulties, my appointment being in the afternoon, I anxiously waited to get it over. The house where Gandhiji stayed was pointed out to me, and I was told that was the place where I should report myself at the appointed time. With a walking stick in one hand and the manuscript in the other I walked down the bank of the Sabarmati at about 2 p.m., and after enjoying the beauty of the bed of the river, walked up the bank again towards Gandhiji's house.

On the way up, I saw an old man seated under a tree on a neatly cleaned cow-dunged floor, spinning. Having never seen a spinning wheel before, I leaned on my walking stick and standing akimbo was watching as there were still ten minutes for the appointment. This old man after about five minutes opened his toothless lips, and with a smile on his face enquired if I was Kumarappa. It suddenly dawned on me that my questioner might be no other than Mahatma Gandhi. So I, in my turn, asked him if he was Gandhiji; and when he nodded I promptly sat down on the cow-dunged floor regardless of the well-kept crease on my silk trousers! Seeing me sitting without stretched legs, more or less in a reclining position, someone from the house came rushing down with a chair for me, and Gandhiji asked me to get up and sit in the chair more comfortably. I replied that since he was seated on the floor I did not propose to take a chair.

Gandhiji told me that he was interested in the essay I had written, and that he proposed to publish that in a series in his journal *Young India*. Then he enquired if I would undertake a rural survey for him in Gujarat, as he found that the approach I had to economics was almost exactly the same as his, and that I was about the first student of economics he had come across with that same viewpoint. I raised the difficulty of language, but he quickly got over that by saying that he would place the professors of economics of the Gujarat Vidyapith with all their students at my disposal to help me with the survey, and suggested that I go to see the Vice-Chancellor of the Gujarat Vidyapith, Kaka Kalelkar, who, Gandhiji informed me, was the very person who came running down the steps with a chair for me!

In the afternoon I went to the Gujarat Vidyapith to see Kaka Kalelkar. Seeing that I was a young man dressed in the most fashionable Western style, Kakasaheb did not feel that I would fit into the sort of work that Gandhiji wanted me to do, and he made my ignorance of Gujarati to be a great handicap and discouraged me. I got into a huff and, even without taking leave of Gandhiji, returned to Bombay, and wrote to him that I should be glad to help him with any work that he wanted done, and reported that Kakasaheb did not feel that I could be of any use. By return post I got back a letter from Kakasaheb to say that he would be most happy if I would go back and do the work Gandhiji wanted. (Years later Gandhiji, in the course of a conversation on the study of characters, referred to this incident and said: 'You remember Kakasaheb was not able to size you up when he first met you. On the other hand, the moment I saw you I felt here is a young man I must grab.' And he succeeded in doing so, as later events proved.)

From: J.C. Kumarappa, "Lessons from his Life", in Chandrashanker Shukla (ed.), *Incidents of Gandhiji's Life, by Fifty-Four Contributors,* Bombay: Vora, 1949, pp.131-143 at 131-134.

POSTSCRIPT:

Kumarappa went on to write countless articles, booklets and books on various aspects of Gandhian economics and rural development. One of the most important, for which Gandhi wrote the foreword, made clear that for Kumarappa (and Gandhi) economics was about far more than material well-being:

> Like his brochure on the "Practice & Precepts of Jesus" Dr. Kumarappa's on "The Economy of Permanence" is a jail production. It is not as easy to understand as the first. It needs careful reading twice or thrice if it is to be fully appreciated. When I took up the manuscript I was curious to know what it could contain. The opening chapter satisfied my curiosity and led me on to the end without fatigue and yet with profit. This doctor of our village industries shows that only through them we shall arrive at the economy of permanence in the place of that of the fleeting nature we see around us at present. He tackles the question — shall the body triumph over and stifle the soul or shall the latter triumph over and express itself through a perishable body which, with its few wants healthily satisfied, will be free to subserve the end of the imperishable soul? This is 'Plain living and High thinking'. (Gandhi in Kumarappa, *Economy of Permanence,* piii)

Despite first appearances, in Kumarappa, the ex-Westernised dandy, the Mahatma had clearly found his ideal economist and village industries advocate.

Further Reading:

Kumarappa, J.C., *Economy of Permanence,* Rajghat, Varanasi: Sarva Seva Sangh, 1948.

Lindley, Mark, J.C. Kumarappa: *Mahatma Gandhi's Economist,* Mumbai: Popular, 2006.

1929 DR. SHERWOOD EDDY

George Sherwood Eddy was born in Kansas in January 1871. After graduating from Yale University at the age of twenty, he went to work for the YMCA and attended Princeton Theological Seminary, graduating in 1896. In 1911 he became YMCA secretary for Asia and travelled widely throughout the subcontinent. During the First World War, he worked with the British and American armies in France as a YMCA secretary. On 3 December 1929, the missionary evangelist visited Gandhi at the Sabarmati Ashram. In 1931 he retired from the YMCA and, in 1936, with the Reverend Sam Franklin, he founded the first Delta and Providence Cooperative Farm to assist sharecroppers in overcoming their entrenched poverty. The farm experiment lasted until 1956. During the Second World War, he favoured military action against the evils of Nazism, but later became a pacifist. He was a prolific writer throughout his life. He died in 1963.

I shall always remember Gandhi at his spinning wheel with the warm light of the Indian sun falling upon him as he sat upon the floor of his simple room and talked with us quietly of the approaching crisis in India's history.

His bodily presence, like that of the Apostle Paul or Socrates, is at first sight weak and unprepossessing; a small emaciated figure, weighing less than 100 pounds, bearing the marks of days of fasting, of five imprisonments and of long hours of work, beginning daily with his hour of prayer at four every morning. Three times he has been beaten by mobs and once left prone in the gutter as one dead.

He has a round, close-cropped head, large ears, a rather long nose, a quiet pensive face, save when it lights in a smile or ripples with laughter, as it so often does. But this only reveals his few remaining front teeth. It is characteristic of the man that he makes use of artificial dentistry at meal-time for practical purposes, but will have no 'false' teeth for the sake of appearance between times.

After three days spent in his Ashram, he impressed us as the most childlike, the most transparent, the most lovable of men. His whole character is centred in his unique passion for truth and reality.

From: Sherwood Eddy, "Dr. Sherwood Eddy", in Joseph John (comp.), *Gandhi as Others See Him*, Colombo: Bastian, 1933, pp.28-30 at pp.28-29. (Originally published in *The Christian Leader*, 1930).
Courtesy: *The New Leader*

POSTSCRIPT:

Eddy, who had had lunch with Lord Irwin not long before, was in fact carrying a message from the viceroy to the Mahatma and was asked to bring back a reply. Eddy noted that the Indians and the British were at this stage 'rapidly drifting apart' and that 'both feared violence'. Irwin, according to Eddy, 'was eager to come to an understanding with the Indian leaders'. Gandhi listened to the message and then gave a reply, which in essence said:

> To be told that India is an equal, but on the level of a beloved child who has not yet reached the age of responsibility and of political majority is not enough. We are offered Dominion status 'in the fullness of time', but this leaves our fate solely to Britain's selfish imperialistic decision. Our position is clear. Unless our demand for Dominion status is accepted on or before December 31, 1929 – that is, before the close of the coming Lahore meeting of the National Congress – we will be compelled, after vainly pleading for Dominion status for forty years, to declare for complete independence and organize a campaign of non-violent non-cooperation to obtain our freedom. (Eddy, *Eighty Adventurous Years,* p.167)

That campaign became the mass Civil Disobedience movement, launched by the celebrated Salt March to Dandi the following year.

FURTHER READING:

Eddy, Sherwood, *Eighty Adventurous Years,* New York: Harper, 1955.

1930 REGINALD REYNOLDS

Born in 1905, the English Quaker, peace activist and writer, Reginald Arthur Reynolds found himself at a loose end following the completion of his schooling. His friend Horace Alexander suggested that he go to India and see Mahatma Gandhi who would find something for him to do. Reynolds duly headed off for India in 1929 and, in the following year, Gandhi gave him something historic to do. Reynolds was given the honour of carrying Gandhi's ultimatum letter to the Viceroy Lord Irwin before the commencement of the Salt March. Due to ill health Reynolds returned to England a few months later. He did not revisit India until the year after Gandhi's assassination (as a delegate of the World Pacifist Conference); however they met in London while Gandhi was attending the Round Table Conference. Reynolds served as the General Secretary of the No More War Movement between 1933 and 1937. He married the writer Ethel Mannin in 1938. As a conscientious objector during the Second World War, he worked in a mobile hospital unit. During the 1950s, Reynolds travelled the world as field secretary to the British Friends' Peace Committee and, on one of those trips, in December 1958, he died suddenly of a brain haemorrhage in Adelaide, Australia.

The moment that I had been waiting for so many months came unexpectedly. [Reynolds came to the Sabarmati Ashram on 24 October 1929.] I knew that Mr. Gandhi has arrived at the Ashram (seminary) late the previous night [4 January 1930] and had caught a dim glimpse of him and heard his voice at the morning prayer. But I was busy in the study of the weaver's art when his 'Well, Stranger!' made me turn round sharply. I knew who it must be.

I was quite prepared for the lack of 'distinction' in the old man's face. I was not prepared for anything quite so typical of the minster's gallery in one of our own Friends' Meetings. Such a dear old man, with his bald head and spectacles, beaky nose, and bird-like lips, with his benign but somewhat toothless smile, I have seen perched at the head of many a silent gathering, and when he spoke there was the same mixture of sense and sobriety and shrewd but economical humour. Kindly practical, sensible, unemotional – the good man's character was obvious immediately, so far as its general lines were concerned.

But of that other thing that gives him power over people and draws them like a magnet from all parts of the country just to look at him, I could see no trace, nor have I got any more light on the matter in the days that have since elapsed. It cannot be his intellect, for though his common sense is acute he is anything but a genius. I suspect it is the simplest and rarest of things – his absolute sincerity.

This first impression of the outstanding characteristic of the Mahatma has been confirmed in the weeks that have followed. He carries his sincerity to the point of bluntness or rudeness if you like, that would shock my Quaker relations; though I should add that he couples it with a simple courtesy of manner that makes the difference between an insult and a reproof. It is typical of him that he dislikes dyed cloth – it is dishonest, he says, because it does not show the dirt. He himself always dresses in white khaddar [course home-spun] which is washed daily.

His scorching passion for truth is almost terrifying – I am always afraid that I shall lapse into one of those silly social lies that we Westerners tell so glibly when we are afraid to give offence or wish to avoid a long explanation, and that he will see through it. He gives to each one who comes in contact with him the impression of a real personal affection, but he can sever every attachment without a sigh of pain. They say that when Mogunlal [Maganlal] Gandhi died he was the coolest man at the Ashram, and ordained 'business as usual' and harder work to make up for the loss of so good a worker. [...]

He never misses his daily hour at the spinning wheel or the long morning and evening prayers. And he is still at the service of everyone, from the delegates of a trade dispute down to Reginald Reynolds or the nonentity of a non-conformist missionary who once wanted a good three-quarters of an hour of his time in telling Mr. Gandhi about himself.

It is a strange thing, but since I have been away from him for a few weeks travelling about India on my own before settling down again at the Ashram for a time, I have felt Gandhi's personality more than I did when with him. I always respected him, but now I feel much more strongly about him. [...]

His last letter lies before me as I write. I had asked him what I could do to help him, and it is typical of his courtesy that in the midst of all his activities he found a minute to reply. 'The real thing,' he writes, 'is not likely to begin before March [the commencement of the Salt March to Dandi]. I know you are doing your work in a thorough manner. Come when you can.' He says he has been thinking about my letter for the last three days, which I hope means that he has a place for me in his scheme of things. Finally, he reminds me that the Ashram is my home to come to whenever I like.

> I no longer wonder at the devotion of the blind masses. Rather am I one with them. If other reasons were lacking, I would follow such a captain for his pure chivalry alone, and so would all the world if they knew him.

From: Reginald Reynolds, "Mr. Reginald A. Reynolds", in Joseph John (comp.), *Gandhi as Others See Him,* Colombo: Bastian, 1933, pp.24-28 (Originally published in *The New Leader*).
Courtesy: *The New Leader*

POSTSCRIPT:

Before setting out on the historic Salt March, Gandhi wrote a letter to the Viceroy Lord Irwin setting out Indian demands that, if met, would forestall another mass civil disobedience campaign to secure political freedom from British rule. In that letter (dated 2 March 1930), Gandhi informed Irwin that, 'This letter is not in any way intended as a threat but is a simple and sacred duty peremptory on a civil resister. Therefore I am having it specially delivered by a young English friend who believes in the Indian cause and is a full believer in non-violence and whom Providence seems to have sent to me, as it were, for the very purpose.' Gandhi also went on to explain the choice of courier to the wider public:

> The messenger selected was a young English friend Reginald Reynolds who came to India some months ago and who has identified himself completely with the Indian cause. For me the sending of the letter was a religious act as the whole struggle is. And I selected an English friend as my messenger, because I wanted to forge a further check upon myself against any intentional act that would hurt a single Englishman. If I have any sense of honour in me, this choice should prove an automatic restraint even upon unconscious error. It pleases me also to have the unselfish and

> unsolicited association of a cultured, well-read, devout Englishman in an act which may, in spite of all my effort to the contrary, involve loss of English life. As for the letter itself, when the reader has the text before him he will see that it is not an ultimatum, but it is a friendly, if also a frank, communication from one who considers himself to be a friend of Englishmen. But the reader must hold himself in patience for a while. ("About that Letter", *Young India,* 6 March 1930)

Reginald Reynolds, in *To Live in Mankind,* observes: 'Before I went Gandhi insisted I should read the letter carefully, as he did not wish me to associate myself with it unless I was in complete agreement with its contents. My taking of this letter was, in fact, intended to be symbolic of the fact that this was not merely a struggle between the Indians and the British. By using an English courier instead of a postage stamp Bapu had deliberately dramatised this fact for all the world to know. But the symbolism would have been false had I merely taken the letter without completely associating myself with what it contained.' (p.51)

FURTHER READING:

Reynolds, Reginald, "Letters from Bapu", in Chandrashanker Shukla (ed.), *Incidents of Gandhiji's Life, by Fifty-Four Contributors,* Bombay: Vora, 1949, pp.278-287.

Reynolds, Reginald, *My Life and Crimes,* London: Jarrolds, 1956.

Reynolds, Reginald, *To Live in Mankind: A Quest for Gandhi,* London: Andre Deutsch, 1951.

Reynolds, Reginald, *White Sahibs in India,* London: Socialist Book Centre, 1946.

1930

NEWTON PHELPS STOKES II

The son of American educator, clergyman, and philanthropist, Anson Phelps Stokes, Newton Phelps Stokes II was born in 1906 into a large well-known philanthropic family. A year after having graduated from Yale University, Phelps Stokes II found himself in India with friends and a letter of introduction to Gandhi from the Mahatma's close friend, Charles Freer Andrews. They went to the half-deserted Sabarmati Ashram, where they were shown around by Mirabehn and Reginald Reynolds. After a day of ashram life, they bought some khadi 'Gandhi caps' and headed off in search of the Mahatma who was then approaching the end of the historical Salt March. Little is known of his life after this except that in 1947 he became president of the Phelps-Stokes Fund, a charity created by the will of a relative, Caroline Phelps Stokes, in 1911 to erect and improve housing in New York for poor families and for the education of 'Negroes' and the needy, deserving poor. He died in 1986.

The next day Gandhi was to march to Surat from a village five miles away. A night train landed us in the city for breakfast, after which we got a motor car and drove out to the village. Many Indians had also come out to see him. All the visitors and the followers of the march were dressed in white *khaddar,* but some of the villagers wore their old clothes. The main street, through which the march was to take place, was festooned with green leaves. At the head of it stood the only house with two floors; here Gandhi was staying. We presented our letter of introduction at the door and were told to come back in an hour, as the Mahatma was bathing. So we wandered around the village and took photographs.

We were the only Westerners there and always the centre of a small crowd. They were glad to hear that we were Americans. Under a large tent we saw the eighty-two 'picked' marchers sitting down to lunch. Many of them were spinning with little hand spindles as they waited for food. These were the men who had been chosen from the Ashram members to go as the first volunteers. They will reach the seacoast today, April 5, and tomorrow will start making salt. If they are arrested a second batch is ready to take on the leadership of the movement.

We went back to Gandhi's house after an hour, and were told to come again at three. In the meantime we returned to Surat for lunch. Large numbers in the streets were wearing *khaddar* caps. This was also true in Ahmedabad, but we had not noticed it anywhere else in India. We ate at the station restaurant. Trains were coming in crowded with white-clad enthusiasts who made the buildings echo to shouts of '*Mahatma Gandhi ki jai!*'

Meanwhile it turned out that the car we had hired for the afternoon had run into a ditch. As it was some time before we could get another, we arrived at the village a few minutes late, to find Gandhi's house crowded with a delegation of Ahmedabad mill-owners. They had come by special train to present a large purse and urge the Mahatma to concentrate his opposition on foreign cloth, rather than machine-made goods. Gandhi thanked them for the contribution but could not change his program.

At four o'clock Gandhi addressed a large gathering in a nearby orchard. Three of us were shown to excellent seats. My first impression of him as he mounted the platform was one of surprising physical vigor. After all one hears of his frailness (except for the fact that he has lost all but three or four teeth and seems to disapprove of false ones as imported luxuries) he does not look his sixty-one years. He was stripped to the waist and looked poorly built but well developed. His mouth, partly due to absence of teeth, is surrounded by deep lines, turning down at the corners with an almost humorous expression. For about ten minutes he sat there, quietly waiting for the meeting to come to order. He pulled out some corded cotton, a little hand spindle, and set to work, seemingly as oblivious to his surroundings as any craftsman in his shop.

At length the meeting was opened with a song accompanied by an Indian stringed instrument. Then Gandhi started to speak. The talk lasted about half an hour – his hands busy spinning cotton throughout. Many of the audience followed his example. At the start he apparently made some humorous remarks, for there was a good deal of laughter, and then he went on in a quiet voice that could hardly have reached the edge of the crowd. We are told that this was just his usual line of argument. I am poor at estimating numbers but my guess would be that the crowd contained about a thousand.

After the meeting we got talking to a young Indian who spoke with a trace of American accent. He had just come back from nearly ten years in the States, where he attended various Midwestern universities. He said it was a bit hard to get used to Indian ways again. As one of the selected marchers he had to dress in *khaddar*, so he sent his American knickerbockers and a knapsack to the tailor to have them copied in homespun! He [the marcher Haridas T. Muzumdar] showed us around the village hotel where the marchers were accommodated. Later, when I took his picture he asked me to send copies with a little news story to a couple of midwestern college papers. It seemed almost unbelievable that a man who has studied and taught economics should be out on such a crusade. While we were talking with him someone came to tell us that Gandhi wanted to see us.

There were several other persons sitting on the floor when we came in. Gandhi was leaning against a pillow at one end, spinning. He was gracious in greeting us, asked a few questions about our travelling, inquired about Mr. Andrews, and wanted to know whether we had any questions to ask – but we must not try to think up any on the spot. I asked him to what extent he thought his program was applicable to the West. He said, 'In its entirety.' He realized that hand spinning would seem preposterous to Westerners, but he was convinced that it is a sound solution of universal problems. A Harvard friend who joined us for this trip asked him to what extent he felt that scientific research should continue. Gandhi replied that he was in favour of all research that could help humanity, but did not see any point in sending expeditions to the North Pole. After this he said pleasantly, 'that will conclude the interview'.

We had sent the car back, deciding to accompany the march to Surat. Promptly at 6 o'clock Gandhi led off, at an amazingly fast pace. He was followed first by the 82 marchers and then by a large crowd. Some of them were enthusiasts, and others were probably just out for a spree. The way lay largely along footpaths till we crossed the river on a railway track and reached the outskirts of town.

From: Newton Phelps Stokes II, "Marching with Gandhi", *Review of Reviews* (1930), vol. 81, pp.34-38 at pp.37-38.

POSTSCRIPT:

From Stokes' account we get a glimpse of how busy the sixty-one-year-old Dandi bound Mahatma actually was. Not only did he walk the whole way (while many of the marchers became ill and were transported by cart or train for at least part of the route) but during the evening hours when the far younger marchers were already asleep or in the early hours before they awoke, Gandhi still had to take care of his correspondence, write articles, deliver speeches, and be available to all those who wanted of his time. During the Salt March, between the morning of 12 March and the night of 5 April, Gandhi wrote an unknown number of letters (of which sixty-two have been preserved), penned at least twenty-nine articles for his papers, gave three formal interviews, and made at least forty-three substantial speeches. Stokes gives us something of the atmosphere, the crowds, and the oppressive adulation which Gandhi had to endure.

FURTHER READING:

Weber, Thomas, *On the Salt March: The Historiography of Gandhi's March to Dandi*, New Delhi: Rupa, 2009.

1930 NEGLEY FARSON

Negley Farson was born in 1890 and brought up by his eccentric American Union Civil War general grandfather. He studied engineering at university but was expelled, so he immigrated to England where he became a journalist (as well as an arms salesman, a Royal Air Force pilot, a beachcomber, and a motor-lorry company manager). He was in Red Square when the Bolshevik Revolution broke out, met Lenin, interviewed Gandhi (just after the completion of the Salt March) and Hitler and became the epitome of the adventurer/correspondent. Between the wars, he was a foreign correspondent for the *Chicago Daily News*, and an inveterate traveller. In the 1920s he was rarely in any one country for more than six months at a time. The travelogue of a sailing adventure across Europe with his wife in 1924-1925 was syndicated in 30 American newspapers (and later became the book *Sailing Across Europe*). The first volume of his autobiography, *The Way of the Transgressor*, became not only a best seller, but was considered a classic of the genre. He also wrote one of the best-known books on fishing. The stress of journalistic life regularly saw him lapse into alcoholism. He died of a heart attack in 1960.

The day after I reached Bombay I went up to Surat and drove across an arm of Baroda State with a Parsee. And there, at Karadi, sitting under a mango-tree, I faced Mahatma Gandhi. He was clad in nothing but a loincloth, a pair of ancient silver-rimmed spectacles, and two hats. Anyone else would have looked ridiculous. But not the Mahatma. I realised, as I sat cross-legged on the ground before the little man, that I was in the presence of a Presence.

'Tell me,' I asked, 'why, do you hate the British so much?'

'Because,' said Gandhi, 'they are sucking the life blood out of India. They do not give us schools, they do not give us roads. That village behind us pays a tax of 1,700 rupees a year.'

'But, 1,700 rupees,' I said, 'would not build a mile of road!'

Gandhi broke the cotton he was spinning into a string on his *takli*. It may have been an accident; I think not, for every time I seemed to get to the point of a convincing condemning statement against the hated British, he broke that thread. Then, with his little monkey-like tongue, he would spend a long time licking the broken ends and splicing the fibres of cotton together again – after which he would resume our conversation, talking about something else.

The students of his *ashram* sat around us.

'But to go back to the loom age,' I asked Gandhi, 'to take all India back to a village life – against the British – isn't that a good deal like sending naked men up against steel?'

Gandhi gave me a toothless grin. 'Well, they aren't doing too badly,' he said. 'As long as we do not hit back, the British do not know what to do. After a while they will become ashamed of themselves.'

What the Mahatma really had his eyes on that day in Karadi, as the grey monkeys swung through his mango-tree, was not the bazaars of India, swarming with young men in Gandhi caps shouting '*Gandhi Ki Jai!*' Nor did he care an iota where [sic] the *sahibs* in the Bombay Yacht Club or up at Simla were thinking about him. Gandhi had his eye on the British House of

Commons, and on the face of American public opinion; both of which he was trying to horrify. That was where he thought he might win his fight. He longed to hold the British up as wife-beaters before a shocked world. The spirituality of his civil disobedience movement rested upon a masochistic base.

'Beat me, you brute!' Gandhi was encouraging Mother India to taunt the British. 'Beat me, beat me, beat me. I won't hit back, and while you are doing it I am going to set up such an outcry that the whole street will know about it; even your own family will be horrified at you. And after you have stood this sort of scandal for a time you will be so ashamed of yourself that you will come to me and say, "Look here, why can't we agree upon something?" And then you will have to give me my liberty of Dominion Status that I want.

'Otherwise you will have to go on beating me until you go crazy.'

Facing the little man that sweltering day on the plain of Karadi this aspect of the Civil Disobedience movement did not present itself to me. I felt abashed in the presence of such apparent simplicity. It was only as I watched him at work that I began to see with what diabolical cunning such simplicity could be used. I saw the British driven almost frantic by it. Gandhi himself may not have started his Civil Disobedience movement with this masochistic intention; but when he failed to get full Civil Disobedience from the Indians (which would have paralysed the British Services within three days), he seems to have exploited this horror side of it. Even a Holy Man it appears must employ guile to triumph. When I asked Lord Irwin, Viceroy of India, what he thought of Gandhi, he replied:

'The first time I saw Gandhi I was tremendously impressed by his holiness. The second time I was tremendously impressed by his legal astuteness. The third time I was sure of it.'

'Of which, Your Excellency?'

Lord Irwin merely smiled and looked down into the Himalayas: 'That is for you to decide,' he said.

From: Negley Farson, *The Way of a Transgressor,* first published in 1984 by Carrol and Graf, New York, pp.415-417. With thanks to Edward Gaskell publishers, www.lazaruspress.com for permission to quote from Negley Farson.

POSTSCRIPT:

Negley Farson wrote two versions of this episode at about the same time. In the other version he focuses on Gandhi's young followers as being the main audience rather than the British House of Commons or Americans:

> During the whole of the two hours and forty minutes that I talked with him I was conscious that Gandhi was directing his replies at the students more than he was to me. He was giving them a demonstration of how to put the case of the Civil Disobedience movement to a white man.
>
> During all this time a conviction was forming in my mind: *Gandhi wanted the English to beat the Indians!*
>
> Things he said made that clear. He admitted, for instance, that he could not control the Bengal terrorists. They would not listen to his non-resistance plea. He admitted that young Jawaharlal Nehru was leading a strong Left Wing movement in the Congress Party that believed in armed resistance and riots against British rule. He admitted that the Mohammedans up in the Punjab would not look on the Civil Disobedience in the way the Gujerat Hindus did, that after they had become inflamed with the movement they would probably riot and kill people – which they did. He admitted that the Pathans and Abdul Gaffar Khan's 'Red Shirts' up on the North-west Frontier would turn to the knife. He finally admitted that he

was even afraid to enter Bombay himself, for fear of the riots his presence would cause in the bazaar.

'Then how,' I asked, 'can you call this a passive resistance movement? Only a small minority of the Indians, as you admit yourself, will allow themselves to be beaten without hitting back. The rest will resist. And if they do that they will come up against British policemen armed with *lathis,* soldiers with bayonets, and, worse – many of them will get killed. My point is that you haven't got a big enough majority in the movement who believe in non-resistance, or passive resistance, to call your movement that.'

The students of his *ashram* stopped their spinning and looked from myself to Mahatma Gandhi. I saw many of them afterwards beaten to a pulp by British police-sergeants. And these particular Gandhi *wallahs* did not hit back. The way they stood up to those *lathi* blows on the Bombay Maidan was one of the bravest things I have ever seen. They blanched a little now as they held their breath, waiting for Gandhi's reply.

But it did not come.

Gandhi did what I had noticed he had done several times when I thought I had put a particularly pertinent question to him during the interview – he broke the thread of cotton he was spinning on his takli. He took time to repair it. When he spoke again it was on an entirely different subject. (Farson, "Indian Hate Lyric", pp.137-138)

Regardless of the above, and somewhat paradoxically, Farson concluded this section of his autobiography with the words 'I still cannot be sure about him in my mind. All that I know is that I have never for one moment doubted his absolute sincerity.'

Further Reading:

Farson, Negley, "Indian Hate Lyric", in E. Lyons (ed.), *We Cover the World: By Sixteen Foreign Correspondents,* London: Harrap, 1937, pp.129-152.

Farson, Negley, *A Mirror for Narcissus,* London: Gollancz, 1956.

1931

WILLIAM LAWRENCE SHIRER

Born in Chicago in 1904, William L. Shirer graduated from college in 1925 and then worked for his passage on a copy editor cattle-boat to France, where he started working as a copy editor for the Paris edition of the *Chicago Tribune* while learning French, German, Italian and Spanish. Then he became a fully-fledged foreign correspondent, and eventually a news-broadcaster, author, and historian. From the mid-1920s to the outbreak of the Second World War, he reported from the main capitals of Europe and spent two years in India reporting on the independence struggle and then, following seven years of reporting from Berlin, chronicling the rise and fall of Nazi Germany. His huge award-winning book *The Rise and Fall of the Third Reich* was the definitive and most famous book on the subject in its day and is still considered a masterpiece of journalism and history. He did a similarly impressive job with *The Collapse of the Third Republic: An Inquiry into the Fall of France in 1940* and wrote three volumes of memoirs. He died in 1993.

It happened the day before my twenty-seventh birthday, on February 22, 1931.

Gandhi sent word he would see me an hour before his daily prayer meeting and invited me to stay on for prayers if I felt inclined. This was a birthday present I much appreciated. When I arrived at the home of Dr. Muktar Ahmad Ansari, an eminent physician and Moslem, which overlooked the river Jumna, a sluggish stream sacred to the Hindus, Gandhi was squatting on the floor in the corner of the verandah, spinning. He greeted me warmly, with a smile that lit up his face and made his lively eyes twinkle. The welcome was so disarming, his manner so friendly and radiant, that my nervousness evaporated before I could say a word. He turned to a tall, pale, white-skinned woman, whose sari, pulled partly back from above her gaunt eyes, revealed a shaved head, and asked her to bring up a chair for me. This woman must be, I conjectured, Mirabai, the former Madeleine Slade, who had shocked her parents, Admiral Sir Edmund Slade and Lady Slade, by forsaking London society to join Gandhi's ashram, taking the vows of chastity and poverty, and throwing herself into the struggle for Indian independence. I sensed at once a strong empathy between Gandhi and her. [...] Kasturbai, Mrs. Gandhi, sat nearby. She had a rather wizened face, but one could see that she must have been a spirited and attractive woman in her younger days. Her large, round eyes were very bright.

'Please don't bother,' I said as Miss Slade started to pull up a chair. 'I would prefer to sit on the floor.'

'If you like,' Gandhi said as I squatted down. There was almost an impish humor in his eyes as he watched me awkwardly sinking to the floor. 'But if it becomes uncomfortable, please tell me.'

As our talk began I tried to take in not only what Gandhi was saying but how he looked. I had seen many photographs of him but I was nevertheless somewhat surprised at his actual appearance. His face at first glance did not convey at all the stature of the man, his obvious greatness. It was not one you would have especially noticed in a crowd. It struck me as not ugly, as some had said – but it was not uncommon either. Age – he was sixty-one – and fasting, an Indian sun and the strain of years in prison, of long, hard, nervous work, had obviously taken their toll, turned the nose down, widened it at the nostrils, sunk in his mouth just a little so that the lower lip protruded, and teeth were missing – I could see only two. His hair was closely cropped, giving an effect of baldness. His large ears spread out, rabbitlike. His gray eyes lit up and sharpened when they peered at you through his steel-rimmed spectacles and then softened when he lapsed, as he frequently did, into a mood of almost puckish humor. I was almost taken aback by the gaiety in them. This was a man inwardly secure, who, despite the burdens he carried, the hardships he had endured, could chuckle at man's foibles, including his own.

He seemed terribly frail, all skin and bones, though I knew that this appearance was deceptive, for he kept to a frugal but carefully planned diet that kept him fit, and for exercise he walked four or five miles each morning at a pace so brisk, as I would learn later when he invited me to accompany him, that I, at twenty-seven and in fair shape from skiing and hiking in the Alps below Vienna, could scarcely keep up. Over the skin and bones was a loosely wrapped *dhoti,* and in the chilliness of a north Indian winter he draped a coarsely spun white shawl over his bony shoulders. His skinny legs were bare, his feet in wooden sandals.

As he began to talk, his voice seemed high-pitched, but his words were spoken slowly and deliberately with emphasis when he seemed intent on stressing a point, and gradually, as he warmed up, the tone lowered. His slightly accented English flowed rhythmically, like a poet's at times, and always, except for an occasional homespun cliché, it was concise, homely, forceful.

For so towering a figure, his humble manner at first almost disconcerted me. Most of the political greats I had brushed up against in Europe and at home had seemed intent on impressing you with the forcefulness of their personalities and the boldness of their minds, not being bashful at all in hiding their immense egos. But here was the most gentle and unassuming of men, speaking softly and kindly, without egotism, without the slightest pretense of trying to impress his rather awed listener.

How could so humble a man, I wondered, spinning away with his nimble fingers on a crude wheel as he talked, have begun almost single-handedly to rock the foundations of the British Empire, aroused a third of a billion people to rebellion against foreign rule, and taught them the technique of a new revolutionary method – non-violent civil disobedience – against which Western guns and Eastern lathis were proving of not much worth. That was what I had come to India to find out. So I simply said:

'How have you done it?'

'By love and truth,' he smiled. 'In the long run no force can prevail against them.'

From: William L. Shirer, *GANDHI: A Memoir,* Reprinted with the permission of Simon & Schuster Publishing Group from, pp.27-29.

POSTSCRIPT:

It is widely accepted that William Shirer was the model for the American reporter named Walker in Attenborough's 1982 epic movie *Gandhi* (although the scenes featuring the raids on the Salt Works at Dharasana surely represented Web Miller whose graphic reporting of the raids brought the incident to the attention of the world). Many journalists interviewed Gandhi but Shirer and Louis Fischer spent considerable time with him and the experience changed both their lives. Fischer moved from being a Marxist sympathiser to Gandhi advocate and Shirer credited Gandhi with getting him through the cold-bloodedness of the Nazi regime, the McCarthyist and communist witch-hunts in America and the horrors of the Vietnam War. What he got from Gandhi 'showed the way to the development of an inner life, which over that considerable time became ingrained enough, and strong and sufficient enough, to ward off all assaults from the outside.' (Shirer, *Gandhi*, p.244) Both he and Fischer, two hard-bitten journalists, wrote of the changes in life that came about through their meetings with the Mahatma.

FURTHER READING:

Shirer, William L., *20th Century Journey: A Memoir of a Life and the Times*, New York: Simon and Schuster, (in three vols.) 1976-1990.

Shirer, William L., *The Rise and Fall of the Third Reich: A History of Nazi Germany*, London: Secker & Warburg, 1960.

1931 JOHN HAYNES HOLMES

Born in 1879, John Haynes Holmes graduated from Harvard Divinity School in 1904. He helped to found the National Association for the Advancement of Colored People in 1909 and the American Civil Liberties Union in 1920. The New York pastor was horrified by the slaughter during the First World War and soon after he discovered in Gandhi a man who practiced Jesus' injunction to return good for evil. On 10 April 1921, he preached his famous sermon 'Who is the Greatest Man in the World Today?' introducing the almost unknown Mahatma to American audiences, doing for America what Romain Rolland had done for Europe. As soon as the weekly newspaper instalments of Gandhi's Autobiography appeared in India, Holmes reprinted them in the American weekly that he edited: the Unitarian paper *Unity*. Holmes kept up a regular correspondence with Gandhi and met him in London in 1931, and again in Delhi in late 1947. He died in 1964.

It was Saturday, the 12th of September, 1931 — a cold, rainy, and dismal day. I was in London, to meet Gandhi. 'Charlie' Andrews, beloved of Gandhi through many years, had sent me word that the Mahatma was landing that very morning at Folkestone, and would I come and join the little group of friends who would be there on the pier to meet and greet him on his arrival. Gandhi's mission in England, as all the world knew, was to attend the impending session of the famous Round Table Conference on Indian affairs.

I had first heard of all this in Switzerland, where I was touring. In an idle moment at the hotel in Constance, I had picked up a newspaper, and there was a dispatch from Bombay, telling of Gandhi's embarkation and his start on his long journey to the West. Instantly I abandoned all my plans for further travel on the continent, and made my way to London to see the distinguished visitor. With him were his son, Devadas, his devout disciple and servant, the former English lady, Mirabehn (Madeleine Slade), his secretary and selfless friend, Mahadev Desai, another secretary and close companion, Pyarelal Nayyar, Mme. Sarojini Naidu, poet and orator, greatest of Indian women, and others less important or less known. Most of them were my friends – but friends I had never seen! Surely, I must not miss this opportunity so unexpectedly laid before me, and would be pardoned for my importunity.

Yet I was appalled at the spectacle of my own audacity in seeking intrusion upon so important, even historic, an occasion. Undoubtedly the affair was official, and therefore in the hands of government which would have no interest in me and my purely personal desires. Distinguished Englishmen and Indians would be waiting in line to see and confer with the Mahatma. At such a time, and under such conditions, would he not be troubled by my unheralded appearance and my insistent expectation of an interview? I was frightened at the mere possibility of bothering him, or of adding by so much as a feather's weight to the burden he was carrying in one of the supreme ordeals of his career. All my life I have instinctively shrunk from imposing myself upon famous and therefore busy men. How many times I have missed the excitement of meeting great personalities because of my reluctance to grasp and seize, for my own satisfaction, some portion of their meagre stores of time and strength. What is it, after all, but sheer impudence to demand attention and therewith interrupt important work or break an irrevocable course of thought? Recall Coleridge and the man from Porlock! No, our business is to protect the great, and not to exploit them for our personal advantage. Yet in this case I clung to the hope, persuaded myself to the conviction, that trespass would be forgiven. Here was Andrews's invitation to come along. Then there was my long relationship with Gandhi in correspondence, which was not voluminous, I may say, since I was as loath to distract the Mahatma with my letters as with my presence, but was invariably on his part kind, cordial, and deeply personal. Very pertinent was a letter written to me in the early summer in which he spoke of the possibility of his journey, and of his hope of seeing me on his arrival in England. Such a letter could surely serve as a spiritual passport at Gandhi's door. Finally, there was the announcement, which had instantly attracted my attention, that the guest from India was to reside during his stay in London, not at St. James's Palace, as the government had planned, but at Muriel Lester's settlement, Kingsley Hall, in the far East End of the city. In the simplicities and informalities of this house, I would surely be received in ways unknown to a royal residence. As a matter of fact, when I reached London, the first thing I did was to hunt out Miss Lester, and state my case. 'I will be a busboy,' I said, 'a dishwasher, a garbage man, if only you will let me in to see and talk with Gandhi.' Miss Lester was wholly sympathetic, bless her heart! She not only gave me entrance, but managed, in kind and clever ways, to bring the Mahatma and me together. So I hoped I was not overreaching myself, nor exacting attention to which I was not entitled.

I went down to Folkestone with Reginald Reynolds, a handsome and ardent young Englishman, a Quaker, who had been useful to Gandhi in India. We were not surprised to learn, on our arrival, that the Channel steamer was late owing to the fog and rain. As time went on, I became chilled to the bone, so cold it was without, and so excited was I within. I began to pace the pier in sheer impatience. Suddenly I found myself talking with a young policeman, posted as a guard for the Mahatma. He was an intelligent man, a college graduate, who recognized me quickly as an American.

'You're at an interesting point on the English coast,' he said. 'Do you see that projection of land over there, just to the north? That's where Caesar landed when he brought his legions to conquer England.' He paused, as though to let me ponder this striking episode of history. Then, pointing in the opposite direction, to the south, he continued, 'And through that fog there, not so far away, is Pevensey, where landed a second conqueror, the great William of Normandy.' Then suddenly, as I gazed upon the sea, there came a moment of inspiration. 'Here is a third conqueror,' I cried within my heart, in expectation of Gandhi's arrival. A very different kind of conqueror, to be sure! He had no armor on his back, no sword at his side. He was accompanied not by a Roman legion or a Norman army, but only by a few scattered secretaries and friends. There was something almost grotesque in Gandhi's appearance later on, as he disembarked, and went splashing up the rain-soaked pier towards the train which was to carry him to London. On one of Britain's rawest days, Gandhi was naked to the thighs, his feet covered only by crude and well-worn sandals. His body was loosely wrapped in a loin cloth and *khaddar* shawl. Over his head was an umbrella, carried by some solicitous person who sought, however desperately, to protect him from the pouring rain. Around and behind him were the members of his entourage, a fluttery flock not knowing just where they were going, or what was likely at any moment to happen. This man a conqueror? The idea seemed completely ludicrous. Yet in the next sixteen years he had defeated England, without violence or bloodshed, and India was free. If there is any parallel in history to this amazing achievement, I do not chance to know what it is.

I wiped the rain from my glasses, and gazed out through the mist to the stormy Channel. Suddenly there appeared a steamer, a little craft in white, emerging from the fog-bound horizon like a sheeted ghost. As she was made fast to the pier, only one man, the official representative of the British Government, was allowed on board. All the rest of us, a shivering and forlorn company, Gandhi's friends, delegates from India, newspaper reporters and photographers, were left standing in the rain, with a great crowd of sightseers behind the barriers. But the delay was brief. In a few moments, which seemed like hours, we were aboard the ship, and I was standing at the door of Gandhi's cabin, awaiting my turn to be received. It was here I had my first glimpse of the Mahatma.

He was sitting cross-legged upon his berth, engaged in earnest conversation with Reginald Reynolds, who was a member of the Quaker group which had been appointed to welcome Gandhi in the name of the English Friends. His head and shoulders were bent forward in a listening attitude, so that I could not see his face. A naked arm, long and lean and wiry, reached out of the shawl, flung lightly about his shoulders, and took a paper from Reginald's hand. There was a quick interchange of words, a flitting smile, and the conference was over.

It was now my turn. I stepped into the little cabin. When Gandhi saw me, he jumped to his feet and, with the lithe quick step of a schoolboy, came forward to greet me. I cannot now seem to remember whether or not he gave me the familiar Hindu salutation. But I felt his hands take mine with a grasp as firm as that of an athlete.

'I wish you might have met me at Marseilles,' he said, referring to his landing at the French port, and taking the train north to the Channel and Folkestone.

I replied that I was afraid that I would be in the way – that I was always reluctant to intrude upon busy and important people. Whereupon he smiled at me gently, and invited me to be with him in London. Then conversation drifted, as conversations have a way of doing on such occasions, to other and more general themes. I do not recall particularly what was said. I was too excited and confused to make note of Gandhi's remarks. But I shall never forget those bright eyes shining through his spectacles, his voice so clear and yet so gentle, his whole presence so simple and yet so strong. We had only a few precious moments together – others were pressing upon us and clamouring for attention. So I withdrew and contented myself with watching this man whose spirit had reached me, years before, across the continents and seas of half the world.

From: John Haynes Holmes, *My Gandhi*, London: George Allen & Unwin, 1954, pp.34-39.

Postscript:

The Holmes sermon that did so much to introduce Gandhi to an American audience began:

I am going to speak to you this morning upon what I hope will be the interesting question as to who is the greatest man in the world today. In seeking an answer to this inquiry, I imagine that all of our minds instinctively go back to the days of the Great War, and run over the names of the men who held positions of vast responsibility and power in that stupendous conflict. Especially do we think of the great gathering of the war-leaders in Paris, in the opening months of the year 1919. Two years ago, at this time, we would all of us have agreed that if the greatest man in the world was anywhere, it was in this council of the premiers and statesmen of the Allied governments. These were the men who had been tested by the most awful peril which had ever threatened the civilization of the world, and who had brought out of that peril a victory which was as complete as it was sudden. Now they were being tested by the challenge of peace – by the great problem as to how to use a victory after it has been won. And it is just here, in this most rigorous of all tests, that these leaders of the nations failed. Who can say, in view of what happened at Versailles, and especially in view of what has happened since the signing of the treaty, that any one of these men responsible for the great disaster of the peace, has any substantial or permanent claims to greatness, in the true sense of the word?

I turn away, therefore, from the storm of the Great War, and from the men who rode that storm to power and place; and I look elsewhere for that man who impresses me as the greatest man who is living in the world today.

What we need is a universal man – a man who combines in perfect balance the supreme qualities of an idealist and a realist, a dreamer and a doer, a prophet who sees 'the heavenly vision' and, 'not unfaithful to (that) vision' makes it come true. Is there any such person living in the world? [...]

I believe that there is – unquestionably the greatest man living in the world today, and one of the greatest men who has ever lived. [...]

The man whom I have in mind is Mohandas Karamchand Gandhi, the Indian leader, of the present great revolutionary movement against British rule in India, known and reverenced by

> his countrymen as Mahatma, 'the Saint'. I wonder how many of you have ever heard of him, or know the story of his life. Listen while I tell this story, and see if I am not right in calling its hero the greatest man in the world today!

Following a somewhat imprecise chronicling of Gandhi's movement in India, Holmes concluded the sermon by declaring:

> Such is Mahatma Gandhi! In this great spirit, he lives among the people. As he moves from city to city, crowds of thirty and even fifty thousand people assemble to hear his words. As he pauses for the night in a village, or in the open countryside, great throngs come to him as to a holy shrine. He would seem to be what the Indians regard him – the perfect and universal man. In his personal character, he is simple and undefiled. In his political endeavours, he is as stern a realist as Lenin, working steadfastly towards a far goal of liberation which must be won. At the same time, however, he is an idealist, like Romain Rolland, living ever in the pure radiance of the spirit. When I think of Rolland, as I have said, I think of Tolstoi. When I think of Lenin, I think of Napoleon. But when I think of Gandhi, I think of Jesus Christ. He lives his life; he speaks his word; he suffers, strives and will some day nobly die, for his kingdom upon earth.

Further Reading:

Gupta, S.P.K., *Apostle John and Gandhi*, Ahmedabad: Navajivan, 1988.

Holmes, John Haynes, "In London and Delhi", in Chandrashanker Shukla (ed.), *Reminiscences of Gandhiji: By Forty-eight Contributors*, Bombay: Vora, 1951, pp.119-124.

Holmes, John Haynes, "Mahatma Gandhi: The Greatest Man Since Jesus Christ", in Kshitis Roy, (ed.), *Gandhi Memorial Peace Number*, Shantiniketan: Visva-Bharati Quarterly, 1949, pp.239-256.

Lavan, Spencer, *Unitarians in India: A Study in Encounter and Response*, Boston: Beacon, 1977.

Seshachari, C., *Gandhi and the American Scene: An Intellectual History and Inquiry*, Bombay: Nachiketa, 1969.

1931

CHARLIE CHAPLIN

The London-born actor and director Charlie Chaplin, who became one of the most important figures in motion picture history, grew up in abject poverty. His salvation came through the theatre where by the age of sixteen he was playing leading roles. In 1914 he toured America with a music hall revue and was spotted by the movie producer Mack Sennett who signed Chaplin to his Keystone Company. Chaplin became famous with his trademark silent film character the Little Tramp, with his moustache, bowler hat, out turned feet and cane. His popularity during his first ten years in America saw him not only signing the first million-dollar film contract and becoming a household name, but also revolutionizing the whole film industry. In 1919, with other leading actors, he formed United Artists to distribute their work and help circumvent studio interference. In the classic 1936 film, *Modern Times,* he bid farewell to his signature character, the Tramp. His leftist sympathies saw him leaving McCarthyist America and its anti-communist witch hunts, to take up residence in Switzerland in 1952. He was knighted in 1975.

I met Gandhi shortly after my stay with Churchill. I have always respected and admired Gandhi for his political astuteness and his iron will. But I thought his visit to London was a mistake. His legendary significance evaporated in the London scene, and his religious display fell short of impressiveness. In the cold dank climate of England, wearing his traditional loin-cloth, which he gathered about him in disorderly fashion, he seemed incongruous. It made his presence in London food for glibness and caricature. One's impressiveness is greater at a distance. I had been asked if I would like to meet him. Of course I was thrilled.

I met him in a humble little house in the slum district off the East India Dock Road. Crowds filled the streets and the press and the photographers packed both floors. The interview took place in an upstairs front room about twelve feet square. The Mahatma had not yet arrived; and as I waited I began to think of what I would say to him. I had heard of his imprisonment and hunger strikes, and his fight for the freedom of India, and vaguely knew of his opposition to the use of machinery.

When at last he arrived there was hooraying and cheering as he stepped out of the taxi, gathering about him the folds of his loin-cloth. It was a strange scene in that crowded little slum street, that alien figure entering a humble house, accompanied by cheering throngs. He came upstairs and showed himself at the window, then beckoned to me, and together we waved to the crowds below.

The room was suddenly attacked by flash-lights from the cameras as we sat on the sofa. I was on the Mahatma's right. Now came the uneasy, terrifying moment when I should say something astutely intelligent upon a subject I knew little about. Seated on my right was a persistent young lady telling me a long story of which I did not hear a word, but I nodded approvingly, wondering all the time what I would say to Gandhi. I knew I had to start the ball rolling, that it was not up to the Mahatma to tell me how much he enjoyed my last film, and so forth – I doubted if he had ever seen a film. However, an Indian lady's commanding voice suddenly interrupted the verbose young woman: 'Miss, will you kindly finish your conversation and let Mr Chaplin talk to Gandhi?'

The packed room grew suddenly silent. And the Mahatma's mask-like expression was one of waiting, I felt that all India was also waiting on my words. So I cleared my throat. 'Naturally I am in sympathy with India's aspirations and struggle for freedom,' I said. 'Nonetheless, I am somewhat confused by your abhorrence of machinery.'

The Mahatma nodded and smiled as I continued: 'After all, if machinery is used in the altruistic sense, it should help to release man from the bondage of slavery, and give him shorter hours of labour and time to improve his mind and enjoy life.'

'I understand,' he said, speaking calmly, 'but before India can achieve those aims she must first rid herself of English rule. Machinery in the past has made us dependent on England, and the only way we can rid ourselves of that dependence is to boycott all goods made by machinery. That is why we have made it the patriotic duty of every Indian to spin his own cotton and weave his own cloth. This is our form of attacking a very powerful nation like England – and, of course, there are other reasons. India has a different climate from England; and her habits and wants are different. In England the cold weather necessitates arduous industry and an involved economy. You need the industry of eating utensils; we use our fingers. And so it translates into manifold differences.'

I got a lucid object lesson in tactical manoeuvring in India's fight for freedom, inspired paradoxically, by a realistic, virile-minded visionary with a will of iron to carry it out. He also told me that the supreme independence is to shed oneself of unnecessary things, and that violence eventually destroys itself.

When the room cleared, he asked me if I would like to remain and see them at prayers. The Mahatma sat cross-legged on the floor while five others sat in a circle with him. It was a curious sight: six figures squatting on the floor in that small room, in the heart of the London slums, as a saffron sun was rapidly sinking behind the roof-tops, and myself sitting on a sofa looking down at them, while they humbly intoned their prayer. What a paradox, I thought, as I watched this extremely realistic man, with his astute legal mind and his profound sense of political reality, all of which seemed to vanish in a sing-song chant.

From: Charles Chaplin, *My Autobiography*, London: The Bodley Head, 1964, pp.367-369.

POSTSCRIPT:

On some accounts it seems that before the meeting, Gandhi, one of the most famous people on the planet, had never heard of Charlie Chaplin, probably the other most famous person. On other accounts he was simply not interested in meeting Chaplin, whom he considered little more than a buffoon, until he was persuaded that Chaplin was in fact a working-class hero. In any event he was not only not enamoured with the cinema (which he regarded as little better than race courses, drinking booths, brothels, opium, and gambling dens, as places that encouraged the waste of money and idleness, spread children's diseases through bad air, and were places where women were molested) but had never visited one. Although many people tried to convince him that movies had an educational potential, the Mahatma was not convinced. He is even recorded as saying that if he had his way, all cinemas and theatres in India would be converted into spinning halls and handicraft factories. However, it does seem that towards the end of his life he did in fact see possibly at least two feature films. On 21 May, 1944, he was apparently persuaded to watch the 1943 Hollywood drama *Mission to Moscow* while he was recuperating at Jehangir Patel's Juhu 'shack' in Bombay following his release from imprisonment. On 2 June, he apparently saw another movie there, the Hindi movie *Ramarajya*. From a letter to his grandson Kanam a few weeks later, he did not seem to have overly enjoyed it: 'I have had enough of watching the cinema all by myself without my compatriots at Sevagram. When I am out and engaged in some good activity I would remember all of you. There was no such thing in the present case. Hence nobody has lost anything by not witnessing the show. On the contrary, I have lost something after having seen the picture.'

FURTHER READING:

Ackroyd, Peter, *Charlie Chaplin*, London: Chatto & Windus, 2014.

Huff, Theodore, *Charlie Chaplin*, New York: Schuman, 1952.

Lynn, Kenneth S., *Charlie Chaplin and His Times*, New York: Simon and Schuster, 1997.

Robinson, David, *Charlie Chaplin: Comic Genius*, London: Thames and Hudson, 1996.

Robinson, David, *Chaplin: His Life and Art*, London: Penguin, 1985, 2001.

1931

JO DAVIDSON

Of Russian-Jewish descent, Jo Davidson was born in New York in 1883. As a nineteen-year-old he set his sights on a career in medicine. While at medical school at Yale University, he concurrently studied art and experimented with clay modelling. Having discovered his passion, he left the Yale Medical School and worked with leading American sculptor Hermon Atkins MacNeil before moving to Paris to study sculpture formally in 1907. In 1911 he had his first solo gallery exhibition and gradually gained an international reputation and following. The flamboyant bearded personality became identified with celebrities and world leaders whose portrait busts he modelled. He lived much of his working life in France but travelled the world to find suitable subjects. He is credited with having probably modelled more notable people than any other sculptor in his time. Celebrities sought him out but he controlled the artistic interaction, except when he came to make a sculpture of Mahatma Gandhi. He retired back to America in 1940 and in later life became involved in political and civil liberties lobbying. He died in 1952.

Mahatma Gandhi was coming to London for the Round Table Conference. My friend Jim Mills of the Associated Press told me that Gandhi had promised him that if the opportunity ever presented itself, he would sit for me. It was decided that I should come over to London and meet Gandhi there.

On their arrival in London, Gandhi and his party were given a house in Knightsbridge, which they used also as offices. Mills took me there.

As we entered, we saw Gandhi squatting on the floor, wrapped in a blanket, with his back to the wall and spinning wheel in front of him. My first impression was: 'What a homely man this is.' His ears stuck out and a front tooth was missing, showing a black space when he grinned. This impression only lasted a split second. Suddenly Gandhi appeared beautiful to me.

I had brought some photos of my sculpture. Gandhi looked at them intently and said:

'I see you make heroes out of mud.'

And I retorted: 'And sometimes vice versa.'

Gandhi laughed and agreed to sit for me the following morning. I had originally intended to make just a head of him. But when I saw him in his white robe, squatting before his spinning wheel, it occurred to me that a life-size figure was a better idea. He looked eternal – a holy man.

In my hotel that evening, I proceeded to build an armature which would hold a life-size figure.

I came back the next morning and went to work. At first, the Mahatma seemed rather upset by my presence. In fact, whenever I caught his eye, he looked pained. However, having promised that he would sit for me, he said nothing. Why had he consented, I do not know but apparently his philosophy was never to refuse anything that was asked of him.

I worked as people came and went, and Gandhi acted as if I were not in the room, as if in fact, I did not exist. He simply continued to ignore me. It generally takes two to make a portrait – the sitter and the artist. In this particular case, however, I had to do it all myself, as I received absolutely no help from my sitter. In addition, I had all the physical difficulty of crawling around the floor, squatting beside him, trying to glance up into the face that was constantly avoiding me, and bending forward. This made the task practically impossible.

By the end of the day, however, I had succeeded in putting up the figure. It was fairly well along before he left me. I pushed my figure into a corner of the room. It was very fragile. The clay was too wet and the armature was not strong. I had built it too hurriedly and feverishly. However, I covered it lightly so the air could get at it and dry it, hoping it would be in better condition the next day. I put a sign on it, 'Please do not touch or move,' and begged the Indians not to touch it.

It was eight o'clock in the evening when I left, and I went back to my hotel exhausted. The next morning when I arrived I was met at the door by Gandhi's son, Devadas.

'I have some bad news for you,' he said.

My heart missed a beat. I thought he would tell me that his father had changed his mind about posing. I followed him upstairs. My figure had been moved into the middle of the room and the head had fallen off and was on the floor. I stood there distressed. Gandhi came in.

As Gandhi stood there I realized for the first time how small and thin he was.

'You see,' he said, 'you should not do it.'

I replied, 'You are quite right, sir. I'll just do a bust.'

I set to work to pull down the figure and put up the bust. Gandhi squatted in his habitual corner of the room. I can never forget the aura around him – his skin actually seemed to glow. I was constantly aware of Gandhi's disapproval, and felt very badly about it, but giving it up was out of the question. I tried to make it as easy as possible for him by keeping away from him and working at rather a long distance. However, it was impossible to work under such trying conditions and I pleaded with him to allow me to work closer so that I could observe him better.

He said, 'You occupy so much room. I am only a pigmy and you will crush me. However, do with me as you like.'

Gandhi's face was very mobile; every feature quivered and a constant change played over his face when he talked. He practised his passive resistance on me all the time I worked; he submitted to my modelling him, but never willingly lent himself to it. Never once did he look at the clay I was working on. But when I stopped for a breather and just sat with him, he was extremely amiable.

There was a constant flow of visitors, or rather pilgrims to seek light who came to worship at his shrine. Some of the visitors asked him rather rude questions. One asked what 'Mahatma' meant. He replied, 'An insignificant man.'

His conversation was not conversation in our sense of the word. He would listen very carefully to the questions they put to him, repeat them to be sure he knew what was asked, and then reply. His language was very simple, almost biblical. He was very patient. Nothing and nobody seemed to irritate him. He liked to play with words, and was brilliant in his repartee. [...]

He did not believe in art for art's sake. He had a great respect for art, but thought it led to nothing unless it had as its motive a religious impulse. Only then did it rise to its highest level.

I wrote to [the American editor, writer and reformer (1866-1936)] Lincoln Steffens:

> 'I am back here once more after my tussle with Gandhi. It was some job. I have met and "busted" all kinds of people in my

> life, but this is the first time that I have ever met such a one as this. He merely allowed himself to be "done". And in the end it is I who was "done". [...] While I was in his presence there was a constant flow of visitors, worshippers, pilgrims, interviewers, cranks and just folks, and they were all received with the same respect and understanding. Yes, he's a politician all right, and he's wise, and courageous. It's rather a childlike courage; perhaps I should not call it courage at all – I think it's merely a total absence of fear which permits him to say anything that enters his mind.'

I spent four or five days with Gandhi and then took the bust back with me to Bécheron, where I completed it. For all the heartaches that I had with the Mahatma, I look back at these sittings with the realization that I had the privilege of recording in clay one of the greatest figures of our time.

From: Jo Davidson, *Between Sittings*, New York: Dial Press, 1951, pp.265-269.

POSTSCRIPT:

During Gandhi's stay in London for the Round Table Conference several painters and sculptors besides Davidson had also asked permission to produce Gandhi's likeness. Sculptor Clare Sheridan got to see Gandhi close up because 'through my friend, Sarojini Naidu, the Mahatma was induced to allow me to model his portrait.' Confirming Davidson's experience, she noted that 'It was not easy. He would not pose. This was either by modesty, through overwork, or because he was not interested in art! Probably all three.' Later she compared notes with Davidson and they agreed that Gandhi stood out among the greats they had modelled; indeed they were 'disappointing to meet'. But, she added, 'Gandhi stands out above all these. In his grandiose simplicity the little bare-legged man, wrapped around in his "Khaddar," is deeply impressive. So impressive is he, such is the respect he inspires, that I reverently kissed his hand at our final parting, when he assured me that he had grown to love me (in the Christ sense) and that he never forgot his friends.' (Sheridan, "The Great Little Mahatma", pp.219-220) Interestingly, nine years later, Gandhi wrote a letter to the viceroy, Lord Linlithgow, relating to Clare Sheridan's work. He had been told that the Maharaja of Darbhanga had given the viceroy a bust of Gandhi done by Sheridan which the viceroy proposed to exhibit in Bombay and then present to the Government of India 'with the suggestion that it should ultimately find a permanent home in the national capital.' Gandhi informed Linlithgow that he may have 'brought a hornet's nest about your ears' because there were sure to be protests against its acceptance and in any case 'nothing is to be gained' by the contemplated steps. (Gandhi to Lord Linlithgow, 7 June 1940)

Were Davidson and Sheridan right about Gandhi's attitude to art? Did he not appreciate art, or only art for art's sake? What about beauty? One of Gandhi's close English associates, Agatha Harrison, kept up a lengthy correspondence with the Mahatma for several years. At one stage they discussed the meaning of beauty. As a replay of Gandhi's debates on beauty with his friend the poet Rabindranath Tagore some twenty years before, in 1946 Harrison asked Gandhi, 'Won't you ask people to grow flowers on a small piece of land? Colour and beauty is necessary to the soul as food is to the body.' She was having a friendly jibe at his suggestion that a millionaire friend should dig up his beautiful flower gardens in order to plant vegetables. Gandhi replied 'No, I won't. Why can't you see the beauty of colour in vegetables? And then there is beauty in the speckless sky. But no, you want the colours of the rainbow which is a mere optical illusion. We have been taught to believe that what is beautiful need not be useful, and what is useful cannot be beautiful. I want to show that what is useful can also be beautiful.' ("Talk with Agatha Harrison", *Harijan,* 7 April 1946) For Gandhi the practical was beautiful. Many commented that the walls of his ashram buildings were not adorned with works of art while Gandhi would respond that buildings are for shelter and that what nature provides is real art. Although he was greatly taken by statues of Christ on the cross he had seen, and claimed that some paintings transported him (while others were just splotches of colour) he was certainly not keen on having himself immortalized in stone or clay. One can only speculate what subtle pressure Naidu and others had to put on him in order to get him to allow Jo Davidson and Clare Sheridan to model him.

Further Reading:

Bose, Nandalal, "Bapuji", in Kalpathi Ganapati Subramanyan and Nandalal Bose (eds.) *The Visva-Bharati Quarterly: Nandalal Centenary Number* (May 1983-April 1984), vol.49, nos.1-4, pp.164-169.

Gandhi, Madan G., *Gandhian Aesthetics*, Chandigarh: Vikas Bharati, 1969.

Sheridan, Clare, "The Great Little Mahatma", in S. Radhakrishnan (ed.), *Mahatma Gandhi: Essays and Reflections on His Life and Work*, Bombay: Jaico, 1956, pp.218-225.

1931

WEBB MILLER

Webb Miller was born in America in 1891. His newspaper career started in 1911 when he became a reporter with a Michigan daily. He joined United Press of America in 1916 covering General John Pershing's punitive raid against the Mexican revolutionary Pancho Villa. Following this he went to Europe, where he stayed until his death in a London Underground accident in 1940. He covered the Irish troubles, and the British and American fronts in the First World War. He went on to cover many of the great stories of the time from the London and Paris offices of United Press, including the Spanish Civil War, the Russo-Finnish War, the Italian invasion of Ethiopia and Stalin's purges. One of his most famous pieces of reportage had a profound impact on the Gandhi-led Civil Disobedience Movement following Gandhi's celebrated Salt March (although he had not yet met the Mahatma at this time). Fellow journalist William Shirer said of Miller that he was one of 'the great American foreign correspondents' who, while being a sensitive man 'somehow managed to keep his emotions more in check than most of the rest of us did' in his dispatches. However, during his reporting of the Dharasana salt raids, 'he could not hold them back.'

I first encountered him at a tea party at the Dorchester Hotel. He cut a bizarre figure among the smart, morning-coated Englishmen in the *de luxe* hotel, for he wore his usual *dhoti* of coarse white homespun cotton that looked like jute sacking. His skinny brown legs were quite bare, but his feet were encased in crude native sandals.

He invited me to sit with him on a silk and gilt sofa, remarking jocularly: 'Why didn't you come to see me when you were in India?' 'But you were in jail then, and they wouldn't let me see you,' I replied. The shrivelled, little brown man grinned toothlessly and blinked through his cheap, steel-rimmed spectacles. 'So I was. I spend a good deal of my time in jails.' 'How much of your life have you spent in jails?' I asked. Gandhi counted thoughtfully on his fingers and pondered a while. 'I don't really know. I've been in jail seven or eight, maybe nine times, but I don't remember how many years. Since about 1907 in South Africa I have spent much time in jail. I don't really mind it much because it gives me a chance to think and write better than when I am out. I am not interrupted so much in jail. They have always treated me well and I shall probably spend a great many more years in jail and may die in jail.'

As a former vegetarian, I was interested in Gandhi's lifelong abstinence from meat and his extraordinarily frugal diet and frequent fasts, during which he drinks salted water. He told me he had tasted meat only once in his life.

'When I was a young man I thought much about the reasons for the superior physical strength of the British. I wondered why they were the dominant race in India and in so much of the world. Finally I thought that perhaps it was because they are heavy meat-eaters; I thought that perhaps they absorbed some of the strength of the animals they ate. As you know, our religion forbids the eating of meat or the killing of any animal. But I decided to start eating meat to see whether it had any useful effect upon me. I ate it once, then my conscience hurt me so much that I never ate it again. I was afraid my mother would be horrified if she knew I had put the flesh of a dead animal in my mouth. As I grew older I began to doubt that the British are the strongest race.'

I asked him about his personal habits and diet.

'I rise at four a.m., pray for twenty minutes, write letters about an hour, take about half an hour's walk, and then breakfast at six o'clock on goat-milk curds, dates, and raisins. Since the civil-disobedience campaign started I card, spin, and sew cotton between six and nine. I made a vow to spin at least two hundred yards of cotton every day. I want to influence our people to spin their own cloth and make themselves independent of importation from England. The largest single item of British importation into India is cotton cloth. At noon I lunch on bread, goat-milk curds, boiled vegetables, raw tomatoes, and almond paste, take a nap, and spend the afternoon in reading, meditation, and receiving visitors. I do not eat at night. Before my bedtime at nine-thirty I write in my diary. Until recently I always slept on the floor, but now I am old (he was then sixty-three) I sleep on an iron bed. Every Monday I have a day of silence; I speak to no person, no matter how urgent the matter may seem.'

From: Webb Miller, *I Found No Peace: The Journal of a Foreign Correspondent*, Harmondsworth: Penguin, 1940, pp.159-160.

POSTSCRIPT:

The incredible scenes of 21 May 1930, the start of the nonviolent raids in the Salt Works at Dharasana not long after Gandhi's arrest following his celebrated Salt March were observed by Webb Miller. He conveyed the news of the 'battle' to the world in moving prose, and his reports helped to swing the pendulum of moral righteousness from the side of the British to that of the nationalists.

The British government in India had instituted a clamp-down on the press as a response to the threatening internal situation during the Salt Satyagraha. The Government however consistently maintained that it imposed no censorship on outgoing messages. Webb Miller was the only foreign correspondent who witnessed bloody scenes at Dharasana, where unarmed and completely nonviolent Gandhi volunteers marched, row upon row, to certain and brutal beatings at the hands of officers guarding the salt works. When he attempted to cable the story from the nearest town with a telegraph office, only three and a half of his five short cables reached the United Press office in London. Soon after that the cable office contacted United Press stating that the Government of India wanted even these messages cancelled as they had been transmitted 'by error'.

From Bombay, Miller wrote a longer cable. An apparent Gandhi sympathizer informed him by way of unsigned note, that his message was not sent. On inquiring at first he could get no information about his message at all. Later at the Government headquarters of Bombay Presidency he was reassured that as there was no censorship his telegram must have gone. After further protests and a statement of intention to fly to Persia if necessary to get his scoop to the world, it was admitted that his message was stopped by the censor. After further arguments most of his message was transmitted.

These actions helped to shift American opinion from continuing its support of British imperialism (the opposite to what happened after Katherine Mayo's reports). Miller's story made an enormous impact. It appeared in 1,350 newspapers around the world and was read out in the U.S. Senate. American supporters of Gandhi printed it as a leaflet and distributed in excess of 250,000 copies.

The British were in an unenviable situation when dealing with the foreign press – either they were criticized for unfair censorship or for the repression which they unleashed and that Miller's uncensored cables made known to the world.

FURTHER READING:

Weber, Thomas, "The Marchers Simply Walked Forward until Struck Down": Nonviolent Suffering and Conversion, *Peace and Change* (1993), vol.18, no.3, pp.267-289.

Weber, Thomas, *On the Salt March: The Historiography of Gandhi's March to Dandi*, New Delhi: Rupa, 2009.

1931 ROMAIN ROLLAND

Romain Rolland was an important French writer and pacifist. He was awarded the Nobel Prize for Literature in 1915 for his ten-volume novel *Jean-Christophe,* which, through the friendship of the leading German and French characters, called for a commitment to humanity between two of the main protagonists in the First World War, and in the longer term for peace between nations. As a pacifist, in self-imposed exile, he settled in neutral Switzerland during the War to devote himself to writing. Rolland was impressed by the Gandhi-led nonviolent struggle for Indian independence, and in 1924 he published a book, *Mahatma Gandhi: The Man Who Became One with the Universal Being,* which offered Europeans a Jesus-like Hindu. During his travels on the continent in 1928, Gandhi's lieutenant Rajendra Prasad came to 'realise to what an extent Romain Rolland's book on Gandhiji had made him known in that part of the world.' Gandhi also admitted that 'All the reputation that I enjoy in the West is borrowed from him [Rolland].' It was through Rolland's book that Mirabehn came to the Mahatma. Rolland and Gandhi finally met in Switzerland when Gandhi was on his way back to India following the 1931 Round Table Conference in London.

How I should have liked to have you here during the visit of the Indians! They stayed five days – from Sunday night until Friday afternoon, the eleventh – at the Villa Lionette. The little man, bespectacled and toothless, was wrapped in his white burnoose but his legs thin as a heron's stilts, were bare. His shaven head with its few coarse hairs was uncovered and wet with rain. He came to me with a dry laugh, his mouth open, like a good dog panting and flinging an arm around me leaned his cheek against my shoulder. I felt his grizzled head against my cheek. It was, I amuse myself thinking, the kiss of St. Dominic and St. Francis.

Then came Mira, proud of figure and with the stately bearing of a Demeter, and finally three Indians, one a young son of Gandhi, Devadas, with a round and happy face. He is gentle, but little aware of the grandeur of his name. The others were the secretaries – disciples – two young men of rare qualities of heart and mind: Mahadev Desai and Pyarelal.

As I had contrived shortly beforehand to get a severe cold on my chest, it was to my house and to the chamber on the second floor where I sleep at Villa Olga – you will remember it – that Gandhi came each morning for long conversations. My sister interpreted, with the assistance of Mira, and I had also a Russian friend and secretary, Miss Kondacheff, who took notes on our discussion. Some good photographs by Schlemmer, our neighbour from Montreux, recorded the aspect of our interviews.

Evenings, at seven o'clock, prayers were held in the first floor salon. With lights lowered, the Indians seated on the carpet, and the little assembly of the faithful grouped about, there was a suite of three beautiful chants – the first an extract from the Gita, the second an ancient hymn on the Sanskrit texts which Gandhi had translated, and the third a canticle of Rama and Sita, intoned by the warm, grave voice of Mira.

Gandhi held other prayers at three o'clock in the morning for which, in London, he used to wake his harassed staff, although he had not retired until one. This little man, so frail in appearance, is tireless, and fatigue is a word which does not exist in his vocabulary. He could calmly answer for hours the heckling of a crowd, as he did at Lausanne and Geneva, without a muscle of his face twitching. Seated on a table, motionless, his voice always clear and calm, he replied to his adversaries open or masked – and they were not lacking at Geneva – giving them rude truths which left them silenced and suffocated.

The Roman bourgeoisie, militarist and nationalist, who had at first received him with crafty looks, quivered with rage when he left. I believe that if his stay had lasted any longer the public meetings would have been forbidden. He pronounced himself as unequivocally as possible on the double question of national armaments and the conflict between capital and labour. I was largely responsible for steering him on this latter course.

His mind proceeds through successive experiments into action and he follows a straight line, but he never stops, and one would risk error in attempting to judge him by what he said ten years ago, because his thought is in constant evolution. I will give you a little example of it that is characteristic.

He was asked at Lausanne to define what he understood by God. He explained how, among the noblest attributes which the Hindu scriptures ascribed to God, he had in his youth chosen the word 'truth' as most truly defining the essential element. He had then said, 'God is Truth.' 'But,' he added, 'two years ago I advanced another step. I now say, "Truth is God." For even the atheists do not doubt the necessity of the power of truth. In their passion for discovering the truth, the atheists have not hesitated to deny the existence of God, and, from their point of view they are right.' You will understand from this single trait the boldness and independence of this religious spirit from the Orient. I noted in him traits similar to Vivekananda.

And yet not a single political ruse catches him unprepared. And his own politics are to say everything that he thinks to everybody, not concealing a thing.

On the last evening, after the prayers, Gandhi asked me to play him a little of Beethoven. (He does not know Beethoven, but he knows that Beethoven has been the intermediary between Mira and me, and consequently between Mira and himself, and that, in the final count, it is to Beethoven that the gratitude of us all must go.) I played him the andante of the Fifth Symphony. To that I added Les Chaps Elysées of Gluck – the page for the orchestra and the air for the flute.

He is very sensitive to the religious chants of his country, which somewhat resemble the most beautiful of our Gregorian melodies, and he has worked to assemble them. We also exchanged our ideas on art, from which he does not separate his conception of truth, nor from his conception of truth that of joy, which he thinks truth should bring. But it follows of itself that for this heroic nature joy does not come without effort, nor even life itself without hardship. 'The seeker after truth hath a heart tender as the lotus, and hard as granite.'

Here, my dear friend, are a few hints of those days of ours together on which I have taken much more detailed notes. What I do not dwell on to you is the hurricane of intruders, loiterers, and half-wits which his visit loosed on our two villas. No, the telephone never ceased ringing; photographers in ambuscades let fly their fusillades from behind every bush. The milkmen's syndicate at Leman informed me that during all the time of this sojourn with me the 'King of India' they intended to assume complete responsibility for his 'victualling.' We received letters from 'Sons of God'. Some Italians wrote to the Mahatma beseeching him to indicate for them the ten lucky numbers for the next drawing of the weekly national lottery!

My sister, having survived, has gone to take ten days' rest at a cure in Zurich. She returns tomorrow. For my part, I have entirely lost the gift of sleep. If you find it, send it to me by registered mail!

From: Romain Rolland, "A Visit from Gandhi", *The Nation* (New York), 10 February 1932. (Reproduced in Homer A. Jack (ed.), *The Gandhi Reader*, Madras: Samata Books, 1984, pp.381-385.)

POSTSCRIPT:

The extract above comes from a letter that Rolland wrote to an American friend who leaked it to the press without permission. Embarrassed, Rolland apologised to Gandhi who laughed it off. Romain Rolland's diary recorded the visit of Gandhi's group in fine detail. For the second day of Gandhi's visit it provides a closely observed description of the Mahatma – again one that was certainly not written for publication:

> The next day, Monday, is Gandhi's 'silence day'. He says nothing, but he listens; he jokingly says that it's the best moment for other people to make him listen to anything they want him to hear. He has to sit through everything without replying (there is just one concession; he allows himself to give some short written answers). He arrives punctually at 10 in the morning, having slept, unusually for him, until 8 o'clock. (In London he allowed only three or four hours' sleep each night for himself and his followers; they would come home at 1 o'clock in the morning and get up again at 3 for prayers. Thus they are all visibly very tired – Gandhi himself the least of them. In addition Gandhi caught a cold in London's November fogs; but his solid constitution very soon overcame it without it interrupting his

business or his meetings.) So he comes up my stairs, heralded by his jerky little laugh, and I settle him in the large folding armchair near my table. I am resting my elbows on the table and leaning towards him from my swivelling desk armchair. He at once takes his bare feet out of his sandals and folds his legs under him, surrounding himself with his burnous. He is wearing his broad spectacles, whose lenses consist of two half-moons formed together for distance and close vision at the same time. His complexion is weathered rather than dark, bronzed by the sun. The profile of his head is elongated, and the impression is accentuated by his missing front teeth which reduce his jaw to something like a rat's muzzle; his lower lip is rather large and protruding, and his upper lip bears a thin grey moustache. His nose is straight, a little sunk, and crushed at the end with his broad nostrils. His ears stick out considerably. His brow is broad and well-formed; deep wrinkles become visible when he is speaking, but his cheeks and the rest of his face are of strong substance and show no signs of the network of wrinkles usually seen on European faces. The first impression he gives of fragility is deceptive; his constitution is solid. His large, skinny hands, clutching at the burnous on his arms, are all bones and protruding, swollen veins and muscles. Their perpetual twitching (together with what one can sense of his feet under the burnous) reveals to me the underlying nervousness of this calm and always self-controlled (though lively) man. (Publications Division, *Romain Rolland and Gandhi Correspondence*, pp.166-167)

FURTHER READING:

Aronson, Alex, *Romain Rolland: The Story of Conscience*, Bombay: Padma, 1946.

Fisher, David James, "Romain Rolland and the Popularization of Gandhi: 1923-1925", *Gandhi Marg* (1974), vol.18, no.3, pp.145-180.

Francis, R.A., *Romain Rolland*, Oxford: Berg, 1999.

Malhotra, S.L., "A Study of Gandhi's Biographies – Joseph J. Doke and Romain Rolland", *Gandhi Marg* (1985), vol.6, no.12, pp.845-861.

March, Harold, *Romain Rolland,* New York: Twayne, 1971.

Publications Division, *Romain Rolland and Gandhi Correspondence (Letters, Diary Extracts, Articles, Etc.)*, New Delhi: Publications Division, Ministry of Information and Broadcasting, Government of India, 1976.

Ramana Murti, V.V., "Romain Rolland and Gandhi", *Gandhi Marg* (1966), vol.10, no.1, pp.38-51.

Rolland, Madeleine, "Some Reminiscences of the Visit of Mahatma Gandhi to Romain Rolland in 1931", in Chandrashanker Shukla (ed.), *Incidents of Gandhiji's Life, by Fifty-Four Contributors,* Bombay: Vora, 1949, pp.292-298.

Rolland, Romain, *Mahatma Gandhi: The Man Who Became One With the Universal Being,* New Delhi: Publications Division, Ministry of Information and Broadcasting, Government of India, 1968.

1931

F. MARY BARR

Mary Barr had been in India for ten years overseeing a mission boarding school in Hyderabad State before she met Gandhi. Until then, she knew very little about him holding 'the average Britisher's feeling that he must be misguided, if not actually bad, to be in any way "agin" the Government.' However, being on leave in England during Gandhi's visit for the Round Table Conference, she began to take an interest in his life and thought. Finding herself on the same India-bound ship as the Mahatma fostered a long and close relationship. She spent time in Gandhi's ashrams and eventually settled with some fellow Gandhian workers in an out of the way village and for some time she served as the warden of the girls' hostel at Rabindranath Tagore's institution Shantiniketan. In the 1940s, while in South Africa to look after her aged father, she was arrested as part of the local Indians' struggle against discriminatory laws. In 1951, the now Quaker Barr returned to India where she worked with other Gandhian Quakers, Marjorie Sykes and Alice Barnes, in the Nilgiri Hills until her death in 1968.

In December I embarked in S.S. Pilsna at Venice to return to India and when I heard that the great Indian leader was to board the vessel at Brindisi two days later, my already awakened interest was enormously intensified [...] and here, all unsought, was the opportunity to meet him.

His party was nine in all, his son Devadas, his two secretaries Mahadev and Pyarelal, and Miraben, the English admiral's daughter, who had already been his devoted helper for some years; also four friends who had joined him by special request. [...]

Although they were all travelling 'steerage' and I was a second class passenger, I soon managed to get to know them all and learned many interesting things about their leader, details about his regular life for instance, as well as further facts about his ideas, work and fasts.

He weighs around about a hundred pounds according to the diet, or absence of diet, which he is on at the time. He is thin, and taller than people generally give him credit for being. He wears ordinary cotton cloth wrapped around his shoulders if the occasion seems to demand it. This is covered by a cream-coloured woollen shawl in very cold weather. He always has sandals for outdoor wear, but nothing on his feet in the house, even in London in December. He sits cross-legged on a small, thin, white mattress – and when I say 'white' I mean white, for dusty, travel-stained feet are not allowed to sully his seat. Feet must always be rubbed or washed on coming in from a walk. This like everything else, is done with an economy of labour which is restful yet somehow rapid – the opposite of fussiness. [...]

On the boat there was no bookshelf or desk, but interviews, writing and spinning occupied Gandhi's time, and the regular life of prayer, exercise and work was adhered to just as if he had been at home – though he has no home of his own in the ordinary sense.

He had booked steerage because he felt that as representative of India's masses, he should travel as simply as possible. So his party had only the open deck on which to live, and on those December days and nights during the early part of the voyage, the wind was often cold. The captain, a kindly man, had a tarpaulin fixed round the hatch on which they slept, but even so, it must have been bitterly cold, and the two Swiss people [Dr. and Madame Privat] who used their little camp cots the first night, dispensed with them afterwards in favour of the floor, which did not allow the wind to blow underneath, as well as all around them. They kept this up later too when the weather became warmer, probably because they wished to experience as much as possible of what it meant to go 'simple-lifing' with Gandhi.

A large hound, the property of some first-class passenger, became devoted to Bapu (as I soon learned to call him) and spent its days and nights in very close proximity to him. I remember it always followed at his heels whenever we walked the deck together and lay at his side at prayer-time. Those deck promenades were real exercise, for his habit it was to walk much faster than most younger men would do, and this practice of rapid locomotion has been commented upon by many people describing walks in Delhi or London. It is interesting to note that he followed this custom even on a lurching boat.

The Captain suggested that he should use the second-class saloon for his meals which were not at the same times as those of the second-class passengers: he also offered him the use of a cabin so that he might not have to use the tap on the deck which seemed to be the only bathroom provided for steerage passengers. Several people brought chairs for him to sit on: but, having chosen to travel 'deck' he would accept none of these privileges. Just once, early in the voyage, he went to the upper deck by special request, as all the first and second-class passengers wished to have an opportunity of seeing him.

After that, if their interest or curiosity drove them to desire an interview, they had to descend to the little steerage deck to get satisfaction. Consequently there was a constant succession of visitors, and sometimes the already limited space was strained to the utmost. One of the people who seemed honestly interested was an English judge, who showed a sincere desire to understand the Gandhian point of view. But the merely curious were far greater in number, some being just 'flappers' who wished to take his photograph. Bapu submitted good-humouredly to the snap-shotting, but would never waste a moment in moving or posing for that purpose, even for members of his own party.

One of the things which amazed me during that voyage was the open-ness, trustfulness and lack of secrecy, displayed by Gandhi and his friends. One day I went to their hatch to speak to somebody, but not one of them was there, yet their unlockable satchels and bundles containing important papers and personal belongings were lying unattended. In addition to the possibility of people's coming from other decks, there were other steerage passengers who were always near at hand, some rough, uncultured Indians, three or four rugged Russians and so on. Yet, as far as I know, nothing was tampered with. Since those days I have become accustomed to the extreme publicity of 'Indian India', and also realized that Gandhi's complete openness is due to the fact that he never has anything to hide, and to his transparent honesty and truthfulness. How many politicians could thus bear the light of such constant publicity?

Another thing which struck me from the first was the amount of joking and laughter which was generally to be heard in any group of which Bapu was the centre. Indeed the general impression which I very soon got was of an intensely human individual, and not the saintly but fanatical person of whom I had read.

From: F. Mary Barr, *Bapu: Conversations & Correspondence with Mahatma Gandhi*, Bombay: International Book House, n.d., pp.2-6.

POSTSCRIPT:

In mid-1939, Barr's mother died and she was not sure whether to leave India to look after her South African based father, or to bring him to India. Gandhi advised her that if she felt the call to go and serve her father, she should do it without hesitation after she had done what was possible to ensure the continuation of the work at her Khedi village 'ashram'. He cautioned her that it would be risky to bring her father out as he would not stand the climate. In 1940, on the way to joining her father Marybehn (as she had become known) spent a few days at Sevagram with Gandhi. At one stage she informed him that she wanted to greet him by touching his feet in the Indian fashion, but that her body was too stiff and that she was too self-conscious. Gandhi joked that the problem was that she really was just not humble enough. On their evening walk, Barr came to the realization that perhaps he was right and she was not humble enough to greet Gandhi the way it was appropriate in the country for a daughter to greet her father. While she was intellectualizing her concerns to Gandhi, he remarked laughingly that 'you had better do it now'. As she stooped to grip his ankles, he gave her the affectionate whack on the shoulders children received from adults, and they both laughed. (Barr, *Bapu*, pp.179-183)

FURTHER READING:

Weber, Thomas, *Going Native: Gandhi's Relationship with Western Women*, New Delhi: Roli Books, 2011.

1932 DR. DINSHAW K. MEHTA

Dr. Mehta was the pioneer of modern naturopathy in India. He started his nature cure clinic in Poona in 1929 and from 1933 he became Gandhi's personal nature cure physician and friend. Several of Gandhi's fasts were undertaken under Mehta's supervision and they often discussed various aspects of nature cure. Gandhi was a regular visitor to Mehta's Poona clinic and Mehta treated the imprisoned Kasturba Gandhi just before her death. In 1945, Gandhi founded the All India Nature Cure Foundation Trust with himself as chairman for life. Mehta followed him as chairperson. Mehta also established a rural clinic in the village of Uruli Kanchan and in 1986 the Government of India established the National Institute of Naturopathy at the site, fulfilling his own dream of founding a nature cure university. However, Dinshaw Mehta's contact with Gandhi did not only revolve around health issues. In early December 1947, not long after the bloody partition and independence of British India, Gandhi sent Parsi followers, Jehangir Patel and Mehta to investigate the plight of Muslims in the Indian state of Junagadh and then, just a few weeks before his assassination, to the interim Pakistani capital of Karachi to pave the way for his intended, but never made, visit. Mehta became a naturopath/sanyasi and died in 1993, aged ninety.

Your interview with Mahatmaji fixed tomorrow seven morning start tonight positively wire decision care Mahatmaji – Anand

I felt very happy that Bapu had called me. Leaving everything, I rushed to Bombay from Poona, and well in advance of the appointed time, I reached Laburnum Road where Mani Bhavan was situated. I was not allowed to enter the building. There was a huge crowd outside, there was a lot of activity inside. I told the volunteers that I had been called by Bapu. They said: 'We shall deliver the message. You give it to us in writing.'

I did so, and waited. Time passed. It was past 7 a.m. I thought there was no more chance of meeting him. I went back and sat in my car.

After some time Anand Hingorani [a member of Gandhi's secretariat] came out and saw me sitting in the car. He was surprised and said: 'Bapu is waiting for you! What are you doing here?' I told him that I was prevented by the volunteers. He immediately took me inside.

We went upstairs to the terrace of Mani Bhavan. It was covered with a big shamiana. As soon as I entered the door frame, I saw Bapu sitting in the centre of the terrace on my left, with a whole group of people around him. He looked at me. Our eyes met. I thought: 'I know this man!' even though we had never met before.

Many a time, Bapu had come to Bombay and Poona, but I had refrained from going to see him. It was my feeling that if it had to happen, it would happen. If not, let it not happen; but if it would happen then it would be some higher force that would bring us together. I knew about his activities. He also knew about me and my work in Nature Cure. He was sending patients to our Poona Nature Cure Home.

Bapu raised his right hand forefinger and, shaking it towards me, smiled and said in Gujarati: '*Main Hahyun hatun ne ke e evshe!*

Avshe!!' (Didn't I say that he would come! He would come!!) Then, he asked me in Gujarati: '*Kem? Wakhat Kem lagadyo.*' (Why? Why are you late?)

I told Bapu that I was prevented by the volunteers from coming inside. He smiled and said jokingly '*Eh bichara mari par daya khare chche na!!*' (Poor volunteers! They also have pity on me.) Then, he said: '*Have tamaro wakhat khalas thayo. Tumne kasha javu hoy to jayee ne avo.*' (Now, your time is over. If you have to go anywhere, you can go and come back.)

I replied: '*Tame mane bolavyo tethi avyo chhun. Mare kethe javanu nathi.*' (I have come because you called me. I do not have to go anywhere.)

He said: '*Tyare tame ahian besi jao. Divas ma koi wakhat aapne kadhishun.*' (Then, you sit here. During the course of the day, we shall find some time.)

Many people were sitting around him: Sardar Vallabhbhai Patel, Mahadev Desai and others. I went and sat with Anand Hingorani in the first row, some distance away from Bapu. Many people were coming and going. They were talking with Bapu for anything from one to five minutes and then going away. Some would talk with his Secretary. Some time an important person would come who would talk with him for a longer time. For instance, Jayakar came. Bapu took him to a shed which had been prepared in a corner of the terrace, talked with him there, and then came out. He was calling public leaders and workers one by one and talking with them – a few minutes with each. The day passed by, then came sunset. The day of his silence had begun.

I thought to myself: 'Now there is no chance.' At that very time, we looked at each other. He called me and wrote on a piece of paper that though his silence had started, I could talk with him freely and he would reply in writing. He asked me: 'Do you want other people to remain here? Or, should they go?' Vallabhbhai was sitting there; Mahadev Desai was also there. Several other leaders were sitting near and far.

I replied in Gujarati: '*Jay to Saru!*' (Better if they go.) He made a gesture to all the people to go. They went and sat at a far distance.

We talked. I spoke. He replied in writing. I must still be having the scraps of paper on which he wrote his replies. After we finished, Anand Hingorani said to me: 'What were you talking all this time with Bapu? I measured the time and it was twenty-one minutes!'

From: Vaswni Sundri, (comp. and ed.), *Mahatma Gandhi the Beloved Patient: Revered Dadaji Dr. Dinshah K. Mehta,* Bombay: Bharatiya Vidya Bhavan, 1992, pp.1-4.

POSTSCRIPT:

A few hours after this discussion, at 3 a.m. on 4 January 1932, Gandhi was arrested at Mani Bhavan and taken to Yeravda Central Prison in Poona.

Uruli Kanchan is still continuing its nature cure work. The history of the clinic is tied up with Gandhi's interest in nature cure. As Gandhi explained in late 1945:

> I had purposely refrained from correcting or contradicting reports about my shifting to Poona and establishing a nature cure hospital on an extensive plot of ground in Poona or even Nasik. All this was wrong, as most unauthentic reports in the Press are. These have always cost me dear, perhaps the public more than me. There was, however, a grain of truth in the ounce of rumour. Dr. Dinshaw Mehta knew me before I knew him and, ever since I have known him, I have liked him. I have been myself a nature cure man before all known to me. Of them, Dr. Dinshaw has made the greatest impression on me and he is a dreamer like me. He wants

a nature cure university; so do I. He has made over to a Trust his concerns at Poona and Sinhgad. Their nominal cost, according to the schedules to the Trust, is, in round figures, Rs. 50,000. I have allowed myself to be one of the Trustees. The other two are Dr. Mehta himself and Mr. Jehangir Patel who is interested in nature cure. Hitherto Dr. Mehta's institution has been meant for monied men and then for as many poor people as he could safely take. Patients have all been residential.

From the 1st of January next, this institution will be devoted to the service of the poor. The rich will be taken only if they can accommodate themselves to remain with the poor, and expect no more space or comforts than the poor will get at this institution. The guarantee will be that the standard of cleanliness, shorn of luxury, will be the highest attainable in any institution of the kind. Treatment will be both indoor and outdoor. Outdoor will naturally be more than indoor.

The Birlas have interested themselves in me for years. And they were prepared to give me in Nasik as much land with buildings as were required for the institution. But Dr. Dinshaw was not wholeheartedly inclined to favour the Nasik idea, unless I consented to include in the Trust the going concerns at Poona too. I could not shoulder the burden. Hence the Nasik project had to be dropped, for the time being at any rate. Dr. Dinshaw will still remain the sole Director so far as the technical part is concerned. This institution, if it is to grow at all, will require the silent blessings of the poor, the financial support of the rich, active co-operation of genuine naturopaths of India and sympathy of the medical fraternity. Its present site is too small for the requirements of the poor. Moreover, it will largely depend upon the leaseholder whether the institution can in any case remain located on the present site. ("Statement to the Press", *The Hitavada*, 22 November 1945)

Further Reading:

Gandhi, M.K., (Anand Hingorani ed.), *The Health Guide*, Bombay: Bharatiya Vidya Bhavan, 1965.

Gandhi, M.K., *Key to Health*, Ahmedabad: Navajivan, 1948.

Patel, Jehangir P., and Marjorie Sykes, *Gandhi: His Gift of the Fight*, Rasulia: Friends Rural Centre, 1987.

1933

NILLA CRAM COOK (NILA NAGINI DEVI)

The twenty-two year old American Nilla Cram Cook was the strangest, most difficult and perhaps most controversial of Gandhi's followers. She came from an unashamedly bohemian background and in the eyes of many was a 'fallen' woman. She travelled across India, counting off her rosary, practising yoga, and taking various vows. She had mystical experiences, visited temples and swamis, lived with a spiritual master in Mount Abu, socialized with the highest of princely society, made influential friends, fell in love with the Maharaja of Mysore, and lived on nothing but orange juice for three months because she did not know how to tell him. While Gandhi's anti-untouchability campaign was in full swing, Nilla became involved in the 'Untouchable' temple entry agitation in Bangalore. She wrote to Gandhi of her work, but Gandhi had been hearing unfavourable reports about her behaviour. He decided to take her under his wing. She stayed for a while in Sabarmati Ashram and then with Gandhi in Wardha, where she had a psychotic episode and disappeared. Gandhi respected her enthusiasm for life and tried to rehabilitate her (she was one of the causes for his May 1933 fast), but in the end he was not up to the task.

Yeravda was a village on the other side of the river that flowed through Poona. In the midst of the bright fields at the edge of it was the prison that had come to be called Yeravda Mandir, the Yeravda Temple, since Gandhiji had taken up residence in it. The guard at the barred outside gate called the jailor, when I said I wanted to see Gandhiji, and I gave him my name. They opened a little door in the bars like the door of a bird cage, and I went through and registered in the prison guest book, putting down my Hindi name, the hour I arrived, where I came from and whom I wanted to see. Then the jailor took me into his office and told me to wait.

In about fifteen minutes he came back, opened the bars of a second gate and led me across a cobblestone road into a courtyard surrounded by high walls. The first thing I saw there was a mango tree. Two white figures were sitting in the shade of it on the other side, so that I could not see them until I went around. One was a well-built and good-looking young man in a jail uniform, writing at a table loaded with papers. I gathered he was Mahadev Desai, Gandhiji's secretary, who was living in the same jail. The other was the ugliest-looking human being I had ever seen. I had heard that Gandhiji was not very beautiful to look at, but had not expected anything like this. My instinct was to turn and run.

'So you came!' he said.

When he spoke he was even uglier. How could anything as ugly as this be beautiful inside? 'Gurudev!' I wanted to shout and run. Gurudev [a Jain monk from Mount Abu with whom Nilla had previously stayed] was majesty and beauty from the first moment, inside and out.

'As I told Mahadev, either you would come right away when you got my letter, or never come at all,' continued Gandhiji. 'Did you check your bag at the station, as I said?'

'Yes,' I replied.

'And what class ticket did you come on?'

'Third class.'

'What did you eat on the way?'

'Fruits and nuts.'

'Did you buy them in the railway stations?'

'Yes.'

'What did you spend on them?'

'Not more than eight annas a day.' Eight annas was about ten cents.

'Well,' said Gandhiji, 'that's pretty good, though eight annas has to feed a whole family in many cases.'

'And I took a bath in the first and second class waiting room at the Poona station this morning!' I added a little belligerently. 'You once let your wife take a bath in the second class waiting room on a third class ticket!'

'So you've read everything I've ever written!'

The story about the illegitimate bath he told in his autobiography, *The Story of My Experiments With Truth*. Some women travelling in the second class invited Mrs. Gandhi to go along with them for a bath. Men in the third class could bathe under the station water pipes, but there were no third class bathing facilities for women, and unless she bathed she could not eat. Gandhiji allowed her to do it and told the story afterwards as a confession. 'Thus,' he wrote, 'one's weakness for one's wife stands in the way of the practice of truth.'

'Have you eaten this morning?' he asked me.

'No, I would not eat before I had seen you.'

I had not fasted all the way from South India, as Gurudev's disciples did, but at least I would not have eaten before seeing him. 'I'll feed you,' he said. 'But first let's get to the reports I alluded to in my letter. Is it true you have had carryings-on with the Crown Prince of Mysore?'

'The Crown Prince?' I gasped, flabbergasted. 'Why, he's only thirteen years old!'

He was a delightful child I had met at the Birthday Durbar and talked with once.

'Or with the Yuveraja?' Gandhiji continued.

'Why, one is the father of the other!' I cried, utterly astounded. 'Which one do you mean, the Yuveraja or his thirteen-year old son?'

'One story was the Yuveraja, the other was the Rajkumar.'

One didn't sound bad enough!

The Yuveraja would have been as amazed as I was. The one time I was seated beside him, at the birthday concert, I fled to Mirza and Madame de Morsier. After the Birthday Festival he had gone to Europe and America and did not return in time for Dasara. I had never seen him again. I was particularly disgusted by the story because during all that time I had secretly worshiped the Maharaja, and it was not very pleasant to hear that I had carryings-on with his brother and brother's son.

'As I wrote you, I hear it from a man of worth,' said Gandhiji.

'I know who!' I exclaimed, and pronounced a name.

'Yes,' said Gandhiji. 'How did you know?'

'By — intuition,' I replied.

I had never met the man, nor had he met me, and I had only heard of him once. He was from Poona, and when he went to Bangalore he stayed with some small-fry officials, pillars of society, who knew more about me than I knew about myself, but whom I did not know. Many others also had been in Bangalore and I had no particular reason to pick on him. But when I read Gandhiji's letter his name flashed across my mind in a peculiar and unmistakable way.

'Well, you're right,' said Gandhiji, and smiled. With his smile all his ugliness vanished. His eyes twinkled like Gurudev's and his smile was like the Dailwarra gods. Not many smile in exactly

> that way. Gurudev, the Dailwarra gods, the Maharaja of Mysore and one Yogi in his kingdom were the only ones I knew. Their smiles were like the byword of a brotherhood, and an admission that they knew more than they told. Such knowledge was in the background of all Gandhiji's writings, whether it was scavenging he was talking about, or making fertilizer of pulverized bones.
>
> Nothing in his talk that first morning would have led me to believe he had Gurudev's wisdom. For the face value of his talk I might have walked out of the jail. But there was no mistaking that smile.
>
> 'How long will you stay?' he asked.
>
> 'As long as it takes to work out what I am to do – as long as you want me to stay.'
>
> 'Very well. There is a man here from the Ashram, and his daughter. They will call for you at noon and take you to where they're staying. And now Mahadev will feed you.'

From: Nilla Cram Cook, *My Road to India,* New York: Lee Furman, 1939, pp.337-339.

POSTSCRIPT:

In her autobiography, Mirabehn summed up Nilla's life with Gandhi, and her disappearance after about five months in his ashrams, most poetically. She wrote that Nilla

> was a young woman from America, with a Greek background of dancing and poetry, the very opposite of my pupil in cooking and washing [Margaret Spiegel 'an extremely earnest young woman from Germany who had fled Nazi persecution of the Jews']. She had come to Bapu previously and had stayed at Sabarmati Ashram just before and during the disbandment of the place, after which

> she had come to Wardha for a time. So she was familiar with her surroundings. Bapu told me simply to look after her in a general way. This time the job was hard for me, because Nilla was a sprite, a spirit, dancing and singing her way through life like a bird. Earnest was she too, but it was an earnestness of exaltation, and one fine morning we found that she had flown from the nest, like the bird that she was. When we next heard of her she was in Brindaban [near Mathura, where the Gopis had danced for Krishna], where she had been taken to a missionary hospital with a poisonous thorn in her leg as a result of dancing all alone in the woods of Lord Krishna. Bapu did his best to extricate her from this predicament, but the Missionaries and the British Government combined to send her all the way back to America. Bapu was pained. It was clear to me that, in spite of the extraordinary escapades, he had seen much more in that passing spirit than the rest of us had at the time. (Mira Behn, *The Spirit's Pilgrimage*, pp.179-180)

Nilla Cram Cook recovered from her mental illness and led a productive but no less extraordinary post-Gandhi life. In 1939 she left America for Europe as a war correspondent in Greece. In 1941 she was in Iran as the censor of theatres and cinemas for the Interior Ministry and, following travels in Afghanistan, as the United States cultural attaché in Tehran. She converted to Islam, translated the Koran and spent years as the director of the Iranian National Ballet and Opera.

FURTHER READING:

Mira Behn (Madeleine Slade), *The Spirit's Pilgrimage*, London: Longmans, 1960.

Weber, Thomas, *Going Native: Gandhi's Relationship with Western Women*, New Delhi: Roli Books, 2011.

1934 NIRMAL KUMAR BOSE

Nirmal Kumar Bose was born in 1901. As a student he was interested in anarchist literature and when he came across Gandhi's writings he saw the Mahatma as belonging to the same tradition as Tolstoy and Kropotkin, and began compiling an anthology of Gandhian writings. He was arrested during the Salt Satyagraha, and in 1934, he finally met and conducted a lengthy interview with Gandhi. That same year, he published the anthology under the title *Selections from Gandhi*. In 1940, he published the first edition of *Studies in Gandhism* and two years later a reworked edition of *Selections*. (Gandhi wrote the foreword to the 1948 edition). Nevertheless, it was not until 1946, when Gandhi asked him to go as his Bengali interpreter to Noakhali that he came into intimate contact with the Mahatma. Following disagreements over Gandhi's brahmacharya experiments, he returned to Calcutta, where he wrote the controversial classic (detailing Gandhi's brahmacharya experiments with Manu Gandhi) *My Days with Gandhi*. He became one of India's leading anthropologists and the Director of the Anthropological Survey of India (between 1959 and 1964). He died in 1972.

We [K.R. Kripalani and Bose] reached the place on the 9th of November 1934, and were accommodated as guests in Jamnalal Bajaj's house, which is not very far from the railway station.

That same day Khan Sahib [Khan Abdul Ghaffar Khan] had an appointment with Gandhiji in the afternoon; and he very kindly asked me to come with him to meet Mahatmaji, with whom I had never had the opportunity of coming into personal contact before. [...] While introducing me [Khan Sahib] said that I was a Congress worker engaged in constructive work among the untouchable castes.

It was about half-past four when we were ushered into a room at the top of the Mahila Ashram or Womens' [sic] Institute in Wardha, where Gandhiji had taken up his residence ever since his abandonment of Sabarmati Ashram. Sevagram had not yet come into being, and he occupied a clean and spacious room with a broad terrace in front in the upper storey of a brick-built building.

When we entered the room, we found Gandhiji seated behind a small desk near the southern end, close to a door which opened into a terrace. A spotlessly clean white sheet of handspun and handwoven khadi was spread over a durrie which covered almost the whole of the floor. The small desk in front had some paper and writing materials neatly arranged upon it. There did not seem to be many men about. Pyarelal, his secretary, was there, and a few women workers were also in attendance. What impressed me at the first glance was the perfect cleanliness and the almost ascetic simplicity of the furnishings of the room.

The time of the interview had been fixed outside the usual hours reserved for that purpose. When all of us had seated ourselves in a semi-circle, Gandhiji opened the conversation. [Khan and his son Ghani were in dispute. Khan wanted Ghani to work on a political journal, while Ghani, who professed no interest in politics, wanted to spend his time in the pursuit of art.] [...]

Gandhiji sat listening in silence, and when the two had finished, he turned to Kripalani and asked him what opinion Ghani's Principal [at Shantiniketan where he was studying] held of him. Kripalani reported that the former had a favourable opinion about his talents but Ghani was never serious in his work but flirted with it. Gandhiji broke into a merry laughter and said, 'Ha! Ha! see that he does not flirt with anything else.' I never imagined Gandhiji could joke in this manner; but when he did, all of us joined in the laughter and the serious atmosphere of the room was appreciably dispelled.

Gandhiji now turned towards Abdul Ghaffar Khan and spoke in a more serious vein. He was of opinion that when God had endowed Ghani with talents in Art, we had no right to harness him to any other purpose. All we could do was to help him in his own growth, and therefore if Ghani promised to spend some time every year in Shantiniketan, he would gladly find work for him in a factory. Kripalani now added that the Principal had also said that Ghani had a special talent for sculpture, and as he personally knew nothing of carving, Ghani could more profitably seek instruction elsewhere. Gandhiji, however, broke in and said, 'No, no. Nandalal knows the poetry of sculpture, and Ghani must imbibe it from him.'

Abdul Ghaffar Khan sat listening in silence and when Gandhiji pronounced his final judgement he took it with calmness, like the good soldier that he ever had been. What, however, appeared surprising to me was the tenderness with which Gandhiji treated the case of an artist in distress. In the midst of the political tension through which the country was passing in 1934, he had perhaps the right to call even an artist to soldier's duty; for had he not once written to the poet

Rabindranath Tagore many years ago that a poet should lay down his lyre when the house is in flames and associate himself in work with the famishing millions of his countrymen?

When Ghani's case was over, Gandhiji turned to me and asked me to 'say something about myself.' It was an embarrassing question, but I succeeded in briefly recounting my antecedents. Then he said that Khan Sahib had informed him how I wanted to discuss a few questions with him. I then handed over to him four questions which had been brought in writing. He went through them carefully, and as none of the questions was of a private nature, asked me if he could discuss them in the present company. Of course, there was no ground for objection, and so he started his discourse.

From: Nirmal Kumar Bose, *My Days with Gandhi,* Bombay: Orient Longman, 1974, pp.8-11.

POSTSCRIPT:

When the forty-year-old Bose took leave from his teaching position at the University of Calcutta to become Gandhi's translator and secretary during the Mahatma's Noakhali pilgrimage to bring peace to war-torn rural Bengal, he had little idea of the controversy that lay ahead of him. At this time Gandhi was engaged in his *brahmacharya* experiments, making sure that he had overcome all lust by sleeping naked with his nineteen-year-old grandniece Manu, to ensure that he had the spiritual strength to undertake the struggle he was engaged in. Bose strongly disagreed with Gandhi's actions and, although a strong admirer and Gandhi philosophy promoter, he left his leader and returned to Calcutta, complaining that although the women were willing partners in his experiment, there was a power imbalance and consequently he was unconsciously exploiting Manu and others who had taken part. Bose thought that it was unfortunate that Gandhi did not know more about Freud and modern psychology. He wrote about these experiments in his memoir of the Noakhali peace effort. Two years after Gandhi's assassination, he submitted his manuscript to Navajivan, which owned the copyright to Gandhi's works. Navajivan refused to publish the work unless he left out reference to Gandhi's *brahmacharya* experiments. He then attempted to self-publish it but was refused permission to include any matter in which Navajivan held copyright. He then spent three years showing the manuscript to friends and publishers to ascertain their opinions. Some thought that it would give rise to misunderstandings and that it might be exploited by Gandhi critics, nevertheless he managed to get the book published in 1953, and in 1974 it was finally published by a mainstream publisher. It has become one of the classics of the literature on Gandhi.

FURTHER READING:

Bose, Nirmal Kumar, *Selections from Gandhi,* Ahmedabad: Navajivan, 1948.
Bose, Nirmal Kumar, *Studies in Gandhism,* Ahmedabad: Navajivan, 1972.
Mehta, Ved, *Mahatma Gandhi and His Apostles,* London: Andre Deutsch, 1977.

1935 HALIDE EDIB ADIVAR

Born into a high-status family within the Ottoman Empire (her father was Secretary to the Sultan) in 1884 in Constantinople, Halide Edib was educated in part at the American College for Girls. She became a leading Turkish writer and feminist political activist working for the emancipation of women in her country. Her writings led to her being given the task of reforming girls' schools in the capital in 1909 and the following year she divorced her first husband when he took a second wife. After the First World War, she took up arms in the Turkish national cause. She lived in France and England and travelled widely in the 1930s, including to India to deliver a series of lectures at the Jamia Millia Islamia. Returning to her homeland in 1939, she became a professor of English literature at Istanbul University and was elected to Parliament in 1950. Following her retirement in 1954, she continued to write until her death in 1964.

I was going to see Mahatma Gandhi for the first time. To me he represented the Hindu of Hindus [...] the essence of the oldest India. Unconscious expectancy made me especially sensitive to my environment during that drive. [...] Our car drew up in an open field where stood a two-storied stone building, flying the Congress flag.

The facade of the house was towards the other side, overlooking a vast field where, in the distance, fires were being lighted and figures in white were moving about. The fires were yet only wreaths of smoke curling upwards lazily. There was a spacious porch before the house into which all the rooms of the first floor opened, including that of Mahatma Gandhi. His was a large room with a concrete floor. In the corner facing the entrance were a mat, and a floor cushion, and a low desk, such as we used in old days in Turkey. Papers and books were on the desk and scattered over the cushion.

The face might be that of any Hindu, I thought. Yet it had none of the mystery and closed-in-ness of Hindu faces. Nothing could be more clear-cut and sharply defined than this triangular, dark, serene face. The mouth was large and toothless except for a single front tooth. The lips were closed over each other tightly, yet they did not give the impression of forbidding grimness or sunken old age. With the long nose and its tip curling over the lips, the mouth made one think its owner might be easily amused, and have a tendency to give and take jokes. As I saw it first, the face was very grave. The eyes were deep-set and clear and slightly drawn towards the narrow temples, somewhat in a Mongolic fashion. But the eye-folds were not Mongolic. They were distinctly Hindu, very tautly drawn towards the raised delicate eyebrows. As the face bent forward, there appeared a baldish dome with a Hindu-lock, a tiny curl, on the top of it.

'He has majestic personality; everyone who comes in touch with him loses all capacity for clear judgment – everyone who knows him becomes too emotional to be trusted to be objective.' [...] I was told that by several people including some English.

As I sat there I thought: 'If people are carried away by emotion, it must be that they are excitable, and in search for emotion instead of truth.' Mahatma Gandhi seemed to me the last person in the world to appeal to the emotional, to make any attempt to capture the fancy or create fantasy and mystery around himself; though his religious nature is undeniable, and some of his talk may occasionally lead one to term him as a mystic. I had gone there with an honest determination to understand him and not to indulge in emotion; and I felt more than ever that I must not give way either to my former prejudice caused by the over-sensational European propaganda or the sympathy and admiration his person inspired. He is so important a happening in twentieth-century history, I said to myself, that every witness must leave as objective and honest report as is humanly possible.

The door opened continually. Men in all sorts of costumes came in and fell on their faces at the fringe of the mat; then sat, their hands folded on their knees. I recognised some of the faces belonging to Congress members or to people in other leading positions, intellectual, spiritual, or otherwise. This sort of salute may appear to the Western eye as servile; but it is not. It is rather the Eastern reverence for those whom they believe to be spiritually great. The wonder of it was that it should survive a modern, a scientific, a materialistically Western education. It was evident that they had submerged themselves in Mahatma Gandhi's personality. That kind talked little. But there were others who came to consult him, or to have his blessings on some enterprise; and some came to tell him what they were going to do. The range of subjects on which he is consulted is infinite. It is almost inconceivable for most of the Hindus and a considerable number of Muslims to do anything without his knowledge. This applies also to political life, though Mahatma

Gandhi has retired from politics. Whether the general desire to consult Mahatma Gandhi is due to a mystical and spiritual adoration, or to a recognition of the excellence of his judgement, or merely a habit of doing what the rest of the world does, it results in taking up an enormous amount of his time and energy. His economy of words, I often thought, was a reaction to being perpetually talked to.

[...] Meanwhile mats were being spread on the left. Men and women were walking towards the mats and then sitting in rows. Mothers brought their children, leading them by the hand or carrying them in their arms. Quite soon a crowd in the form of a great horseshoe had gathered. At the open end of the horseshoe a few carpets had been placed. No more gold in the sky, but the dusk was velvety. The fires, which had been smoking, were now flames licking the dusk, while tiny groups of people appeared as white smudges on a mat. A gong sounded when I also was settled on a mat. Mahatma Gandhi descended the steps of the porch, and sat at the centre of the opening.

Children moved and whispered, mothers leaned over and tried to silence them. There was something contagious in the happiness of the little ones; they seemed more aware of what was happening than their elders. No wonder, for there was a childlike simplicity about the whole scene. Behind me a mother was feeding her baby at her breast. I could hear the cluck, cluck of the tiny throat as it swallowed. And the old pandit opposite was tuning his sitar. I could distinguish a few faces from Jamia. At the moment it was the atmosphere rather than the motionless figure of Mahatma Gandhi that took hold of the crowd. He was only a unit. Yet I watched him. By some freak of light, or rather because of the thinness of his shoulders, his draperies stood out both sides in sharp angles. Everything about him seemed to have fallen into geometrical shape. Wrapt in the white mantle, his shoulders two edges, his face immobile, he looked like Buddha. [...]

The crowd rose with a gentle rustle, women dragging their chattering babies, men adjusting their draperies. All were hurrying towards the steps of the porch where Mahatma Gandhi was trying to go up. But he was stopped by the surging crowd, especially by the women, who pushed their babies towards his feet, asking for his blessings, or perhaps asking him to heal some of their sick ones. We stood in the open. The moon had come out from behind the clouds. The Jamia professors in their tightly buttoned coats and white Gandhi-caps were sharply outlined; others in their draperies vaguely outlined. This perhaps is the fundamental difference between the Muslim and the Hindu. Hinduism has a vague outline, so that it is difficult to say where it begins and where it ends; while Islam is sharply defined, compact. [...]

'Now, now, now [...]' was saying Mahatma Gandhi to the women, 'you don't mean that [...]' trying all the time to prevent those who embraced his knees from kissing his feet. At least so it seemed to me from where I was. There were both friendliness and a slight chiding in his voice. He was amused, but also was perhaps scolding them for the incurable idolatry which abides in man's heart, strongest in that of the simple Hindu.

From: Halide Edib, "My First Visit to Mahatma Gandhi", in Chandrashanker Shukla (ed.), *Reminiscences of Gandhiji: By Forty-eight Contributors,* Bombay: Vora, 1951, pp.87-91. This is more or less a reprint of pp.55-63 of Halidé Edib, *Inside India,* London: Allen & Unwin, 1937.

POSTSCRIPT:

Halide Edib gave eight lectures at Jamia Millia Islamia. They were presided over by eight notable Indians, four Muslims and four Hindus, one of whom was Mahatma Gandhi. She recalled the atmosphere in the packed hall that evening with eyes riveted on Gandhi: it 'vibrated with a mixture of profound affection and mystic fervour' with the fragile figure out front 'being more like a Buddha than ever'. Her mind wandered from her lecture topic to thinking about the 'quality of Mahatma Gandhi's greatness.' There was the greatness of Napoleonic figures with their love of power, ambition and cruelty, and the greatness in the mould of Buddha and Christ, with Gandhi belonging to this second category. She thought that these types seemed to have lived only in the times of the saints and prophets, or, did the fact of Gandhi 'mean the opening of a new era?' By way of conclusion, she asked:

> Otherwise why should he be so much loved by millions, and revered by the Intelligentzia of this materialistic world of ours? For the moment Mahatma Gandhi revived my faith in the infallibility of the better nature of Man. Not only Gandhi, but the Indian masses who take sides with this ancient type of leader who represents love, seemed to me worthy of the world's gratitude. For in following Mahatma Gandhi the Indian has no hope of worldly reward. On the contrary he is often persecuted for it. In the hall that night there was a sense of fraternity and friendliness: the feeble old man had turned the light on the human qualities of us all without which we must all perish. (Edib, *Inside India,* pp.81-82)

FURTHER READING:

Adivar, Halide Edib, *The Memoir of Halide Edib,* New York: Century, 1926.

Adivar, Halide Edib, *The Turkish Ordeal,* New York: Century, 1928.

Edib, Halide, *House with Wisteria: Memoirs of Halide Edib,* Charlottesville, VA: Leopolis Press, 2003.

Edib, Halidé, *Inside India,* Delhi: Oxford University Press, 2002.

1935

PARAMAHANSA YOGANANDA

Paramahansa Yogananda was born Mukunda Lal Gosh in 1893 in the north Indian town of Gorakhpur. He was absorbed by spiritual concerns since his childhood, and became a disciple of Shri Yukeshwar Giri at the age of seventeen. Following his graduation from Calcutta University in 1915 he entered a monastic order and assumed the name Yogananda. In 1917, he established a yoga school in Ranchi. Three years later, his guru sent him as an emissary to America where Yogananda founded the Self-Realization Fellowship and became the first Indian swami to live in the West for a lengthy period of time. The Fellowship had the aim of disseminating 'among the nations a knowledge of definite scientific techniques of attaining direct personal experience of God.' Yogananda's teachings were based on traditional yoga texts and his method, 'kriya yoga', combined deep meditation and the direction of life energy from outer to inner concerns in order to 'serve mankind as one's larger Self.' He visited Gandhi on a trip to India in 1935 and was present at the death of his guru (who had invested him with the highest spiritual title of Paramahansa). Yogananda passed away in Los Angeles in 1952. His book, *Autobiography of a Yogi* is perhaps the classic text of its genre. It has been translated into many languages.

'Welcome to Wardha!' Mahadev Desai, secretary to Mahatma Gandhi, greeted Miss Bletsch, Mr. Wright and me with these cordial words and with the gift of wreaths of *khaddar* (homespun cotton). Our little group had just arrived at the station of Wardha on an early morning in August, glad to leave the dust and heat of the train. Consigning our luggage to a bullock cart, we entered an open motor car with Mr. Desai and his companions, Babasaheb Deshmukh and Dr. Pingale. A short drive over the muddy country roads brought us to 'Maganvadi', the ashram of India's political saint.

Mr. Desai led us at once to the writing room where, cross-legged, sat Mahatma Gandhi. Pen in one hand and scrap of paper in the other, on his face a vast, winning, warm-hearted smile!

'Welcome!' he scribbled in Hindi; it was a Monday, his weekly day of silence.

Though this was our first meeting, we beamed at each other affectionately. In 1925 Mahatma Gandhi had honoured the Ranchi school by a visit, and had inscribed in its guest book a gracious tribute. [...]

'The ashram residents are wholly at your disposal; please call on them for any service.' With characteristic courtesy, the Mahatma handed me this hastily written note as Mr. Desai led our party from the writing room towards the guest house.

Our guide led us through orchards and flowering fields to a tile-roofed building with latticed windows. A front yard well, twenty-five feet across, was used, Mr. Desai said, for watering stock; nearby stood a revolving cement wheel for threshing rice. Each of our small bedrooms proved to contain only the irreducible minimum – a bed, handmade of rope. The whitewashed kitchen boasted a faucet in one corner and a fire pit for cooking in another. Simple Arcadian sounds reached our ears – the cries of crows and sparrows, the lowing of cattle, and the rap of chisels being used to chip stones. [...]

Two hours after our arrival, my companions and I were summoned to lunch. The Mahatma was already seated under the arcade of the ashram porch, across the courtyard from his study. About twenty-five barefooted *satyagrahis* were squatting before brass cups and plates. A community chorus of prayer; then a meal served from large brass pots containing *chapatis* (whole-wheat unleavened bread) sprinkled with *ghee*; *talsari* (boiled and diced vegetables), and lemon jam.

The Mahatma ate *chapatis,* boiled beets, some raw vegetables, and oranges. On one side of his plate was a large lump of very bitter *neem* leaves, a notable blood cleanser. With a spoon he separated a portion and placed it on my dish. I bolted it down with water, remembering childhood days when Mother had forced me to swallow the disagreeable dose. Gandhi, however, was eating the *neem* paste bit by bit, without distaste. [...]

Our trio enjoyed a six o'clock supper as guests of Babasaheb Deshmukh. The 7.00 P.M. prayer hour found us back at the Maganvadi ashram, climbing to the roof where thirty *satyagrahis* were grouped in a semicircle around Gandhi. He was squatting on a straw mat, an ancient pocket watch propped up before him. The fading sun cast a late gleam over the palms and banyans; the hum of night and the crickets had started. The atmosphere was serenity itself; I was enraptured.

A solemn chant led by Mr. Desai, with responses from the group; then a *Gita* reading. The Mahatma motioned to me to give the concluding prayer. Such divine unison of thought and aspiration! A memory forever; the Wardha roof-top meditation under the early stars.

Punctually at eight o'clock Gandhi ended his silence. The herculean labours of his life require him to apportion his time minutely.

'Welcome, Swamiji!' The Mahatma's greeting this time was not via paper. We had just descended from the roof to his writing room, simply furnished with square mats (no chairs), a low desk with books, papers, and a few ordinary pens (not fountain pens); a nondescript clock ticked in a corner. An all-pervasive aura of peace and devotion. Gandhi was bestowing one of his captivating, cavernous, almost toothless smiles.

'Years ago,' he explained, 'I started my weekly observance of a day of silence as a means for gaining time to look after my correspondence. But now those twenty-four hours have become a vital spiritual need. A periodical decree of silence is not a torture but a blessing.'

I agreed wholeheartedly. The Mahatma questioned me about America and Europe; we discussed India and world conditions.

'Mahadev,' Gandhi said as Mr. Desai entered the room, 'please make arrangements at Town Hall for Swamiji to speak there on yoga tomorrow night.'

As I was bidding the Mahatma good night, he considerately handed me a bottle of citronella oil.

'The Wardha mosquitoes don't know a thing about *ahimsa* [nonviolence] Swamiji!' he said, laughing.

The following morning our little group breakfasted early on whole-wheat porridge with molasses and milk. At ten-thirty we were called to the ashram porch for lunch with Gandhi and the *satyagrahis*. Today the menu included brown rice, a new selection of vegetables and cardamom seeds.

Noon found me strolling about the ashram grounds, on the grazing land of a few imperturbable cows. The protection of cows is a passion with Gandhi. [...]

Returning to the guest house I was stuck anew by the stark simplicity and evidences of self-sacrifice which are everywhere present. The Gandhi vow of non-possession came early in his married life. Renouncing an extensive legal practice which had been yielding him an annual income of more than Rs. 60,000, the Mahatma dispersed all his wealth to the poor.

At three o'clock that afternoon in Wardha, I betook myself, by previous appointment, to the writing room of the saint who had been able to make an unflinching disciple out of his own wife – rare miracle! Gandhi looked up with his unforgettable smile.

'Mahatmaji,' I said as I squatted beside him on the uncushioned mat, 'please tell me your definition of *ahimsa*.'

'The avoidance of harm to any living creature in thought or deed.'

'Beautiful ideal! But the world will always ask: May one not kill a cobra to protect a child, or one's self?'

'I could not kill a cobra without violating two of my vows – fearlessness, and non-killing. I would rather try inwardly to calm the snake by vibrations of love. I cannot possibly lower my standards to suit my circumstances.' With his amazing candour, Gandhi added, 'I must confess that I could not carry on this conversation serenely were I faced by a cobra!' [...]

On the previous night Gandhi had expressed a wish to receive the *Kriya Yoga* of Lahiri Mahasaya. I was touched by the Mahatma's open-mindedness and spirit of enquiry. He is childlike in his divine quest, revealing that pure receptivity which Jesus praised in children, '[...] of such is the kingdom of heaven'.

The hour for my promised instruction had arrived; several *satyagrahis* now entered the room – Mr. Desai, Dr. Pingale, and a few others who desired the Kriya technique.

I first taught the little class the physical *Yogoda* exercises. The body is visualised and divided into twenty parts; the will directs energy in turn to each section. Soon everyone was vibrating before me like a human motor. It was easy to observe the rippling effect on Gandhi's twenty body parts, at nearly all times completely exposed to view. Though very thin, he is not unpleasingly so; the skin of his body is smooth and unwrinkled.

Later I initiated the group into the liberating technique of *Kriya* Yoga. [...]

On my last evening in Wardha I addressed the meeting which had been called by Mr. Desai in Town Hall. The room was thronged to the windowsills with about 400 persons assembled to hear the talk on yoga. I spoke in Hindi, then in English. Our little group returned to the ashram in time for a good-night glimpse of Gandhi, enfolded in peace and correspondence.

Night was still lingering when I rose at 5.00 A.M. Village life was already stirring; first a bullock cart by the ashram gates, then a peasant with his huge burden balanced precariously on his head. After breakfast our troop sought out Gandhi for farewell *pranams*. The saint rises at four o'clock for his morning prayer.

'Mahatmaji, good-bye!' I knelt to touch his feet. 'India is safe in your keeping.'

From: Paramahansa Yogananda, *Autobiography of a Yogi*, Bombay: Jaico Publishing House, 1985, pp.428-439.

POSTSCRIPT:

When Gandhi had visited Yogananda's school in Ranchi ten years previously, he had written in the visitors' book that 'I wish this institution to progress in every way. It has made a good impression on me. I hope more knowledge will spread through the plying of the spinning-wheel.' For Gandhi's version of the 26/27 August 1935 discussion with Yogananda, see Mahadev Desai's account in his 'Weekly Letter' published in Gandhi's paper *Harijan* on 7 September 1935.

FURTHER READING:

Yogananda, Paramahansa, *Journey to Self-Realization: Discovering the Gifts of the Soul,* San Francisco: Self-Realization Fellowship, 1997.

Zeleski, Philip, *The 100 Best Spiritual Books of the Century,* San Francisco: HarperCollins, 1984.

1935 MARGARET SANGER

Margaret Sanger was one of the international leaders of the birth control movement. She was the sixth of eleven children of a devout Irish Catholic mother who endured eighteen pregnancies in twenty-two years. Sanger wanted to become a doctor but a lack of finances led her to study nursing instead. The tuberculosis-suffering Sanger had three children by the time that she was thirty. She decided that she did not want to slip into the usual domesticity that was often the lot of wives and mothers. During nurse training, she came to realise the degree to which many women lived in fear of constant childbearing, and working in New York City, she discovered the relationship between poverty, uncontrolled fertility, unwanted pregnancies, and high death rates from botched illegal abortions. This led her to become a life-long crusading feminist for women's rights, championing contraception to avoid unplanned pregnancies. Invited to speak at the All-India Women's Conference, she toured India over the winter of 1935-1936. She had asked New York Reverend John Haynes Holmes to write to the Mahatma on her behalf requesting an interview. Gandhi responded: 'Do by all means come whenever you can, and you shall stay with me, if you would not mind what must appear to you to be our extreme simplicity; we have no masters and no servants here.'

We were met at the station at Wardha by a covered, two-sided cart, a tonga, very clean with little steps leading up and drawn by a cream-colored bullock. Since there were no seats, we sat flat on the bottom and were pulled leisurely and slowly along dusty roads to the *ashram*.

Gandhi was cross-legged on the floor of a room in a large squarish structure, a white cloth like a sheet around him. He rose to greet me as I entered with an armful of books and flowers and magazines and gloves that I had not realized were there until we tried to take each other by both hands. He beamed and I laughed.

Perhaps even more exaggerated than his pictures was Gandhi's appearance: his ears stuck out more prominently; his shaved head was more shaved; his toothless mouth grinned more broadly, leaving a great void between his lips. But around him and a part of him was a luminous aura. And once you had seen this, the ugliness faded and you glimpsed the something in the essence of his being which people have followed and which has made them call him the Mahatma.

This was Monday, Gandhi's day of silence, of meditation and prayer. He was so besieged by problems and difficulties on which he had to decide that this one twenty-four hours he reserved for himself without interruption. Therefore, he merely smiled and nodded his head and then [Sanger's assistant] Anna Jane [Philips] and I were escorted along a gravel path to the guest house perhaps a hundred yards away, a building of four rooms, rough-hewn, white-plastered wall, the upper section open for ventilation. On the uneven stone floor stood two mattress-less cots on which our bedding was spread. A roof pole in the centre had a circular shelf which served as table or chairs according to need.

Bowls of porridge and milk were brought, sweetened with either honey or burned sugar – I could not tell which, but it was very pleasant. I asked no questions about its being boiled, or whether it was goats' or cows' milk; although I happened not to be hungry, down it went just the same.

From tiffin on we inspected the cotton-growing, the paper-making, the oil press, and the irrigation by means of old-fashioned turn wheels. I was not enthusiastic. It seemed so pitiable an effort, like going backward instead of forward, and trying to keep millions labouring on petty hand processes merely in order to give them work to do by which they might exist.

In the evening Gandhi wrote on his slate that next morning I could join him in his walk. This was his regular exercise, occupying about an hour. He took quite good care of himself physically, observing rules of health and diet rigidly and strictly. He had to in order to perform the tremendous quantity of labor always facing him.

After we had ascended to the roof for evening prayers, our cots were moved out on the terrace under the moon and stars and the glorious, limitless sky overhead. Lights shimmered along the path to the main house but, for the rest, all was darkness. I never was more conscious of nature's stillness or of more constant stirrings from human beings – the echoing chant from the village near by, singing, calling, laughing, dogs barking, the sounds wafted clearly through the cool and crisp air while not a leaf on the trees trembled. At four the bells rang out for morning prayers and at six [Sanger's Indian assistant] Joseph came to tell me the hour and I arose and dressed.

Gandhi and I walked with his other two women guests; they deemed sacred every moment they spent with him. Men, women, and children waited for him as he passed, several prostrating themselves as to a holy person. Stepping over the debris we traversed narrow byways through the open fields where families huddled in their tiny huts together with dogs and goats. People were bathing and washing and cleaning their teeth. Little spirals of smoke were drifting from the fires for the morning meal.

At eleven we all went to our breakfast across the court, leaving our shoes outside. Everybody was ready, and great shining trays of silver-looking metal were placed before us on the floor. Gandhi was trying to persuade the Indians to utilize native-grown vegetables in different ways and thus increase their vitamin consumption. Mrs. Gandhi supervised the culinary department, and herself served the meal, of which there was a goodly and varied supply – no meat, but plenty of fruits and vegetables in curious combinations, such as tomatoes and oranges in a salad. All picked up their food with their fingers, mixing it and scooping it in very cleverly without dropping a morsel.

So numerous were Gandhi's adherents, so deep his influence that I was sure his endorsement of birth control would be of tremendous value if I could convince him how necessary it was for Indian women. After breakfast I set myself to the task.

He spoke fluent English in a low voice with accurate intonations, never lacking for a word, and could apparently discuss any subject near or far. Nevertheless, I felt his registering of impressions was blunted; while you were answering a question of his, he held to an idea or a train of thought of his own, and, as soon as you stopped, continued it as though he had not heard you. Time and again I believed he was going along with me, and then came the stone wall of religion or emotion or experience, and I could not dynamite him over this obstacle. In fact, despite his claim to open-mindedness, he was proud of not altering his opinions.

Gandhi maintained that he knew women and was in sympathetic accord with them. Personally, after listening to him for a while, I did not believe he had the faintest glimmering of the inner workings of a woman's heart or mind. He accused himself of being a brute by having desired his wife when he was younger, and classed all sex relations as debasing acts, although sometimes necessary for procreation. He agreed that no more than three or four children should be born to a family, but insisted that intercourse, therefore, should be restricted for the entire married life of the couple to three or four occasions.

I suggested that such a regimen was bound to cause psychological disturbance in both husband and wife. Furthermore, when respect and consideration and reverence were a part of the relationship I called it love, not lust, even if it found expression in sex union, with or without children.

Gandhi referred me to nature, the great director, who would solve our problems if we depended on her, but said what we were doing was to inject man's ideas into nature.

To this I replied, 'How can you differentiate? Here is cotton growing on your land and lemons also. That's nature. Would you object to dipping cotton into lemon juice and using that as a contraceptive?'

He said positively that he would. For every argument I presented he countered with 'I would devise other methods,' but proposed none that was not based on continence. He reiterated that women in order to control the size of their families must 'resist' their husbands, in extreme cases leave them.

Those who listened to the interview declared that the Mahatma made concessions he had never made before. He himself said to me, 'This has not been wasted effort. We have certainly come nearer together.' Nevertheless, I knew it was futile to count on Gandhi to help the movement in India; his state of mind would not change. After reading his autobiography, I thought I saw the cause of his inhibitions. He himself had had the feeling which he termed lust and he

> now hated it. It formed an emotional pivot in his brain around which centered everything having to do with sex. But there remained his kindness, his hospitality, his arrangements for your comfort, which he duplicated again and again for visitors who gave nothing, but instead received inspiration from him. And, furthermore, since humanity as a rule does little for itself and the inert mass has to be upheaved to a point where it can gain initiative, anyone who can arouse a nation of all classes and ages out of the incredible lethargy into which it has long been sunk and can stir up a people to hope is a great, even noble, person.

From: Margaret Sanger, *An Autobiography*, New York, Dover, 1971, pp.467-471.

POSTSCRIPT:

In the 22 February 1936 issue of Gandhi's weekly *Harijan*, in his "Weekly Letter" Gandhi's secretary Mahadev Desai wrote of the Gandhi/Sanger interview that 'as Mrs. Sanger was so dreadfully in earnest Gandhiji did mention a remedy which could conceivably appeal to him. That method was the avoidance of sexual union during unsafe periods confining it to the "safe" period of about ten days during the month. That had at least an element of self-control which had to exercised [sic] during the unsafe period. Whether this appealed to Mrs. Sanger or not I do not know. But therein spoke Gandhiji the truth-seeker.'

Although Sanger had no luck in convincing Gandhi of her position, her lecture tour of India led to the opening of several birth control clinics in the country. When, in 1959, Prime Minister Nehru declared that a large sum of money would go to family planning in India, Margaret Sanger was standing at his side.

FURTHER READING:

Chesler, Ellen, *Woman of Valor: Margaret Sanger and the Birth Control Movement in America*, New York: Simon and Schuster, 1992.

Douglas, Emily Taft, *Margaret Sanger: Pioneer of the Future*, New York: Holt, Rinehart and Winston, 1970.

Gray, Madeline, *Margaret Sanger: A Biography of the Champion of Birth Control*, New York: Richard Marek, 1979.

Lader, Lawrence, *The Margaret Sanger Story and the Fight for Birth Control*, Westport, Con.: Greenwood Press, 1955.

Sanger, Margaret, "A Summit Meeting on Birth Control", in Norman Cousins (ed.), *Profiles of Gandhi: America Remembers a World Leader*, Delhi: Indian Book Company, 1970, pp.35-41.

Weber, Thomas, *Going Native: Gandhi's Relationship with Western Women*, New Delhi: Roli Books, 2011.

1935 YONE NOGUCHI

Yonejiro Noguchi (1875-1947) left his studies at Keio University in Tokyo before graduation to travel from Japan to San Francisco in 1893 in order to take up work at a Japanese-American newspaper. He became part of the Bay Area literary scene and had published several books of poetry before the end of the century. He then moved to New York to engage in a career as a novelist. 1904 saw his return to Japan to teach English at his old university. In 1935, he went to India in order to gain support for Japanese activities in East Asia. In late December, against doctor's orders, an ailing Gandhi invited Noguchi to visit him at the Wardha ashram. Up to the height of the war, ten years after his visit to Gandhi, he was one of the few who wrote that it was incorrect to understand satyagraha as being a quietistic form of resistance, noting its assertive elements that could confront Britain. However, by 1942, Noguchi started re-evaluating Gandhi, calling his activities 'nonresistance' and 'gradualist', and stating that they would not be sufficient to achieve Indian independence. He supported the Japanese cause during the war. His home in Tokyo was destroyed by allied bombing in 1945. He died two years later.

Leaving Nagpur for Bombay towards the end of December 1935, I stopped at Wardha, an insignificant country town but the spiritual centre of the Gandhi movement. I was glad to see Gandhi with a fitting background in his Ashram, a monastery or refuge, where, unlike the ancient ascetic, this modern prophet responds to every pulsation of hope or pain in his nation's life. In view of his illness he was lying down in a tent pitched upon the flat room of a two-storeyed concrete house, square in form with a yard in the centre. I found him with a saintly little smile revealing his broken teeth, stretching out his bare legs, as lean as a cricket's and as stiff as steel wire, which one of his disciples was shampooing. I found difficulty in connecting this seemingly simple and unaffected man with the heroic fasts that had made the mammoth soul of England once tremble in fear. Noticing that he put on his head something wrapped in cotton cloth, I asked him what it was. He said it was wet earth which, according to his doctors' advice, was good for a man like him whose blood pressure was high. Then with a smile in which cynicism and philosophy commingled, he explained: 'I sprang from Indian earth. So it is Indian earth that crowns me.'

After a little talk, I bade him farewell and descended the stairs to meet three or four of his disciples, who were waiting to take me round the Ashram. Passing by a place containing beehives, I was taken into a shed to see a bull turning a stone mortar and making oil out of rapeseeds. Then I went to another place where paper-making experiments were in progress. One of the disciples said: 'How simple it is to make paper! If this paper-making becomes popular in our country as a subsidiary industry, we shall be able to keep a great deal of money at home.' It need hardly be said that the spinning-wheel, the Charkha holds an important position in the Ashram. A little flat wooden box was brought out, which revealed when uncovered a miniature wheel invented by Gandhi himself during his leisure moments in prison. The explainer said: 'You can put it even into a handbag and carry it in the train to fill the vacant hours by turning it.'

Then he said further: 'Gandhi is remarkably scientific. And his patience always brings his inventive mind to complete success. Had he been a watchmaker he would have the best watch in the world to his credit. As a surgeon or a lawyer he would also fill the highest place. But describing himself as a farmer and a weaver by profession at his trial in 1922 he pledged himself to the sacredness of manual labour. Among the various kinds of such work he regards weaving most highly because it gives on a habit of exactitude and a mental training in keeping strictly to the law of economy. Gandhi hates waste more than anything else. Believing that manual labour alone can give a new life to India, he makes the Charkha his own symbol and calls the people to the holy banner of an independent life.' It is only incidental that his movement appears to be a rebellion against the British yoke, because, while seeking to save India from corruption, it would also save the other countries of the world through its great lesson of creative energy, the propagation of life close to the soil. The importance of service within one's immediate surroundings as against a groping after distant ideals, is not limited to India only: the manliness of the 'self-supporting and self-sufficing' Swadeshi spirit must be recognized through all time and throughout the world.

Gandhi cannot find any higher way of worshipping God than by serving the poor and identifying himself with them. When he goes on a railway journey, for instance, he always takes a third-class ticket, reminding himself that he also belongs to the lower orders of mankind where humanity and love are found to be the richest. As one who has spent the best part of his life with working-class people and has shared joys and sorrows with them equally. Gandhi offers to his friends the spinning-wheel as an inspiration of the 'self-supporting and self-sufficing' life.

Lying alone in my compartment of the train for Bombay, I could not put away from my mind for some time the image of Mahatma Gandhi. Once I had the pleasure of reading his little essay entitled 'Voluntary Poverty,' in which he expressed his joy at discarding the things that belonged to him before. For anybody in a country like India to live with anything more than the bare necessities, he believes, means living like a robber. Unless you be like one who sleeps outside with nothing on his body, you have no right to declare that you can save India and the Indians. I am told that even the cloth with which Gandhi covers his loins is reduced to the very minimum. It was natural that Gandhi should advance from his eulogy of poverty into asceticism through which one's five senses are to be controlled as a method of self-purification.

From: Yone Noguchi, "A Visit from the Far East" in S. Radhakrishnan (ed.), *Mahatma Gandhi: Essays and Reflections on His Life and Work,* Bombay: Jaico, 1956, pp.159-162 at p.159-161.

POSTSCRIPT:

In their discussions, Gandhi admitted to Noguchi that he knew very little about Japan except what he had read forty-five years ago in Edwin Arnold's weekly letters in an English journal that had described Japanese life. Gandhi made a comment on the 'darker side' of Japan as seen through its 'traffic and trade rivalry' but then quickly added that he also knew Japan's brighter side through Joseph Kagawa, a Japanese Christian missionary who had stayed at the ashram the previous year. There had also been, and would continue to be, a steady stream of Japanese Nichiren Buddhist monks visiting Gandhi's ashrams (the prayers at Sevagram still start with the thrice repeated 'Nam Myoho Renge Kyo' ['I devote myself to the Supreme Law of the Lotus Sutra'], followed by two minutes of silence before the prayers proper start, as part of this legacy). When Noguchi asked for a message for Japan, Gandhi merely replied that his message was included in the message from India's poet Rabindranath Tagore. Probably Gandhi was referring to the criticisms Tagore had made of Japan when he first visited the country in 1916. Tagore had criticised the Japanese approach to modernisation as an imitation of Western nationalism. ("Interview to Yone Noguchi", *Harijan,* 11 January 1936)

FURTHER READING:

Ishida, Takeshi, *Japanese Political Culture: Change and Continuity,* New Brunswick: Transaction Books, 1983, especially the chapter "Japan's Changing Image of Gandhi", pp.137-146.

Noguchi, Yone, "Indian Impressions", *Contemporary Japan* (1936), vol.5, no.2, pp.225-235.

1936

SHRIMAN NARAYAN (AGARWAL)

Shriman Narayan Agarwal was born in 1912 and, after he had obtained an M.A. degree in English literature and economics, in 1935 he went to London to take the Indian Civil Service examination. Missing out by a few marks, he returned to India and became an active worker in Gandhi's educational and constructive programs at Wardha and Sevagram. In 1937 he married one of the daughters of Gandhi's 'fifth son' Jamnalal Bajaj. He was arrested and imprisoned for a year and a half during the 1942 Quit India movement. He was the founder and principal of Seksaria Commerce College in Wardha and then Dean of Commerce at Nagpur University near Wardha. He wrote on Gandhian plans for the economic development of India and on what a Gandhian constitution for a free India might look like. Following Gandhi's death, he toured the world to spread the message of Gandhi. He became a member of parliament and general secretary of the Indian National Congress in 1952, following which he served in various posts as a public servant, diplomat, and leading figure in many Gandhian institutions as well as being involved in Vinoba Bhave's land-gift Bhoodan movement. He dropped 'Agarwal' from his last name in the 1950s.

After my return from England towards the end of 1935, a friend of mine closely connected with Gandhiji and other leaders of the Indian National Congress suggested that I should visit the Congress Session at Lucknow early in 1936. A year's stay in England had made me deeply interested in the national movement for political freedom and I did go to Lucknow to have a glimpse of the leaders from a distance. I was, however, casually introduced to Seth Jamnalal Bajaj whom Gandhi had often called 'the fisher of men'. On meeting me, Jamnalalji expressed his joy that I had missed the I.C.S. by a few marks, and desired that I should join national service and work for Indian freedom.

Jamnalal Bajaj also invited me to visit Wardha and meet Gandhiji. Frankly, I had never heard of Wardha before, and on detecting my ignorance, Jamnalalji informed me that Wardha was only fifty miles away from Nagpur and located almost in the heart of India. I thanked him for the invitation, but quietly replied: 'I do not feel like wasting the time of a great leader like Gandhiji. He is too busy a person to find time for meeting an ordinary young man like me.' But Jamnalalji would not easily take 'no' from me. He enquired about my subjects of special interest. 'Literature and education,' I put in. He promptly added: 'The All-India Hindi Sahitya Sammelan is meeting at Nagpur in April this year. Why not attend it?'

This appeared to be a fairly attractive proposition, and so I reached Nagpur in the first week of April and was happy to meet a number of well-known Hindi poets and writers at the Sahitya Sammelan. I was also asked to recite one or two Hindi poems of mine at the open session and was glad to find that my poems, written mostly in London, received good appreciation from the audience. [...]

After the concluding session of the Sammelan I went to Jamnalalji to take my leave of him and return home. He was surprised at my reluctance to proceed to Wardha for meeting Gandhiji. He informed me that a special bus was going directly from Nagpur to Wardha and he would very much like me to spend a few days there as his guest. I could not decline the kind invitation and joined the bus party. [...]

We reached Wardha in the evening and I was accommodated in the guest house of Bajajwadi. At the community dinner in the back veranda, I was able to meet a number of constructive workers of different institutions in Wardha. The next morning, Jamnalalji took me to Maganwadi where Gandhiji was staying. [...]

I was experiencing great hesitation in meeting Mahatma Gandhi whom I had seen several times as a student from a distance, but never at close quarters. I had imagined that he would be a very serious and reserved type of a leader and would hardly care to meet an unknown young man like me. Jamnalalji, however, insisted that I should meet the Mahatma who was at that time preparing to have his bath after the daily massage. When I touched Gandhiji's feet with deep respect, he looked at me with great affection as though he had known me for years. I was deeply touched by this gentle treatment. The Mahatma looked so human and loving. After preliminary enquiries he asked me: 'Will you not like to work for me?'

'Bapuji, I will try my best,' I humbly replied.

From: Shriman Narayan, *Memoirs: Windows on Gandhi and Nehru*, Bombay: Popular Prakashan, 1971, pp.3-5.

POSTSCRIPT:

In another place, Shriman Narayan tells us a little more of what happened immediately after the initial meeting at Maganwadi:

I felt greatly disillusioned – disillusioned not because I was disappointed, but because I found Gandhiji very much different from what I had expected him to be. I, like so many others, was under the impression that the Mahatma must be full of reserve and unchanging seriousness. But to my great surprise, within a few minutes of my first personal acquaintance, I found him to be eminently human, with an ever-flowing fountain of sparkling wit and cheering humour.

'What work will you like to do for me here?' asked Gandhiji.

'I am at your service, Bapuji. Please give me orders!'

'I know that you have recently returned from England and can do good literary work; but I will not give you that work. Do you know the science of the charkha? Here is my charkha which is out of order. Can you set it right?'

'I am afraid I do not know anything about the charkha. I shall have to learn its technique first!'

'Has all your education not been to waste then? As the Hindustani idiom expresses it, your education has amounted to "sieving out sands" (*Khak Chhanana*),' remarked Gandhiji with a hearty laugh.

'I agree, Bapuji,' I smiled out.

'All right, then. I will give you the same work, in a very real sense. Good sand has to be sieved out for the trench latrines here. Why not assist Sjt. M.S. in that work?'

'I will do the job with pleasure,' was my prompt reply. 'I have done a lot of gardening, and the work will, therefore, not be new to me.'

'O.K.,' smiled Gandhiji. And I did do the job on each Sunday for some months. (Agarwal, 'Gandhi Anecdotes', p.1-2)

Further Reading:

Agarwal, Shriman Narayan, *Gandhian Constitution for Free India*, Allahabad: Kitabistan, 1946.

Agarwal, Shriman Narayan, "Gandhi Anecdotes", in Chandrashanker Shukla (ed.), *Incidents of Gandhiji's Life, by Fifty-Four Contributors*, Bombay: Vora, 1949, pp.1-3.

Narayan, Shriman, *India Needs Gandhi*, New Delhi: Chand, 1976.

Narayan, Shriman, *Mahatma Gandhi: The Atomic Man*, Bombay: Somaiya, 1971.

Narayan, Shriman, *Principles of Gandhian Planning*, Allahabad: Kitab Mahal, 1960.

Narayan, Shriman, *Relevance of Gandhian Economics*, Ahmedabad: Navajivan, 1970.

1936 HERBERT FISCHER

As a student, Herbert Fischer came into contact with peace activists and new age reformers. With the coming to power of Hitler, he left his native Germany for France and then Spain. Following the start of the Spanish Civil War he undertook an adventurous journey to India to meet Gandhi. He stayed on to take part in several of Gandhi's constructive programs. Following the outbreak of the Second World War, he was interned as an 'enemy alien'. After the war, with his family, he was deported to Germany. He wanted to take part in the rebuilding of his shattered country and worked as a teacher and educational institution director until, in 1953, he commenced working for the German Democratic Republic Foreign Ministry in India, eventually as ambassador. In all, Fischer spent over twenty years in India and wrote several books on Gandhi (in German). In 2003 he received the Padma Bhushan from Prime Minister Vajpayee during the latter's visit to Germany. He died in Berlin in 2006, aged ninety-one.

It was in 1936 that I first met Mahatma Gandhi. It was the time that war seemed imminent in Europe. In my own country – Germany – Hitler had not only come to power but was actively preparing for war. In such a situation, a man, like Mahatma Gandhi, working to bring independence to his country by new methods, attracted the attention of quite a few people in Germany and other European nations. The vast majority, however, influenced by the official Nazi ideology, had nothing but contempt for this strange little man. Those who saw the danger of a new world war, and all the misery it would bring to Germany and other countries, were in anguish. It was among those who took an active interest both in the political objectives of independence for India and Mahatma Gandhi's way of life and philosophy.

After some correspondence, I managed to come to India with high expectations. The first letter I wrote was addressed simply to 'Mahatma Gandhi, India'. The fact that it reached him was proof enough that he was unique and known to everyone in India. The reply came from Wardha, and that is where I went on a cool December morning. I found my way to Maganwadi (in Wardha) but was disappointed when I heard that Gandhi had left for the Congress session in Faizpur. Some people were leaving for this destination, so I gladly joined them.

It was in a bamboo hut in Faizpur that I met Gandhiji. I was so excited that I do not even remember exactly what his first words were. But I think that when I was introduced to him, he just said: 'So you have arrived.'

Naturally, during the Congress session, Gandhiji did not have much time to waste on a young man from Germany who had just come to India.

In the turmoil of the Congress session, I lost my coat with all my money. Gandhi, when informed about it, found time to enquire about what I needed. He ordered a khadi blanket to keep me warm during the cold nights. I foolishly told him that I did not worry much about the money. That provoked him. He explained that money was very important and that many people could be helped by using it in a proper way. I then realised that he was not a utopian or one who had renounced the world, but a man with a strong sense of reality wanting to do something for the world or, rather, for his fellow beings. His main concern was to help the poor and the handicapped and, most of all, to secure a full and dignified life for every individual.

Even in periods of great national importance, he found the time to look after a sick child or to settle a quarrel say, between two inmates of this Ashram. I slowly began to understand why he was called Bapu by those who knew him, and why he meant so much to so many.

There were important issues I wanted to discuss with Gandhiji after he returned to Wardha or, rather, to his hut in the village which was later to be called Sevagram.

We dealt with the possibility of combating militarism and Nazism. Of course, he was not familiar with the details of the situation in Nazi Germany. One thing however he was clear about – he abhorred the very idea of this worst and most aggressive form of imperialism based on racial arrogance, a desire to subjugate and exterminate other races. He realised that Nazism was not the madness of one or several individuals, but an imperialist tradition kindled by thoughts of economic and political domination. What impressed me most about Gandhiji was his respect for the other man's point of view.

While he discussed and tried to drive his point home, he never sought to impose his ideas on others. Often I got the impression that he preferred hearing many different viewpoints.

He did not like those who said 'yes' to all that he expressed, which is the reason why so many people, sometimes holding opposite views, enjoyed meeting Gandhiji.

Another facet of his charismatic personality was his insistence on fearlessness, or to put it in a positive way, of sticking to one's conviction without fear of consequences.

I have learned, on meeting this great personality, that peace is worth fighting for and that the best way of doing it is by eradicating the roots of strife and war. I was fortunate enough, after the Second World War, to be able to work for the achievement of a society in the German Democratic Republic; and, looking back, I think my first encounter with Gandhiji paved the way for this lofty ideal.

From: H. Fischer, "My First Meeting with Gandhiji", *The Illustrated Weekly of India* (1969), vol.90, no.18, p.21.

POSTSCRIPT:

In 1946, following his internment, Herbert Fischer was to be deported to Germany. He requested to see his friend Gandhi beforehand, so the Mahatma wrote to the Viceroy's private secretary for permission: 'Mr. Herbert Fischer, a German of Friends' Settlement, Itarsi, is known to me. He was for some time in the Village Industries Association in Wardha. His wife is a lady of Jamaica but in India, also of Friends' Settlement. I understand that Mr. Fischer and his wife are due to be sent to Germany in virtue of some plan. Mr. Fischer is now in a concentration camp in Satara. I wonder if it is possible for him to meet me before being sent to Germany. I wonder, too, if this matter falls within the Viceroy's department or whether I should write to some other.' The Fischers were allowed to meet Gandhi before leaving for Germany.

FURTHER READING:

Fischer, Herbert, "Living and Working with Gandhiji", in Manmohan Choudhuri and Ramjee Singh (eds.), *Mahatma Gandhi 125 Years,* Rajghat, Varanasi: Sarva Seva Sangh, 1995, pp.73-75.

Fischer, Herbert, *Mahatma Gandhi: Personality and Leader, of his Time,* Calcutta: K.P. Bagchi, 1983.

1937 JOSEPH JEAN LANZA DEL VASTO (SHANTIDAS)

Lanza del Vasto was born to a French-speaking Italian noble family in 1901. He led a privileged early life, studying in Paris, Florence and Pisa. He obtained a Ph.D. for a dissertation on the question of the Christian Trinity. However, academic life did not suit him and his scholarly reading led him to become a dedicated Catholic. He turned his back on high society and embraced voluntary poverty and the life of a vagabond. In 1936 he travelled to Asia. The trip is detailed in his classical work *Return to the Source*. In 1937 he met Gandhi at Sevagram Ashram. The Mahatma gave him the name Shantidas, and his life was changed yet again. In 1939 he returned to France and set up a rural Christian/Gandhian community that became known as the 'Community of the Ark'. He and other members of the Community campaigned against the French use of torture during the Algerian war of independence, for peasant land rights, and against French nuclear weapons. He fasted for his causes, and, until his death in 1981, became known as the person who 'keeps Gandhi alive in the West'.

Dawn already streaks the sky, but our path still twists and turns in the dark countryside. We meet a group of disciples returning from the ashram and greet them by joining our hands against our closed lips. The Mahatma has already spoken to them. We are among the last to arrive.

Daylight has come by the time we reach the little close. In the middle of the parched field is a small clay hut, open and so low that it makes no break in the countryside.

In the doorway under the slope of the thatched roof, a little, half-naked old man is seated on the ground. It is he!

He waves to me – yes, to me! – makes me sit down beside him and smiles to me. He speaks – and speaks of nothing else but me – asking me who I am, what I do and what I want.

And no sooner has he asked than I discover that I am nothing, have never done anything and want nothing except to stay like this in his shadow.

Here he is before my eyes, the only man who has shown us a green shoot in the desert of this century.

A man who knows the hard law of love, hard and clear like a diamond.

The captain of the unarmed, the father of the pariahs, the king who reigns by the divine right of sainthood.

He has come to show us the power over this earth of absolute innocence. He has come to prove that it can stop machines, hold its own against guns and defy an empire.

He has come into the world to bring us this news from beyond, where nothing changes, to teach us the truth that we have always known, being Christians. Truth so ill-assorted with us, so strangely contradictory to everything that the world and men had taught us, that we did not know what to do with it. We kept it between the four walls of the church and in the dark of our hearts. He, the Hindu, had to come for us to learn what we had always known.

While the old man questions me and smiles, I am silent, trying not to weep.

From: *Return to the Source* by Lanza del Vasto, published by Random House Children's Publishing, reprinted by permission of The Random House Group Limited, 1971, pp.100-101.

POSTSCRIPT:

A little further on in *Return to the Source,* Shantidas offers a description of the Gandhi he has just met. The Mahatma 'walks with a very lively step [...] carrying a long bamboo stick. His bare head is shaven, he is naked to the waist and wears no holy cordon, his legs are bare and his loin-cloth is tucked up between them. [...] His thinness is not dry and bony but resembles youthful slenderness, being slight and supple.' And further:

> His skin is the colour of old ivory. To tell the truth, he is far from handsome. His shaven skull has great wings of ears, his nose dips over his toothless mouth and sometimes, when he ponders, his lower lip hangs down over his short chin; but there is something touching in his ugliness, rather like that of the newly-born child when it opens its mouth wider than its whole face.
>
> His black, almond-shaped eyes hide behind small metal-framed spectacles; faint, mischievous lines prolong their upward slant.
>
> He is at all times friendly and cheerful. But there is no beating around the bush when he gives an order (or advice, which is the same thing) or makes a rebuke. (God keep us from ever deserving one.) (del Vasto, *Return to the Source,* p.101)

Further Reading:

del Vasto, Lanza, *Gandhi to Vinoba: The New Pilgrimage,* London: Rider, 1956

del Vasto, Lanza, *Principles and Precepts of the Return to the Obvious,* New York: Schocken, 1974.

del Vasto, Lanza, *Warriors of Peace: Writings on the Technique of Nonviolence,* New York: Knopf, 1974.

Hope, Marjorie and James Young, *The Struggle for Humanity: Agents of Nonviolent Change in a Violent World,* Maryknoll, NY: Orbis, 1977.

Shepard, Mark, *The Community of the Ark,* Arcata, CA: Simple Productions, 1990

Weber, Thomas, *Gandhi as Disciple and Mentor,* New Delhi: Cambridge University Press, 2004.

1942

LOUIS FISCHER

Born in the Philadelphia slums in 1896, after a stint as a school teacher and a member of the Jewish Legion in Palestine, Louis Fischer became a journalist covering Europe from Germany and then, in 1922, became a correspondent based in Moscow. His disillusionment with the West and longing for an alternative to capitalism that put people before profits meant that he had sympathetic feelings for the communist experiment and hoped for its eventual success. He lived for a lengthy period in the Soviet Union and wrote several books about the country and its leaders. Following the mass trials and executions of the late 1930s and the cynical Soviet-Nazi Pact of 1939, disenchantment set in. Realising that the 'system' was more concerned with self-preservation rather than caring for its citizens, he broke with his past and turned from Stalin to Gandhi. He first came to India in 1942 and in June he spent a week at Sevagram Ashram with the Mahatma. Later he wrote a book comparing Gandhi and Stalin and in 1950 he published the first complete, and probably still the most popular, biography of Gandhi's life. During the 1960s he lectured at Princeton University. He died in 1970.

I was up early and took a tonga with Gandhi's dentist for Sevagram, the village which is Gandhi's home when he is not in jail. The dentist said that England had been 'an understanding master.' I tried to make him talk about Gandhi. He insisted on talking politics.

The tonga stopped. I jumped out and there stood a tall, brown-and-white figure – Gandhi. I walked towards him with long, quick steps. He held his hand on the shoulders of two women who walked on either side of him. His thin brown legs were bare up to his loincloth. Leather sandals on his feet; a cape of cheesecloth around his shoulders; a folded white kerchief on his head. He said, 'Mr. Fischer,' with an English accent, and we shook hands. He greeted the dentist, turned about, and I followed him to a flat, thick board resting on two metal trestles. He sat down, put his hand on the board, and said, 'Sit down.' He said, 'Jawaharlal has told me about your book and the type of person you are, and we are glad to have you here. How long will you stay?' I told him I could stay a few days.

'Oh,' he exclaimed, 'then we will be able to talk much.'

A young man walked over to him, bowed low to his feet, and swayed up and down. 'Bas, bas,' Gandhi muttered. I imagined it meant 'Enough,' and later found that my guess was right. Soon two other young men did the same thing, and again Gandhi shooed them off.

I asked him why he had chosen this village to live in. He said so-and-so, and he mentioned a name which I didn't get, had chosen it for him. I made no comment, but he noticed that I didn't catch the Indian name, and so he said Mira Ben was Miss Slade, an Englishwoman who had long been associated with him. He explained that it was her idea that he should live in a village in the centre of India, and he had asked her to find the place. He did not wish to live inside the village because it was too unhygienic and noisy. 'It is better here, on the outskirts.' The dentist started talking about false teeth, and Gandhi explained to him that the bite in the sets he wore was imperfect. A woman brought out a brass bowl filled with water and three sets of artificial teeth, and I decided to go. Gandhi said, 'You will walk with me in the evening and morning, and we will have other opportunities to talk.' I bowed and went away. [...]

At eleven A.M., when I was starved, [ashram member] Kurshed [Naoroji] took me over to Gandhi's house, which is about a hundred yards from the guest house. It is a one-story affair with walls of matting and a roof of poor red tiles. I left my bedroom slippers on the outside cement step and walked in and remained in the tiny anteroom from which I could see the one chief room of the house. Gandhi was lying on a white pallet on the earthen floor, and one of his disciples sat on the ground near this bed and pulled a rope which moved a board, with a black cloth hanging from it, suspended from the ceiling. This is supposed to take the place of an electric fan. There is no electricity in the village. Gandhi got up and said to me, 'Now put on your shoes and hat. Those are the two indispensable things here. Don't get sunstroke.' A woman brought him a folded, moistened cheesecloth for his head. Then, putting one hand on Kurshed, who walked one step in front of him, he said to me in friendly fashion, 'Come along.' We passed two houses and came to a common dining hall built of matting. I left my shoes outside, as Gandhi did, gave my sun helmet to Kurshed, who found a place for it on a peg in the wall, and took a seat on the ground which Gandhi indicated, two removed from him. [...]

The dining hall has two long walls connected by a third back wall. Where one enters, it is open to the elements. Near the entrance is a table covered with jars and trays of food. The women sit apart. I watched some bright-eyed, brown-faced children, some of them three, five or eight years old, the children of the members of the ashram. Soon every person had a brass tray in front of him, and several waiters were moving noiselessly on bare feet, depositing food on the trays. Several pots and pans were placed before Gandhi. He opened them and started dishing out food to his neighbours. I had been given a metal tumbler full of water. Gandhi handed me a bronze bowl filled with a vegetable mush in which I thought I discerned chopped spinach leaves and pieces of squash. Then he uncovered a metal container and gave me one hard, paper-thin wheatcake. A woman poured some salt into my tray and handed me a bowl of hot milk. Soon she came back with two boiled potatoes in their jackets and some soft, flat wheatcakes baked brown. Gandhi turned to me and said, with a smile, 'I am serving you, but you must not eat until the prayer.' I told him I had noticed that the children were not touching their food and so I knew I mustn't. [...]

Gandhi ate continuously, only stopping to serve food to his wife, Kurshed, Dev, and me. His hands are big and his fingers are big and well-formed. His knees are pronounced bulges and his bones are wide and strong. His skin is smooth and clean. His hands do not shake as he digs into the pots. His wife fanned him frequently with a straw fan. She looks the symbol of silent self-effacement.

Once Gandhiji interrupted to say, 'You have lived in Russia for fourteen years. What is your opinion of Stalin?'

I felt very hot, and my hands were sticky, and so I replied briefly, 'Very able and very ruthless.'

'As ruthless as Hitler?' Gandhi asked.

'At least,' I replied. [...]

I was discovering my ankles. Too much of my weight was resting on them. The Indians know how to distribute their bodily weight, but I hadn't learned. I stood one leg on its foot, and felt a bit more comfortable. Gandhi said to me, 'I see you have come to a standstill.'

'No,' I replied, 'I find the food surprisingly good.'

'You can have all the water you want,' he said. 'We take good care that it is boiled. And now you must eat your mango.'

I said I had been observing others eat it, and would now, for the first time in my life, try one. Kurshed suggested that I would need a bath when I was through. I started peeling the mango. Gandhi and the others laughed. Gandhi explained that they usually turned it in their hands and squeezed it to make it soft, and then sucked out the contents, but I was right to peel it to see whether it was good. He said, 'You will earn a medal of courage for being ready to eat as we do.' I had finished the meal and Kurshed indicated with her head that I could go before Gandhi got up. I bowed to him, and got my hat and shoes, and left. Kurshed said Gandhi would see me at three. [...]

At a few minutes to three, I walked across the hundred yards of hot gravel and sand which separated my house from Gandhi's. The heat made the whole inside of my head feel dry. The temperature was a hundred and ten. When I entered Gandhi's room, six men in white were sitting on the floor in his room. A woman in a black sari was pulling the rope of a fan. There was only one decoration in the room, a glass-covered, black-and-white print of Jesus Christ, on which were printed the words, 'He is our peace.' Gandhi sat on the pallet which is his bed. There was a board behind his back and a pillow between the board and his back. He was wearing gold-rimmed glasses, and writing a letter with a fountain pen. His legs were crossed scissors-fashion. He held a small board on one knee and on the board was the pad on which he wrote. Three other fountain pens stood in holes in a hand-made wooden stand. Left of his bed were some books piled neatly on the floor. He said to me, 'Come sit down in the coolest place here beside the woman working the fan.' I sat down in a corner and leaned my back against the matting. Gandhi said, 'If you do not mind, these people will remain here. They will not speak. If you object, they can go.' Dev was there and Desai, and several other members of the ashram, including Kurshed. I did not very much like the idea of an interview in company, but I said, 'No,' and got settled.

'Now I am fully at your disposal,' Gandhi announced.

From: Louis Fischer, *A Week with Gandhi,* London: HarperCollins, 1943, pp.5-14. Reprinted with permission of HarperCollins Publishers Ltd.

POSTSCRIPT:

In 1946 Fischer returned to India and spent another six days with the Mahatma at the hill station of Panchgani near Poona. Every morning at 5.30 he took a walk with Gandhi, noting that his host was not walking quite as fast as he had been four years before, during their previous meeting. However, it seems that Gandhi's mind was as sharp as ever and his sense of humour had not diminished:

> The first morning he asked me how I slept. I said I had slept badly; a mosquito had stung me. 'How did *you* sleep?' I inquired.
>
> 'I always sleep well,' he replied.
>
> The next morning he again inquired how I had slept. I said, 'Fine and you?'
>
> 'Don't ask,' he answered. 'I always sleep well.'
>
> The third morning I asked him how he had slept. 'I told you not to ask,' he declared.
>
> 'I thought you had forgotten,' I teased.
>
> 'Ah,' he commented, 'you think I am deteriorating. How did *you* sleep?'
>
> 'Don't ask,' I said.
>
> 'One or two swallows don't make a summer,' Gandhi laughed.

Several mornings it drizzled. 'Surely, you are not going to walk in the rain,' I protested.

'Oh, yes,' he replied. 'Come along. Don't be an old man.' (Fischer, *Gandhi and Stalin*, p.15.)

FURTHER READING:

Fischer, Louis, *The Essential Gandhi: His Life, Work and Ideas: An Anthology*, New York: Random House, 1962.

Fischer, Louis, *Gandhi and Stalin: Two Signs at the World's Crossroads*, London: Victor Gollancz, 1948.

Fischer, Louis, *Gandhi: His Life and Message for the World*, New York: New American Library, 1954.

Fischer, Louis, *The Life of Mahatma Gandhi*, New York: Harper, 1950.

Seshachari, C., *Gandhi and the American Scene, An Intellectual History and Inquiry*, Bombay: Nachiketa, 1969.

1942

EDGAR SNOW

The American journalist Edgar Snow is best known for his reporting on the rise of communism in China. He was born in Kansas City in 1905 and attended the University of Missouri and the Columbia School of Journalism before starting his professional life at the *Kansas City Star* in 1927. The following year he visited China, which was to become his base for the next dozen years while he reported on East Asia for American papers and magazines. In 1931 he had a brief meeting with Gandhi in a group of several others. In 1936 he was invited to the headquarters of the Chinese communists in Yen-an, where he spent several months with Mao Zedong and the rest of the Party's leadership. Following this, he gave the outside world the first realistic reports of what was happening with the revolution and the resistance to the Japanese invasion. His book *Red Star over China* is the best first-hand account of the early history of the communist movement. He returned to America in 1941. Soon after he ventured on a world assignment during which he spent seven months in Russia and six months in China and India, where he had his first full interview with the Mahatma, reporting the Second World War from their perspectives. Following accusations of being a communist, he migrated to Switzerland where he died in 1972. Half of his ashes are interred at Peking University where he taught in the early 1930s.

That day I went to Sevagram to visit the little generalissimo himself. Arch Steele (the *Chicago Daily News*) and I bumped out on the back of that instrument of primitive torture, the Indian *tonga*, or two-wheeled cart. Gandhi had a very special one, I noticed, pulled by a fine beast which stamped and noisily stirred the bells round its neck. On its sides were painted portraits of the Congress leaders. Gandhi's own face was on the front, right behind the horse's tail.

Sevagram was a cross between a third-rate dude ranch and a refugee camp, a colony of mud huts with thatched roofs set in a cactus-sprinkled countryside. A dirt path led through the cluster to a hut that looked like the rest, except that it was surrounded with a fence of sticks and there was a *charka*, or spinning-wheel, adorning the wall in crude bas-relief. A cow wandered by morosely (cows in India are as rude and insolent as camels) and scrawny chickens strutted about the yard. Inside, squatting barefoot on the matted floor, sat the toothless seventy-four-year-old Messiah whom all India was waiting to hear speak the word of command.

Amidst this collection of simple buildings, chickens and cows, in a place infested by scorpions and poisonous snakes, and kindly spinners and toilers carrying out his creed, the Mahatma had, between sessions at prayers, spinning, administering purgatives to relieve the aches and pains of patients in his own hospital, thought up his last headache for Churchill. Gandhi hated science almost as much as he hated machines, and he specially welcomed anyone who came to get his own personal mud-pack cure for high blood pressure. Here, also, he edited *Harijan*. A combined Dorothy Dix and Dorothy Thompson, he offered everything from advice to young maidens on how to avoid being raped to recommendations to Churchill, Stalin and Tojo on how to win the war.

And now, as he spoke to us out of this background, his words were so incongruous you could hardly take in their meaning. He sat there leaning against a big white pillow, his brown body naked except for a few yards of cheesecloth round his middle (and how we envied him in that withering heat) and over his big, gold-rimmed glasses he peered down at us now kindly, now a bit petulant. He was going to lead a mass movement, he explained, on the broadest scale. It would be the biggest of his life, his 'last struggle'. But it would be non-violent, in so far as he could make it so.

'And do you really expect the British to withdraw in answer to your threat?' I asked.

'Of course,' he said, 'if the British wish to withdraw that would be a feather in their caps. But I want to stress this point. There is no room left in the proposal for negotiations.' He wagged his bald pate determinedly. 'Either they recognize the independence of India or they do not. After that many things could happen. Once independence is recognized the British would have altered the face of the whole landscape.'

But he did not, he emphasized, mean any statement on paper; he wanted a physical withdrawal now. 'Next it would be a question of who would take over India, God or anarchy.' In one breath he said that Free India would make common cause with the Allies. In the next he said, 'If I can possibly turn India towards non-violence then I would do so. If I could succeed in making 400,000,000 people fight with non-violence it would be a great gain.'

What a stubborn and honourable old saint he was! Not even now would he personally endorse that part of the resolution promising to fight Japan. Yet if he had influence enough to bring Congress into line behind him there, was there not every possibility that he would later be able to bring a Free Indian government round to withdrawal from the war? But he denied to me that he would ever use soul-force against his 'own' government to get it to obey his will. Absently pulling on his big toe and looking down at us, in his child-like, innocent way, the old man touched off his heavy artillery.

'This time it isn't a question of (giving the British) one more chance,' he said. '*It is open rebellion!*'

And that was that. Gandhi certainly intended his remark to be taken literally, as he later repeated it several times. With the rope the British had given to him he now surely hung Congress for the rest of the war. He played the game of the men 'on the hill' just as they had foreseen he would.

As I left I had a feeling that he was right about one thing, anyway. Whatever happened, it would probably indeed be the 'last struggle' in which Gandhi would lead a great nationalist struggle. It was the biggest gamble of his life and the old man knew it. You may not agree with a lot of things about Gandhi, but no one could deny the honesty of his convictions, nor his fighting courage in defence of them. And these, too, are qualities of his greatness.

As Gandhi said elsewhere, he had not much time left and he wanted to see India free before he died.

From: Edgar Snow, *Glory and Bondage* [US title: *People on Our Side*], Sydney: Angus and Robertson, 1946, pp.38-39. For a slightly different recounting of this story, see Snow, *Journey to the Beginning*, pp.273-275.

POSTSCRIPT:

This was not strictly Edgar Snow's first meeting with Gandhi. In May 1931 he had accompanied Congress Party stalwart Pandit Madan Mohan Malaviya to Simla where Gandhi was in discussions with the Viceroy, Lord Irwin. As Snow explains, 'Gandhi was much too busy to suffer the presence of young greenhorns. I had no formal interviews with him at that time. Instead, I had to be content to trot along on his visits to his associates or to the Viceregal Lodge.' He did not 'get much out of [their] fragmentary talks, held on the fly, to enable [him] to grasp the essence of Gandhi's method, his "strange mixture" of religion and politics. That was to come much later.' He had a great deal of trouble understanding how Gandhi's political power related to love and nonviolence and the quest for the ultimate truth. After all, 'politics was the art of the possible' while religion was the 'art of the impossible.' During that first meeting, he had the opportunity to ask Gandhi a question 'which revealed my doubts along these lines'. In response Gandhi gently advised him to 'study some more'. He concluded that 'Gandhi's attempt to combine the two, in his honest search for truth, was the nexus of his genius.' (Snow, *Journey to the Beginning*, pp.75-76)

FURTHER READING:

Hamilton, John Maxwell, *Edgar Snow: A Biography*, Bloomington: Indian University Press, 1988.

Snow, Edgar, *Journey to the Beginning*, London: Victor Gollancz, 1960.

Snow, Edgar, *Red Star over China*, New York: Modern Library, 1944.

1945

HERMON OULD

Hermon Ould was a British playwright and short story writer. Born in 1886, he became a professional singer at ten, and at fourteen he became an office boy in the City of London and had his first play produced in 1913. He was a pacifist and imprisoned as a conscientious objector during the First World War. He became Secretary of the International P.E.N. (the association of poets, playwrights, editors, essayists and novelists) Club between 1926 and his death in 1951. Along with British writer Margaret Storm Jameson, he was concerned with the plight of writers under Nazi and Fascist dictatorships and started writing letters, organising visas, and raising money to help them escape and then provide funds so that they could continue their work in England. His pacifism was shaken during the Second World War because of the evils of Nazism which he believed had to be stopped. He put his duties to P.E.N. ahead of his own work and displayed great diplomatic skills in keeping various centres around the world from being drowned in internecine squabbling and kept up a vast correspondence with writers from around the globe.

When I was in Bombay I had an opportunity of experiencing this upsurge of mass emotion. An Indian friend of mine, frankly calling himself a follower of the Mahatma, came to me one day with the exciting news that Gandhi would shortly be spending a day in Bombay. He was very anxious that I should come face to face with one whom he regarded with such reverence and promised to do his best to arrange an interview. My friend was a truly saintly person to whom I was sincerely attached, and I was loath to upset him by displaying less enthusiasm than the occasion seemed to call for, but I felt compelled to say that the last thing I wished was to inflict my presence on a man who was always besieged by people of all kinds, many of whom no doubt had greater claims to his attention than I. I was quite content to admire at a distance. But my friend had made up his mind, and a few days later I heard that the Mahatma would see me if I could come to Petit Hall where he was staying and accompany him to his usual prayer meeting. [...]

As we entered the ante-room I received my first shock, for my friend murmured something about taking off one's shoes. Now I had often enough taken off my shoes on entering a mosque, and this had not come amiss to me, for a mosque is the house of God, but something in me revolted against removing my shoes in the presence of another human being, however worthy of respect. I was spared a decision, luckily, by the appearance of the Mahatma himself, accompanied by a number of men and women. The atmosphere of awe was almost tangible. Voices were hushed; all eyes were turned on Gandhi, who was accompanied by his wife [Kasturba in fact had died in 1944] and a young girl, on both of whom he lent. Before introducing me to him, my friend had prostrated himself before the Mahatma and kissed his feet – an action which I found distasteful. When Gandhi heard my name he returned my clasped-hand salute – which had become second nature to me – and then with a smile he shook hands with me, European fashion, but said nothing. By this time we were moving in a kind of procession to the door, Gandhi still leaning on the young girl and followed by a row of women in white saris and the men who had been awaiting him.

As we proceeded down the path lined by boy scouts, who saluted us, our numbers swelled and I found myself at the head of a procession some fifty or sixty strong. The Mahatma indicated to me that I should stay by his side, and turning to me he pursed his lips and tapped them with his index finger. 'He means it is his silence day,' explained Mrs. Gandhi, and my friend walking behind me murmured reverently that although Gandhi could not speak to me I might speak to him. I confess the situation embarrassed me. If I had been alone with Gandhi, or anybody else, I might have been induced to speak in the hope of interpreting his reactions by the look in his eyes; but walking down a public thoroughfare, with policemen keeping the crowd at a distance, and boy scouts extending their staves in salute, I felt quite incapable of uttering a monologue for which I was unprepared. I decided that my time would be more profitably spent in observing the Mahatma, who seemed to be in excellent health. Supported by the two women, he held himself very erect; his body was taut and wiry, and his rather spindly legs were quite equal to carrying him along at a good pace. He wore a *dhoti* and a shawl and no shoes. His spare body was glowing like polished copper and his shiny head was shaven. Although he did not speak, his rather small shrewd eyes were active, to charm, to please, to impose silence, to admonish, but chiefly, or so it seemed to me, to charm.

As we drew near the grounds of the mansion where the prayer meeting was to be held, the crowd grew considerably, and the guard of scouts and policemen was in closer formation: A platform had been erected behind the house, facing the green sward going down to the sea. On the platform were a couple of couches covered with white material and a large square cushion on which Gandhi sat cross-legged; behind him, an erection of pillows, against which, however, he did not lean. He sat there, like an ancient sculpture, his eyes closed, motionless, and raying out from the dais some hundreds of people, men, women and children, were assembled, most of them sitting on the grass.

The service began by somebody intoning a hymn, in the somewhat whiney voice characteristic of Indian sacred singing, further songs were sung, and finally one in which a leader sang a phrase which was repeated by the congregation as they clapped their hands rhythmically. There were amplifiers, but I don't think they were in use. A carpet had been spread near the platform on which I was invited to squat, but I remained standing, looking at the immobile figure on the dais, impressed by the profile with its thrusting lower lip, the very symbol of determination. All around me was a lively excited crowd; reporters and photographers were everywhere, as well as men with movie-cameras; there were hawkers with sweetmeats and flowers; one wild-eyed woman carried a vessel containing a mixed assortment of foods, a handful of which she offered to me; but a journalist at my elbow told me not to eat it, so with tact I allowed the wet and sticky mess to trickle through my fingers. The service over, the autograph-hunters crowded around the Mahatma and those who were lucky enough to get his signature paid five rupees to the *Harijan* fund. Reporters besieged me too, begging for interviews: What was my opinion of the Mahatma? They drew a blank, but I heard from them and from others a series of little stories of Gandhi which revealed the attitude of awe which they shared with my saintly friend and the masses surrounding us.

From: Herman [sic] Ould, "Gandhi", in S. Radhakrishnan (ed.), *Mahatma Gandhi: Essays and Reflections on His Life and Work,* Bombay: Jaico, 1956, pp.357-363, at pp.359-362.

POSTSCRIPT:

After the War had ended, in October of 1945 Ould went to India to attend the first post-war International P.E.N. Congress, held in Jaipur. He was accompanied by E.M. Forster, the renowned author of *A Passage to India.* The Jaipur meeting included the first All-India Writers' Conference where Jawaharlal Nehru and Sarojini Naidu spoke. It would appear that Ould managed to catch up with Gandhi on the evening of 19 November, three weeks after the closing of the conference.

FURTHER READING:

Birkett, Jennifer, *Margaret Storm Jameson: A Life,* Oxford: Oxford University Press, 2009.

Iyengar, K.R. Srinivasa, *Jaipur, '45: A Milestone for Indian Letters,* Bombay: The International Book House, 1947.

Storm Jameson, Margaret, "In Memory of Hermon Ould", in *Hermon Ould: A Tribute,* Slough: Kenion Press, n.d., pp.8-13.

Ould, Hermon, *Shuttle: An Autobiographical Sequence,* London: Andrew Dakers, 1947.

Ould, Hermon (ed.), *The Book of the P.E.N.,* London: Arthur Barker, 1950.

1945

R.G. CASEY

Born in Brisbane in 1890 and educated in Melbourne and Cambridge, Richard Gardiner Casey became an engineer before being appointed Australian Liaison Officer in London in 1924. He was elected to the Australian House of Representatives in 1931 and served in various conservative governments. The Right Honourable R.G. Casey was appointed the Australian Minister in Washington (1940-1942), the Minister of State Resident in the Middle East, and served as a member of the British War Cabinet (1942-1943) before becoming the Governor of Bengal (1944-1946), during which time he had several meetings with Gandhi. In 1949, he re-entered the Australian House of Representatives and five years later, he became Australian Minister for External Affairs. Following his retirement from politics in 1960, a life peerage was conferred on him, giving him the title of Baron Casey. He was Governor General of Australia between 1965 and 1969. He died in 1976.

By far the most outstanding and interesting individual that I met in India was Mr. Gandhi. Although I believe he is 76 years old, he shows no outward sign of the weight of years.

His personality is real and lively and he has great charm. He is not, on ordinary standards, a good-looking man; yet his bearing and his appearance warm one to him. You feel that here is a human being of consequence, and likeable as well.

Mr. Gandhi gave me the unusual feeling, the first time I met him, that he was a man with whom one could discuss one's most intimate personal problem, and get wise and understanding advice.

He is innately courteous, tactful and a good listener. He has a good sense of fun and I think, probably, also a good sense of humour. His physical gestures are simple and dramatic. A discussion with him is enlivened by a good deal of relevant and entertaining reminiscences. [...]

Mr. Gandhi is a lawyer by profession, but not, as he takes pains to point out, a man of great learning. His command of English is very good, almost perfect, but slightly coloured by the almost universal Indian habit of pronouncing certain words differently from the way we pronounce them.

Mr. Gandhi is credited by many of his followers with being a Saint and a Statesman. Whilst I have a considerable regard for him, I do not believe he is either. He has protested for many years against being called 'Mahatma' (holy man), but in vain. He is almost universally referred to in the Congress Press as Mahatma or Mahatmaji, the respectful and affectionate diminutive.

Mr. Gandhi is an intensively religious man. Apart from his spiritual convictions he has made more than a passing study of all religions. His daily evening prayers are attended by thousands of people, and have something of the flavour of open-air revivalist meetings. To emphasise his universal approach to religion, he introduces Muslim prayers in Arabic, hymns in English, and selections from other religions.

What claims has Mr. Gandhi to statesmanship? There is a simple criterion for determining whether a man is a statesman; the passage of time should show that he was right in his major political decisions three times out of four. I do not think Mr. Gandhi can claim this record.

Perhaps one might say that amongst saints he is a statesman, and amongst statesmen a saint.

From: R.G. Casey, *An Australian in India,* London: Hollis & Carter, 1947, pp.58-60.

POSTSCRIPT:

On the first day of December 1945, Bengal's Governor R.G. Casey sent a note via Gandhi's emissary Sudhir Ghosh to the Mahatma, explaining that he looked forward to meeting Gandhi when the latter had rested up from his long journey from Sevagram. Ghosh relays what happened after that:

> Gandhiji said he was not going to wait for a day or two; he was going to call on the Governor that very evening. So I rang up the Governor to say that Gandhiji was coming within an hour. Casey did not imagine that the number one enemy of British rule in India could be so deeply courteous to a representative of the British Raj. Gandhiji, too, was touched by the solicitude of a British ruler. They went on talking with each other from 7 to 9.30 about everything under the sun – about Gandhiji's South African days, the inmates of Tolstoy farm, his experiences with General Smuts – cabbages as well as kings. At 9.30 I intervened and said, 'Well, Bapu, I think that we had better go now. I am sure the Governor has had no dinner yet.' He was distressed to hear that he had kept the poor man

from his dinner; he had forgotten that British Governors did not have their dinners before sunset as he did.

The Governor's study, where he received Gandhiji, was on the first floor of the great mansion (it was the residence of British Viceroys before the capital moved from Calcutta to Delhi in 1911) and, as we got up to leave, Casey very politely came downstairs with us and escorted Gandhiji to his car in the porch. To reach the porch, he had to walk with Gandhiji from one end of the great hall on the ground floor to the other and to his great surprise the Governor found that the entire community of servants of Government House – gardeners, cooks, cleaners, messengers – about 200 in number, were silently standing in the hall in two long rows with their palms folded in reverence. Many of them were barebodied and such clothes as they had on them were not the clothes in which they were fit to be seen by the Governor. The news had gone around the servants' quarters of Government House that the Mahatma had come to see the 'Lord Sahib', and the servants thought it was their great chance to have a glimpse of the great father. But they had not counted on the 'Lord Sahib' himself coming downstairs to bid farewell to the visitor; it was not done. They looked rather sheepish when they saw the Governor. Casey was surprised. Flourishing his hand at the assembled congregation he said to Gandhiji 'Look at all this. I assure you I did not arrange this.' Next day when I met Casey he said, 'You know I had the shock of my life – because most of these Government House servants are Muslims! I never knew that Gandhi had that kind of a place in the hearts of Muslims in this country.' (Ghosh, *Gandhi's Emissary*, pp.58-59)

FURTHER READING:

Casey, R.G., *Personal Experience 1939-1946*, London: Constable, 1962.
Ghosh, Sudhir, *Gandhi's Emissary*, London: Cresset, 1967.

1946

MARGARET BOURKE-WHITE

Margaret Bourke-White was one of the world's most famous photographers. In 1929 she became the chief photographer for the newly created *Fortune* magazine and in 1936 she became one of the first staff photographers for *Life* magazine and one of her pictures was featured on the cover of its first issue. As a fearless photo-journalist, she pioneered the concept of the photo-essay and chalked up many other 'firsts': she was the first western photographer allowed into the Soviet Union, she was the first woman war correspondent covering the Second World War, she was the first woman photographer attached to the US armed forces, she was the only foreign photographer in Moscow when the Germans attacked the city, she crossed the Rhine with General Patton's First Army, she was the first woman to fly on a combat bombing mission, and was present with U.S. troops when they liberated Buchenwald concentration camp in 1945, becoming one of the first to document the Nazi death camps. After the war she went to India to photograph and write about the coming of independence. Many of her photographs have iconic status, and some of the best known portraits of the elderly Mahatma were taken by her.

Photography demands a high degree of participation, but never have I participated to such an extent as I did when photographing various episodes in the life of Gandhi.

I shall always remember the day we met. I went to see him at his camp, or ashram in Poona where he was living in the midst of a colony of untouchables. Having thought of Mahatma Gandhi as a symbol of simplicity, I was a bit surprised to find that I had to go through several secretaries to get permission to photograph him. When I reached the last and chief secretary, an earnest man in horn-rimmed spectacles, and dressed entirely in snow-white homespun, I explained my mission. I had come to take photographs of the Mahatma spinning.

'Do you know how to spin?' asked Gandhi's Secretary.

'Oh I didn't come to spin with the Mahatma. I came to photograph the Mahatma spinning.'

'How can you possibly understand the symbolism of Gandhi at his spinning wheel? How can you comprehend the inner meaning of the wheel, the charka, unless you first master the principles of spinning?' He inquired sharply. 'Then you are not at all familiar with the workings of the spinning wheel?'

'No. Only with the workings of a camera.'

The secretary fell into rhapsody. 'The spinning wheel is a marvel of human ingenuity. The charka is machinery reduced to the level of the toiling masses. Consider the great machines of the factories, with all their complex mechanisms, and consider the charka. There are no ball bearings; there is not even a nail. The spinning wheel symbolizes what Gandhi calls "the proletarianism of science".'

It was useless for me to protest that I had a deadline to meet, that this very evening a package of film must be at the airport to be placed on a certain transoceanic plane that would be met at the airfield in New York, rushed to the *Life* photo lab, processed through the night, and in the morning, a scant forty-eight hours after the taking of the photograph, finished prints of the Mahatma at his spinning wheel would be lying on the *Life* editor's desk.

As the secretary became more involved in his oratory, I grew desperate. 'The charka illustrates a major tenet of Gandhi's. When individually considered, man is insignificant, even like a drop of water; but in the mass, he becomes mighty and powerful, like the ocean.'

'You will make me drop photography and take up spinning,' I said politely, wondering when we could get back to the appointment.

'That is just what I wish to do,' said Gandhi's secretary.

I know when I'm licked. 'How long does it take to learn to spin?' I asked wearily.

'Ah,' said the secretary, 'that depends upon one's quotient of intelligence.'

I found myself begging for a spinning lesson.

'I must compose editorials for Gandhiji's weekly magazine, *Harijan*,' said the secretary. 'I have a deadline to meet. Come back again next Tuesday.'

Somehow I persuaded Gandhi's secretary that my spinning lesson must start this very afternoon. It embarrassed me to see how clumsy I was at the spinning wheel, constantly entangling myself. It did not help my opinion of my own I.Q. to see how often and how awkwardly I broke the thread. I began to appreciate as never before the machine age, with its ball bearings and steel parts, and maybe an occasional nail.

Finally, my instructor decided I could spin well enough to be brought into the presence of the Mahatma. There were two injunctions I must faithfully follow. I must not speak to the Mahatma, and this was Monday, his day of silence. And I must not use any form of artificial light, as Gandhi disliked it. I could see from the outside that Gandhi's hut was going to be very dark indeed (a perfect job for Tri-X and souped-up developers, which we did not have). I pleaded with Gandhi's secretary to allow me some lighting equipment, and finally he allotted me three peanut flashbulbs.

I found the inside of the hut even darker than I had anticipated. A single beam of daylight shone from a little high window directly into my lens and into my eyes as well. I could scarcely see to compose the picture, but when my eyes became accustomed to the murky shadows, there sat the Mahatma, cross-legged, a spidery figure with long, wiry legs, a bald head and spectacles. Could this be the man who was leading his people to freedom – the little man in a loincloth who had kindled the imagination of the world? I was filled with an emotion as close to awe as a photographer can come.

He sat in complete silence on the floor; the only sound was a little rustling from the pile of newspaper clippings he was reading. And beside him was that spinning wheel I had heard so much about. I was grateful that he would not speak to me, for I could see it would take all the attention I had to overcome the halation from that wretched window just over his head.

Gandhi pushed his clippings aside, and pulled his spinning wheel closer. He started to spin, beautifully, rhythmically and with a fine nimble hand. I set off the first of the three flashbulbs. It was quite plain from the span of time from the click of the shutter to the flash of the bulb that my equipment was not synchronizing properly. The heat and moisture of India had affected all my equipment; nothing seemed to work. I decided to hoard my two remaining flashbulbs, and take a few time exposures. But this I had to abandon when my tripod 'froze' with one leg at its minimum and two at their maximum length.

Before risking the second flashbulb, I checked the apparatus with the utmost care. When Gandhi made a most beautiful movement as he drew the thread, I pushed the trigger and was reassured by the sound that everything had worked properly. Then I noticed that I had forgotten to pull the slide.

I hazarded the third peanut, and it worked. I threw my arms around the rebellious equipment and stumbled out into the daylight, quite unsold on the machine age. Spinning wheels could take priority over cameras any time.

The secretary was waiting outside, all smiles. I had been in the 'presence'; I belonged. He asked graciously if I would like to see a demonstration of spinning on Gandhi's own personal spinning wheel – the portable one carried when he travelled.

'I would enjoy that very much,' I replied. I enjoyed it even more than I had anticipated, for, in the middle of the secretary's demonstration, the spinning wheel fell to pieces. That made me feel better about the machine age.

This was the first of many occasions on which I photographed the Mahatma. Gandhi, who loved a little joke, had his own nickname for me. Whenever I appeared on the scene with camera and flashbulbs, he would say, 'There's the Torturer again.' But it was said with affection.

From: Margaret Bourke-White, *Portrait of Myself*, New York; Simon and Schuster, 1963, pp.273-278.

POSTSCRIPT:

During an interview the day before he was assassinated, Bourke-White asked Gandhi about his thoughts on nuclear weapons which had been first used in anger not that long before. She recalled that:

> As we began to speak of these things, I became aware of a change in my attitude toward Gandhi. No longer was this merely an odd little man in a loincloth, with his quaint ideas about bullock-cart

> culture and his vague social palliatives – certain of which I rejected. I felt in the presence of a new and greater Gandhi. My deepening appreciation of Gandhi began when I saw the power and courage with which he led the way in the midst of chaos. [...] Gandhi went on to stress the importance of choosing righteous paths, whether for a nation or for a single man; for bad means could never bring about good ends. He spoke thoughtfully, haltingly, always with the most profound sincerity. [...] Since that momentous day, many people have asked me whether one knew in Gandhi's presence that this was an extraordinary man. The answer is yes. One knew. And never have I felt it more strongly than on this day, when the inconsistencies that had troubled me dropped away, and Gandhi began to probe that dreadful problem which has overwhelmed all. (Bourke-White, *Portrait of Myself*, pp.295-296)

FURTHER READING:

Bourke-White, Margaret, *Halfway to Freedom*, New York: Simon and Schuster, 1949.

Goldberg, Vicki, *Margaret Bourke-White: A Biography*, London: Heinemann, 1986.

Weber, Thomas, *Going Native: Gandhi's Relationship with Western Women*, New Delhi: Roli Books, 2011.

1946 HALLAM TENNYSON

Born in December 1920, Beryl Hallam Augustine Tennyson was the great grandson of the celebrated poet Alfred, Lord Tennyson. He was educated at Eton, where he discovered a dislike for blood sports but sympathy for Marxism and pacifism. He went to Oxford as a seventeen-year-old but, two years later, at the height of the Second World War, he left his studies and registered as a conscientious objector and spent two years in the Friends' Ambulance Unit in Egypt and Italy. His two elder brothers joined the army and were killed in action. A year after his marriage, he went to India to head up the Rural Development Program in West Bengal. In July 1946 he was again doing ambulance work in Calcutta. Following three years in India, Tennyson became a productive writer and adapter of works for radio, television and the stage. In 1956 he joined the BBC World Service and then moved on to be Assistant Head of Drama in radio at the BBC. In 1969, with the writer and broadcaster Francis Watson, Tennyson published a book, *Talking of Gandhi*, based on radio documentaries of the previous decade. Although homosexual, he made strong efforts to be heterosexual, including spending twenty-five years seemingly happily married. Following his divorce in 1971, he became a gay rights activist. After his retirement he turned to full-time writing. He was murdered in December 2005.

My wife and I had admired Gandhi from afar for many years, and had decided in advance that our visit to him was likely to prove one of the most interesting and inspiring of our lives. If it had proved otherwise, we would, I suppose, have had the courage to admit it. Luckily, no such readjustment was necessary.

Not that the visit, apart from being good, was at all what we had expected: but then half the fun of life consists in having one's predictions proved wrong – in detail at least. The day of our arrival at the small country town of Wardha – Sevagram is some six miles to the south of it – was bleak and overcast. A totally inert sky had dug itself into the edges of the undulating plain which we had to cross to reach Gandhi's community. The prospect was not unlike certain stretches of the East Anglian coast, whose total dreariness still preserves them from trippers. At length the *Ashram* appeared a huddle of low-tiled huts in a dusty dip of the land. Beyond it was the once scruffy, now neat and industrious, village of Segaon, renamed Sevagram, or Village of Service.

We had come, as it happened, from the midst of the Hindu-Moslem riots which had broken out in Calcutta – the first portent of the catastrophe that was to split India in two. For a whole fortnight the country's premier city had been a living nightmare – as if an atom bomb had paralysed its municipal nerve-centre at the height of a deadly plague. [...]

All these horrors gave us, we could not help feeling, a special if grim importance, for we were the first to arrive at Sevagram direct from the beleaguered city. My wife had worked in soup kitchens and evacuation centres; I had helped rescue isolated minority pockets and had driven an ambulance. We thought that our experiences entitled us, not only to views on the subject of the riots, but also to a long and important interview with the Mahatma in which we could air them. The events in Calcutta would surely be preying on his mind. Was not the India of his dreams vanishing even before it had a chance to materialise? And the harmony between different faiths for which he had worked so long, where was that? We expected he would trace the failures of the past or estimate his hopes for the future in our presence. Perhaps we would be privileged with some classic restatement of faith. Messengers, we thought, even though they bring bad news, contribute their mite to history.

Our interview was indeed memorable, but not for the reason we had expected.

Gandhi lived in the centre of the community in one of the smallest huts. The room in which he conducted his business, sitting on the floor with a canvas back-rest, was about 8 feet square. Framed mottoes and mud mouldings decorated the walls. Its simplicity had an extraordinary elegance and style about it, much as the Canadian log cabins must have had in the days before pin-ups and glossy magazines. The hut was crowded with secretaries, disciples and wraith-like female attendants, and Gandhi was reading our letter of introduction as we came in. The letter told him of some of our exploits in the riots – among them the fact that I had been attacked by a Hindu crowd who had mistaken me for a Moslem because of my 'imperial' (the Hindus do not normally wear beards and, if they do, they prefer them unkempt and prophetic). 'You are preceded by a very loud blast of trumpets,' the old man said, grinning toothlessly and somehow projecting his grin over the top of his spectacles. 'All the same, I can imagine why those Hindus made their little error. And,' he added, giving the English language one of the twists he delighted in: 'I myself would certainly not have *mis*taken you for an Englishman.' The next moment he was asking me about my religious convictions and congratulating my wife on looking so comfortable when she sat cross-legged. It was not until we left the hut nearly an hour later that we realised that he never mentioned the riots again. Instead, he had prompted us to talk

> about ourselves. To him we two ordinary mortals were of more importance than the news we might be bringing or the events in which we had been accidentally involved. That incident taught us more of the essential greatness of Gandhi than we had ever learnt from studying his speeches or his life. India called him *Bapu* or 'Father'. Before we met him this merely seemed part of India's passion for personalisation. But afterwards we realised that it was because Gandhi himself had such an amazing gift for personalising that he had become *Bapu* to others.

From: Hallam Tennyson, *Saint on the March: The Story of Vinoba,* London: Victor Gollancz, 1955, pp.14-16.

POSTSCRIPT:

In his 'Introduction' to the newly added second part to the book of radio broadcasts originally published in 1957 as *Talking of Gandhiji,* Hallam Tennyson gives a shorter version of the first meeting with Gandhi. However, it also adds some additional material:

> [...] My wife and I, aged 24, had been asked to organise a project of rural development in a group of villages about fifty miles from Calcutta. We had studied Gandhi's 'Constructive Programme' and had made a date to travel to Sevagram to discuss our plans with him. On the way, in Calcutta, we got caught by the 'Great Calcutta Killing'. The city was paralysed: all outgoing trains were cancelled and corpses lay piled on every street corner. I helped to man an ambulance and was attacked by a Hindu mob when I tried to dissuade them from slaughtering a trio of helpless Muslims– they thought I was a Muslim too, it seemed, because I spoke Bengali and because of my pointed beard. I repelled the mob, who were clearly even more frightened than I, with a hot-water bottle. I recall this incident because it had an

unexpected relevance to my meeting with Gandhi. My wife and I were the first visitors at the Ashram at Sevagram with news about what had happened in Calcutta. Gandhi knew that it was the beginning of the end of his dream of a united India, and as messengers, even if messengers of doom, we thought ourselves lit with a kind of lurid importance. In the event, things turned out quite differently. Gandhi squatted on his mat reading through the long letter of introduction which we had brought with us and which chronicled my recent adventures in some detail. When he had finished he looked up and giving the English language one of those characteristic little tweaks he was so fond of, he said: 'But my dear Hallam Tennyson, how could you ever expect those Hindus to mistake you for an Englishman!' It was the only time during the week of our stay that he referred to what had happened in Calcutta. In a moment he had plunged into our life story: why we had come to India, what our religious beliefs were, what we had done so far in our villages. To Gandhi it was not the message but the messenger that was important. All my subsequent meetings with him took place in the midst of tragedy and suffering; first in devastated Noakhali in East Bengal in November of the same year, and then in the storm of rioting that broke out in Calcutta soon after Independence. On all these occasions there was the same self-mastery, the same invincible humour, the same ability to go straight to the heart of those with whom he was talking. (Watson and Tennyson, *Talking of Gandhi*, pp.131-132)

FURTHER READING:

Tennyson, Hallam, *The Haunted Mind: An Autobiography*, London: Andre Deutsch, 1984.

Watson, Francis, and Hallam Tennyson, *Talking of Gandhi*, New Delhi: Sangam Books, 1976.

1947

LORD LOUIS MOUNTBATTEN

Louis Francis Albert Victor Nicholas, Prince of Battenberg, great-grandson of Queen Victoria, was born in 1900. He joined the royal navy as a teenager and married Edwina Ashley in 1922. Ten years later he had achieved the rank of captain and by the outbreak of the Second World War, he was in command of a destroyer flotilla. By 1942, he was Naval Chief of Combined Operations Command and the following year Supreme Allied Commander for South-East Asia. He oversaw the campaign against Japan in Burma and received the Japanese surrender in Singapore. In 1947, he was sworn in as the last Viceroy of India. It was his task to oversee the dissolution of the Raj and the transfer of power to the independent states of India and Pakistan. He then stayed on as the Governor General of free India until the position of President was filled by Rajendra Prasad. He was created a viscount in 1946 and 1st Earl of Burma in 1947. Following his return to the navy in 1950, Lord Mountbatten filled various high-ranking positions, becoming First Sea Lord and finally, until his retirement in 1965, chairman of the British Chiefs of Staff Committee. In 1979, he was assassinated by Irish terrorists while fishing at his summer home in Ireland.

Far and away the most outstanding man in India – a world figure and (although a Hindu) revered by hundreds of millions of his fellow-countrymen, Muslims and Hindus alike – was Mahatma Gandhi, known affectionately and reverently to them as Gandhiji.

At my first meeting with Gandhi we didn't talk any business at all. We just chatted. I told him how the Prince of Wales and I had tried to meet him when we were here in 1921, and how we were not allowed to – he was really interested in that. Then I got him to tell me about his early life, his political beginnings in South Africa, and how he built up the non-violent Independence movement. We spent two hours talking in this way, and the Press could hardly believe that we had not been deciding the fate of India. Well, perhaps we had – indirectly.

Gandhi's purely political power was on the wane. He was a modern-day saint, really, and saints cannot thrive for ever in a political atmosphere. It was characteristic of Gandhi that at our very next meeting, the next day, he proposed as a solution to India's problems that I should ask Jinnah to form an administration. He really meant it, even though he must have realised that this would give the Muslims virtual control – anything rather than see India divided, or have a civil war.

Of course, it was quite impractical. I told him he must first get the support of the Congress Party, and this he naturally failed to get. But that was Gandhi! His personal popularity and influence were enormous. We might not be able always to take Gandhi along with us – but we would get nowhere if he came out against us. When he started calling Edwina and me 'dear friends' I began to have the feeling that we were half-way home.

From: John Terraine, *The Life and Times of Lord Mountbatten*, London: Arrow, 1980, pp.149-150.

POSTSCRIPT:

Mountbatten's butler remembers an interesting incident that occurred at that first meeting (but which in fact appears to have happened on the following day during the second meeting between the two):

> One morning Gandhi, the man Winston Churchill had called 'a half-naked fakir', came to the house, recognizable only because of the loin cloth that he wore. He stayed on for afternoon tea, which was arranged on the lawn with scones and sandwiches served by our Indian houseboys – my staff having enlarged considerably at Government House! The Indian leader did not touch either the cakes or sandwiches, but chose to eat a bowl of goat's curd which he had brought with him. He even persuaded Lord Louis to sample a mouthful. His Lordship bravely swallowed it, but gracefully declined the offer of more.
>
> Once back in his room he said, 'I can think of a lot of things I would rather do before eating goat's curd again!'
>
> But of Gandhi there was nothing but homage. Said Lord Louis, 'He is one of the most remarkable men I have met in my life, Charles. There is not another man to compare with him in the world. No man has such faith.' (Smith, *Fifty Years with Mountbatten*, p.82)

FURTHER READING:

Campbell-Johnson, Alan, *Mission with Mountbatten*, Bombay: Jaico, 1951.

Collins, Larry and Dominique Lapierre, *Mountbatten and the Partition of India: Volume 1: March 22 - August 15, 1947*, New Delhi: Vikas, 1982.

Das, Manmath Nath, *Partition and Independence of India: Inside Story of the Mountbatten Days*, New Delhi, Vision, 1982.

The Earl Mountbatten of Burma, "Mahatma Gandhi – A Real Friend", in S. Radhakrishnan (ed.), *Mahatma Gandhi 100 Years*, New Delhi: Gandhi Peace Foundation, 1969, pp.246-249.

Smith, Charles, *Fifty Years with Mountbatten: A Unique Personal Memoir by his Valet and Butler*, London: Hamlyn, 1981.

1948 VINCENT SHEEAN

Born in 1899, James Vincent Sheean was a foreign correspondent, writer, translator and traveller who seemed to have a knack of being present when momentous world events were occurring. His most famous work was the award-winning biography *Personal History,* which formed the basis for Alfred Hitchcock's film *Foreign Correspondent.* As an air force officer, in 1944 he went on a mission to India to cover the trans-Himalayan operations of a B-29 squadron based in Calcutta. India overwhelmed him and, although he originally had little time for Gandhi's nonviolence, he returned to the sub-continent in 1947 in order to be with Gandhi until he had found 'all the answers'. The War and the emptiness of western materialism had left him in a state of spiritual crisis. In preparation, he spent months of patient study and was finally ready at the end of January 1948 to become Gandhi's disciple. As fate had it, he managed only two interviews with the Mahatma, on January 27 and 28 at Birla House. Sheean was in the crowd at the prayer meeting where Gandhi was assassinated on the 30th. He died in his home in Italy in 1975.

Rangaswami [secretary to *Time* and *Life* magazines] spoke to Mr. Pyarelal and introduced me; after a few moments, as we stood on the steps, Mr. Pyarelal came back to the glass doors and signalled to me. 'You must take off your shoes,' said Rangaswami. 'I know there will be a hole in my sock,' I said in terror to Madame Cartier-Bresson, and removed my shoes, and there was a hole. I went into the room.

It was a small rectangular room with glass doors or French windows on one side, where the steps were, and long windows on the other two. The fourth wall was the wall of Birla House, against which this room was a sort of annex, but an almost transparent annex; curious persons were peering through the windows or doors at all times and the Mahatma, through long training, did not even notice.

As I came in he was walking up and down on a rectangular blue carpet which covered less than half the floor. This, and his white pallet in the corner, made the only furniture of the room. In the corner at the right were three or four of 'the girls', grand-daughters, grand-nieces, seated on the floor and talking in whispers.

I began by saying that I wanted to make a rather extensive study of his system of thought and action. (I think I actually said 'Good evening, sir,' at the outset.) He said: 'Yes, Pandit Nehru told me.' He paused and looked up at me with a curious birdlike motion (I was much taller). 'Pandit Nehru did not tell me,' he said, 'whether you wished to see me *absolutely* alone.' The delicate emphasis on *absolutely* was full of meaning; I knew quite well that Mr. Gandhi never saw anybody 'absolutely' alone.

'No, sir,' I said. 'I make no conditions.'

'Very well,' he said. 'Would you like to walk or to sit?'

'Whatever you wish,' I said. 'Perhaps you are tired after the meeting?'

'On the contrary,' he said with a sort of gentle decision (oddly, I can still hear this phrase when some more important ones are preserved only by written notes). 'At this hour I prefer to walk a little.'

We walked up and down the blue carpet. I was absurdly conscious of the hole in my sock, which I hardly suppose Gandhi saw. I was also aware that his swift steps up and down the carpet were much more numerous than mine. For me walking up and down the carpet was hardly walking at all; in three steps I had reached the end of it and turned back with him.

'Then you would not object,' he went on, 'if some notes were taken…?' He motioned with his hand towards Mr. Pyarelal, who was keeping pace with him on the other side.

'No, sir,' I said. 'On the contrary…'

'They might even be useful?' He finished the sentence for me on a rising note, with a curious half-smile.

'I have been reading your edition of the Gita,' I said, 'and my questions are based on that.'

He smiled and exclaimed something ('*Acha, Acha!*' I believe, conveying assent). I went on:

'I propose to begin with action and the fruits of action.'

He stopped still in his walk and looked up at me with his head slightly on one side. This is the characteristic motion I have called birdlike. He then straightened his head and pointed a long finger at the carpet.

'Let me get one thing clear,' he said, 'I have typhoid fever. Doctors are sent for and by means of injections of sulpha drugs or something of the kind they save my life. This, however, proves nothing. It might be that it would be more valuable to humanity for me to die.'

He stopped again for a few seconds; we were both standing still now. The moment was of tremendous importance.

'Is that quite clear?' he asked, looking at me with his head up. 'If it is not, I will repeat it.'

We resumed the walk.

'What I wish to ask is this: how can a righteous battle produce a catastrophic result?' I said. 'This battle is righteous in terms of the Gita. The result is a disaster. How can this be?'

'Because of the means used,' he said. 'Means are not to be distinguished from ends. If violent means are used there will be a bad result.'

'Is this true at all times and places?' I asked.

'*I* say so,' he said with his curious lisp, and rather shyly, too, as if he had never gone quite so far before (as indeed he had not). Then he produced a statement which was much bolder.

'As I read the Gita, even the first chapter, the battlefield of Kurukshetra is in the heart of man. I must tell you that orthodox scholars have criticized my interpretation of the Gita as being unduly influenced by the Sermon on the Mount.'

He took a few more steps and then made a really defiant profession of faith.

'There is one learned book in existence,' he said, 'which supports my interpretation of the Gita. But even if there were no such book, and even if it could be *proved* that my interpretation was wrong, I would still believe it.'

I was so taken aback by this certainty that I could not get out another question for the moment. Gandhi smiled and said: 'Now I think we might sit down. Shall we?'

He made his way over to the pallet in the corner and sat near the end of it, leaning against the wall. I sat cross-legged on the floor beside him, with Mr. Pyarelal, in front of him. I was now quite close to him and saw that his face had assumed an expression of concern, almost of anxiety.

> 'You should not be sitting there,' he said, inclining his body forward a little, as if to emphasize the offer. 'We can send for a chair.'
>
> 'No, sir, I'm comfortable, thanks,' I said.
>
> The question of the chair came up twice more, I think, as he imagined me to be uncomfortable on the floor. As a matter of fact, I did begin to get a bit cramped before the end, but I could never have admitted it. The idea of sitting on a chair with Mr. Gandhi on the floor at my feet was something impossible for me to conceive. I was finally obliged to tell him that I did not want a chair; and after that he abandoned the notion.

From: Vincent Sheean, *Lead, Kindly Light*, London: Cassell, 1950, pp.194-197.

POSTSCRIPT:

Three days after first walking the blue carpet with Gandhi, Vincent Sheean hired a taxi to take him to Birla House in time for Gandhi's five p.m. prayer meeting. What he witnessed and then put down on paper became one of the most memorable pieces of writing on the slaying of the Mahatma:

> As I came to the prayer ground at the end of the garden I ran into Bob Stimson, the Delhi correspondent of the B.B.C. We fell into talk [...] It was unusual to see any representatives of the Press at the prayer-meeting; Bob explained that he had submitted some questions to the Mahatma for the B.B.C. and thought he might as well stay for the prayers, since he was on the premises. He looked at his watch and said: 'Well, this is strange. Gandhi's late. He's practically never late.'

We both looked at our watches again. It was 5.12 by my watch when Bob said: 'There he is.' We stood near the corner of the wall, on the side of the garden where he was coming, and watched the evening light fall on his shining dark-brown head. He did not walk under the arbour this evening, but across the grass, on the open lawn on the other side of the flower-beds. [...] It was one of those shining Delhi evenings, not at all warm, but alight with the promise of spring. I felt well and happy and grateful to be here. Bob and I stood idly talking, I do not remember about what, and watching the Mahatma advance towards us over the grass, leaning lightly on two of "the girls," with two or three other members of his "family" (family or followers) behind them. I read afterwards that he had sandals on his feet, but I did not see them. To me it looked as if he walked barefoot on the grass. It was not a warm evening, and he was wrapped in homespun shawls. He passed by us on the other side and turned to ascend the four or five brick steps that led to the terrace or prayer-ground.

Here, as usual, there was a clump of people, some of whom were standing and some of whom had gone on their knees or bent low before him. Bob and I turned to watch – we were perhaps ten feet away from the steps – but the clump of people cut off our view of the Mahatma now: he was so small. Then I heard four small, dull, dark explosions. 'What was that?' I said to Bob in sudden horror. 'I don't know,' he said. I remember that he grew pale in an instant. 'Not the Mahatma!' I said, and then I knew.

What followed must be told as it happened (to *me* – *me*), or there is not truth in it.

Inside my own head there occurred a wavelike disturbance which I can only compare to a storm at sea – wind and wave surging tremendously back and forth. I remember all this distinctly; I do not believe that I lost consciousness even for a moment, although there may have been an instant or two of half-consciousness. I recoiled upon the brick wall and leaned against it, bent almost in two. I felt the consciousness of the Mahatma leave me then – I know of no other way of expressing this: he left me. The storm inside my head continued for some little time – minutes, perhaps; I have no way of reckoning. Then I was aware of two things at once: a burning and stinging in the fingers of my right hand and a similar burning and stinging in my eyes. In the eyes it was tears, although of some more acid mixture than I had known, and on my fingers I did now know for a while what it was, because I put them in my mouth (like a child) to ease the burning. In the wildness and confusion of that moment a young Indian – unknown to me – came to where I was doubled up against the wall and said: 'Is he dead? Is he dead?' The young Indian had staring eyes and was as filled with horror as I was, I suppose, although I do not know why he asked me such a question. 'I don't know,' I said, taking my fingers out of my mouth to do so.

Then I looked at my fingers. On the third and fourth fingers of my right hand blisters had appeared. They were facing each other, on the sides of those fingers which touch. The blister on the third finger was rather large and was already filled with water. The blister on the fourth or little finger was smaller. They had not been there before I heard the shots. [...]

It was during this time, apparently, that many things happened: a whole external series of events took place in my immediate neighbourhood – a few yards away – and I was unaware of them. A doctor was found; the police took charge; the body of the Mahatma was carried away; the crowd melted, perhaps urged to do so by the police. I saw none of this. The last I saw of the Mahatma he was advancing over the grass in the evening light, approaching the steps. When I finally took my fingers out of my mouth and stood up, dry-eyed, there were police and soldiers and not many people [...] The room with the glass doors and windows, by the rose-garden at the end of the arbour, had a crowd of people around it. Many were weeping. (Sheean, *Lead, Kindly Light,* pp.215-218)

FURTHER READING:

Seshachari, C., *Gandhi and the American Scene, An Intellectual History and Inquiry,* Bombay: Nachiketa, 1969.

Sheean, Vincent, *Mahatma Gandhi: A Great Life in Brief,* New Delhi: Publications Division, Ministry of Information and Broadcasting, Government of India, 1954.

Sheean, Vincent, *Nehru: The Years of Power,* London: Gollancz, 1960.

Sheean, Vincent, *Personal History,* New York: Doubleday, 1935.

Concluding Remarks

As noted in the Introduction, personal observation does not guarantee an objective revelation of immutable facts. Occasionally Gandhi's guests got things wrong or implied that things were different to what history tells us they were. For example, Newton Phelps Stokes gives us an excellent portrait of Gandhi on the Salt March. However, he estimates a crowd of 1,000 in the village where he caught up with Gandhi, when even the police reports, which tended to downplay numbers, put the crowd at 5,000. Hermon Ould was convinced that he had a brief conversation in a large crowd with 'Gandhi's wife' (who in fact had died two years earlier). While there may be some factual errors, these are eyewitness reports and important for that fact alone. And they provide us with a wealth of new material about Gandhi and elucidate the affect he had on those around him.

As can be expected from first meeting accounts, we are provided with detailed descriptions of the Mahatma. We are offered an individual who is variously described as someone with kind eyes and warm smile, someone who is simple, childlike, selfless, humble, gentle, unassuming, considerate, friendly, courteous, punctual, tireless, sincere, truth-seeking, vigorous, joyful, direct, open, loveable, wise, homely, transparent, courageous and saintly. Gandhi comes across as having strong powers of persuasion but also as an active listener; he has integrity and a sense of humour. He seems to be an astute judge of character and is eager to learn. He does not speak badly of others. This is an impressive list of attributes. Is it too good? Halide Edib pointed out that 'those who know him become too emotional to be trusted to be objective.' Can anyone then, following a meeting with the Mahatma, remain trustable enough to be objective?

As I mentioned in the Introduction, these accounts were not selected because they were pro-Gandhi or in some way sensationalist. They were simply the best accounts available. Naturally, most of those who came to see the Mahatma were Gandhiphiles. That is why they came. Those who were not sympathetic to him would presumably not have sought him out. The exceptions were some of the big-named newspapermen of the time (like Negley Farson and Edgar Snow). They were hardened individuals who had seen a great deal of the underbelly of world politics. They were not about to write a hagiography and were tough in their assessments of Gandhi, noting his political realism and even diabolical cunning. However, even they could not help saying something positive in the end, mentioning his sincerity, integrity, courage, and honest search for truth. This makes for a pretty impressive score card and could perhaps be fruitfully kept in mind by those who see it almost as their duty to debunk the 'myth' of the Mahatma.

Perhaps what becomes most obvious from these descriptions is how, after the Salt March, the demands on Gandhi's time become extreme. Very few people seemed to have the type of selfless disposition which could trump their desire to impinge on the Mahatma's time for their own edification. In short, while there were not many considerate souls like John Haynes Holmes, Shriman Narayan and Ould, or extremely shy ones like Muriel Lester, there were plenty of overzealous darshan seekers. Charlie Chaplin and Jo Davidson in London, Romain Rolland on the Continent, and Edib back in India, give us a glimpse of the circus of which the Mahatma had become the prime star. From about that time on, it would be rare that anyone could merely walk into Gandhi's Ashram and find him spinning alone under a tree as J.C. Kumarappa did, or be allowed to visit him in prison and find him almost alone as Nilla Cram Cook did. His schedule, to say the least, had become hectic.

Yet he managed to cope. The way Gandhi interacted with people who may have carried introductory letters but were nevertheless strangers may provide a clue as to how. Hallam Tennyson discovered that Gandhi was more interested in him than in the news he was carrying. This led him to discover 'more of the essential greatness of Gandhi than we had ever learnt from studying his speeches or his life. India called him *Bapu* or "Father". Before we met him this merely seemed part of India's passion for personalisation. But afterwards we realised that it was because Gandhi himself had such an amazing gift for personalising that he had become *Bapu* to others.'

Perhaps it could be argued that the way Gandhi charmed his interlocutors is little more than a practiced technique that he learned from Gokhale: a skill that seems to be a primary implement in the toolbox of any successful politician. After all, who knows how useful the person being talked to might become in the future? However, reading these accounts, Gandhi's way of interacting does not seem to be a cynical exercise for possible future gain. None of those who recorded their first meetings with him mentioned that they felt manipulated. As I discovered when I interviewed the remaining elderly participants in Gandhi's Salt March in the early 1980s, Gandhi's attitude to, and focus on, the individuals he was interacting with came naturally and was to a large degree what made him special. In my previous account I mentioned that

> Gandhi taught the essence of nonviolence in the way he related to others. The marchers often made the point that they were something special to Gandhi: 'I was like a son to him' or 'he was like a father to me' were common responses. Others added 'when he had problems with his spinning he always came to me for advice', 'I took care of his correspondence for him while Pyarelal was away because he thought that I was the best secretary', 'he always came to me for a haircut', and so on. Naturally everyone would like to be able to say that he or she was close to one such as the Mahatma – name dropping crosses the boundaries of time and culture – but these were old, generally well grounded and secure individuals who did not seem to have any need to impress me. They actually believed that they were favoured by Gandhi and for a while it puzzled me: how could so many think that *they* were specially

> favoured? Eventually I realised that they held such beliefs because they were based on fact, Gandhi treated every person as someone special. (Weber, *On the Salt March*, pp.539-540)

Although Margaret Sanger occasionally felt that the Mahatma was not necessarily listening to her argument (and she may have added that, given the topic and his background, psychologically he could not afford to), I think that these first meetings with Gandhi reinforce this aspect of his personality, an aspect that did not change with time. From the examples of the first meetings with Gandhi reproduced here, it seems obvious that regardless of his fame or pressure on his time, he gave pretty well every visitor, high or low, the gift of his full attention. And they felt it.

References

Weber, Thomas, *On the Salt March: The Historiography of Gandhi's March to Dandi*, New Delhi: Rupa, 2009.

Acknowledgements

The reproduced selections in this book are from the following sources. Every reasonable effort has been made to contact the copyright holders to obtain permission for the use of the extracts, and where possible the selections have been reproduced with the permission of the publishers or copyright holders. Where this has proven impossible, the publisher would be pleased to receive information that would enable more complete acknowledgements in subsequent printings of this book. In the meantime, the publisher extends their apologies for any omission.

Agarwal, Shriman Narayan, "Gandhi Anecdotes", in Chandrashanker Shukla (ed.), *Incidents of Gandhiji's Life, by Fifty-Four Contributors,* Bombay: Vora, 1949, pp.1-3.

Alexander, Horace, "My First Meeting with Gandhiji", *Illustrated Weekly of India* (1969), vol.90, no.17, p.17.

Barr, F. Mary, *Bapu: Conversations & Correspondence with Mahatma Gandhi,* Bombay: International Book House, n.d.

Bhave, Vinoba, (Marjorie Sykes trans. and Kalindi ed.), *Moved By Love: The Memoirs of Vinoba Bhave,* Dartington, Totnes, Devon: Resurgence, 1994.

Borkar, G., (ed.), *Selected Speeches and Writings of Rajkumari Amrit Kaur,* New Delhi: Archer, 1961.

Bose, Nirmal Kumar, *My Days with Gandhi,* Bombay: Orient Longman, 1974.

Bourke-White, Margaret, *Portrait of Myself,* New York; Simon and Schuster, 1963.

Brockway, A. Fenner, *A Week in India (and Three Months in an Indian Hospital),* London: The New Leader, 1928.

Casey, R.G., *An Australian in India,* London: Hollis & Carter, 1947.

Chaplin, Charles, *My Autobiography,* London: The Bodley Head, 1964.

Cook, Nilla Cram, *My Road to India,* New York: Lee Furman, 1939.

Davidson, Jo, *Between Sittings,* New York: Dial Press, 1951.

Diwakar, R.R., *My Encounter with Gandhi,* New Delhi: Gandhi Peace Foundation, 1989.

Doke, Joseph J., *M.K. Gandhi: An Indian Patriot in South Africa,* Rajghat, Varanasi: Akhil Bharat Sarva Seva Sangh, 1956.

Eddy, Sherwood, "Dr. Sherwood Eddy", in Joseph John (comp.), *Gandhi as Others See Him,* Colombo: Bastian, 1933. (Originally published in *The Christian Leader,* 1930), pp.28-30.

Edib, Halidé, *Inside India,* London: Allen & Unwin, 1937.

Edib, Halide, "My First Visit to Mahatma Gandhi", in Chandrashanker Shukla (ed.), *Reminiscences of Gandhiji: By Fortyeight Contributors,* Bombay: Vora, 1951, pp.87-91.

Farson, Negley, *The Way of the Transgressor,* New York: Carroll & Graf, 1984.

Farson, Negley, "Indian Hate Lyric", in E.Lyons (ed.), *We Cover the World: By Sixteen Foreign Correspondents,* London: Harrap, 1937, pp.129-152.

Fischer, H., "My First Meeting with Gandhiji", *The Illustrated Weekly of India* (1969), vol.90, no.18, p.21.

Fischer, Louis, *A Week with Gandhi,* London: Allen & Unwin, 1943.

Fischer, Louis, *Gandhi and Stalin: Two Signs at the World's Crossroads,* London: Victor Gollancz, 1948.

Gandhi, M.K., "A Confession of Faith", *Young India,* 13 July 1921.

Gandhi, M.K., *An Autobiography or The Story of My Experiments with Truth,* Ahmedabad: Navajivan, 1940.

Ghosh, Sudhir, *Gandhi's Emissary,* London: Cresset, 1967.

Holmes, John Haynes, *My Gandhi,* London: George Allen & Unwin, 1954.

Husain, Zakir, "Moral Awareness", in S. Radhakrishnan (ed.), *Mahatma Gandhi 100 Years,* New Delhi: Gandhi Peace Foundation, 1969, pp.123-128.

Jones, E. Stanley, *The Christ of the Indian Road,* London: Hodder and Stoughton, 1926.

Jones, E. Stanley, *Mahatma Gandhi: An Interpretation,* London: Hodder and Stoughton, 1948.

Kripalani, J.B., "My First Meeting with Gandhiji", *The Illustrated Weekly of India* (1969), vol.90, no.22, p.17.

Kumarappa, J.C., "Lessons from his Life", in Chandrashanker Shukla (ed.), *Incidents of Gandhiji's Life, by Fifty-Four Contributors,* Bombay: Vora, 1949, pp.131-143.

Lanza del Vasto, J.J., *Return to the Source,* London: Rider, 1971.

Lester, Muriel, *Gandhi's Signature,* Los Angeles: Fellowship of Reconciliation, 1949.

Miller, Webb, *I Found No Peace: The Journal of a Foreign Correspondent,* Harmondsworth: Penguin, 1940.

Mira Behn (Madeleine Slade), *The Spirit's Pilgrimage,* London: Longmans, 1960.

Mayo, Katherine, *Mother India,* London: Jonathan Cape, 1927.

Naidu, Sarojini, "The Father of Modern India: An Appreciation by Her Excellency Sarojini Naidu", in H.S.L. Polak, H.N. Brailsford and Lord Pethick-Lawrence, *Mahatma Gandhi,* London: Odhams Press, 1949, pp.6-8.

Narayan, Shriman, *Memoirs: Windows on Gandhi and Nehru,* Bombay: Popular, 1971.

Natesan, G.A., "Reminiscences", in D.G. Tendulkar (ed.), *Gandhiji: His Life and Work,* Bombay: Keshav Bhikaji Dhawale, 1944, pp.208-215.

Noguchi, Yone, "A Visit from the Far East" in S. Radhakrishnan (ed.), *Mahatma Gandhi: Essays and Reflections on His Life and Work,* Bombay: Jaico, 1956, pp.159-162.

Ould, Herman, "Gandhi", in S. Radhakrishnan (ed.), *Mahatma Gandhi: Essays and Reflections on His Life and Work,* Bombay: Jaico, 1956, pp.357-363.

Polak, H.S.L., "Some South African Reminiscences", in Chandrashanker Shukla (ed.), *Incidents of Gandhiji's Life, by Fifty-Four Contributors,* Bombay: Vora, 1949, pp.230-247.

Polak, Millie Graham, *Mr. Gandhi: The Man,* London: Allen & Unwin, 1931.

Prasad, Rajendra, *At the Feet of Mahatma Gandhi,* Westport, Con: Greenwood Press, 1961.

Prasad, Rajendra, *Autobiography*, Bombay: National Book Trust, 1957.

Publications Division, *Romain Rolland and Gandhi Correspondence (Letters, Diary Extracts, Articles, Etc.)*, New Delhi: Publications Division, Ministry of Information and Broadcasting, Government of India, 1976.

Rajan, T.S.S., "Since My Student Days", in Chandrashanker Shukla (ed.), *Incidents of Gandhiji's Life, by Fifty-Four Contributors*, Bombay: Vora, 1949, pp.259-264.

Ramachandran, G., "My First Darshan", *Gandhi Marg* (1957), vol.1, no.1, pp.43-46.

Reynolds, Reginald, "Mr. Reginald A. Reynolds", in Joseph John (comp.), *Gandhi as Others See Him*, Colombo: Bastian, 1933 (Originally published in *New Leader*, 1930), pp.24-28.

Rolland, Romain, "A Visit from Gandhi", *The Nation* (New York), 10 February 1932, pp.381-385. (Reproduced in Homer A. Jack (ed.), *The Gandhi Reader*, Madras: Samata Books, 1984.)

Sanger, Margaret, *An Autobiography*, New York, Dover, 1971.

Sheean, Vincent, *Lead, Kindly Light*, London: Cassell, 1950.

Shirer, William L., *Gandhi: A Memoir*, New York: Touchstone, 1980.

Smith, Charles, *Fifty Years with Mountbatten: A Unique Personal Memoir by his Valet and Butler*, London: Hamlyn, 1981.

Snow, Edgar, *Glory and Bondage* [US title: *People on Our Side*], Sydney: Angus and Robertson, 1946.

Stokes II, Newton Phelps, "Marching with Gandhi", *Review of Reviews* (1930), vol. 81, pp.34-38.

Tennyson, Hallam, *Saint on the March: The Story of Vinoba*, London: Victor Gollancz, 1955.

Terraine, John, *The Life and Times of Lord Mountbatten*, London: Arrow, 1980.

Vaswni Sundri, (comp. and ed.), *Mahatma Gandhi the Beloved Patient: Revered Dadaji Dr. Dinshah K. Mehta*, Bombay: Bharatiya Vidya Bhavan, 1992.

Watson, Francis, and Hallam Tennyson, *Talking of Gandhi*, New Delhi: Sangam Books, 1976.

Yogananda, Paramahansa, *Autobiography of a Yogi*, Bombay: Jaico Publishing House, 1985.

www.ingramcontent.com/pod-product-compliance
Ingram Content Group UK Ltd.
Pitfield, Milton Keynes, MK11 3LW, UK
UKHW041842190726
13854UKWH00002B/668

9 788174 369970